EAST COAST MAIN LINE DI

Adrian Gray

CONTENTS

© Adrian Gray and Pendragon Publishing, 2013

Published by Pendragon Publishing, PO Box 3, Easingwold, York, YO61 3YS

Cover design by Barry C. Lane

Page Layout by Highlight Type Bureau Ltd, Bradford, BD8 7HB

Printed by The Amadeus Press, Cleckheaton, BD19 4TQ

British Cataloguing-in-Publication Data: a catalogue reference for this book is held by the British Library.

ISBN No. 978-1-899816-19-4

INTRODUCTION

The East Coast route from London to Edinburgh has provided countless millions of travellers with safe journeys for over 150 years but, given the volumes of travel involved, there have been many 'accidents' and disasters although only a small number of great severity. It is not possible to cover all the incidents in this book, so the narrative mainly concentrates on those where passenger fatalities were involved and a few less serious occurrences which usefully illustrate the themes of the story. It should also be borne in mind that, although it was the passenger train accidents which attracted the attention, the majority of serious incidents and deaths involved railwaymen working on the line, especially in the early days.

The East Coast Main Line was not built as a single entity but was formed by the efforts of several separate companies which only finally joined together in 1923. Working from the south, the Great Northern Railway (GNR) opened from a temporary station at Maiden Lane to Peterborough on 7th August 1850 but at first used a lengthy loop via Boston and Lincoln to get to Doncaster; the direct route via Grantham only opened in 1852. King's Cross opened on 14th October 1852.

The Great Northern dropped its plans for its own line into York and at first entered that city by using the tracks of the York & North Midland (YNMR) via Burton Salmon, thereafter effectively terminating at Shaftholme, north of Doncaster. The YNMR was itself an amalgamation of the York & Newcastle and the Newcastle & Darlington Junction Railway.

The YNMR merged with the Leeds Northern and, more significantly, the York Newcastle & Berwick (YNBR) to form the North Eastern Railway in 1854. The YNBR had opened its line at first to Tweedmouth in 1847 and then to Berwick using a temporary viaduct across the Tweed which was replaced by the famous Royal Border Bridge in July 1850.

Of the three main constituents, the North Eastern had had the most complex genesis and its route was the least suited to trunk traffic. Various improvements were made later, such as the direct route from Durham to Gateshead, the shortened route from Doncaster to York via Selby following the opening of the new section through Riccall in 1871 and the new King Edward VII Bridge at Newcastle in 1906.

At the Scottish end of the line, the route from Berwick-upon-Tweed into Edinburgh was opened by the North British Railway in 1846.

The North Eastern, Great Northern and North British were brought together into the London & North Eastern Railway from 1923 and then nationalised into British Railways from

King's Cross locomotive depot from the coaling plant in 1956, with the main line shed in the foreground and the 'Met' shed behind it; the goods depot is in the background. Noise, steam, smoke, pits between the rails, tripping hazards on the ground, moving engines and wagons, poor lighting – all combined to make a dangerous workplace.
(Pendragon Collection)

LNER D16 4-4-0 No.8787 with an up express passing Welwyn North station and, it seems, a totally unperturbed shunting horse and shunter. It is not difficult to see how staff were killed or seriously injured when such working practices prevailed.
(Allan Sibley)

1948. A minor deviation to the route was made in 1979, after the collapse of Penmanshiel Tunnel. In 1983 British Railways opened a new section from Temple Hirst to Colton Junction, south of York, to avoid possible dislocation by the development of a coalfield around Selby. This meant that the direct route from Selby to York was closed entirely. Following privatisation, the main line service became a franchise operated by the Great North Eastern Railway from 1996 to 2007, following which it became a service of National Express East Coast until financial issues forced it to hand back the franchise to the Government. At the time of writing principal express services are operated mainly by East Coast Trains, a wholly owned subsidiary of the Government-backed Directly Operated Railways but several other companies operate over parts of the route.

During this period control of the infrastructure was separated from that of running the trains and from 1994 to 2002 the line was maintained by contractors on behalf of Railtrack, which was in turn replaced by Network Rail.

This book concentrates on operating accidents where it is the train that comes to grief because of technical or human failure, with the greatest focus on accidents where there were passenger fatalities. In general it does not attempt to cover the most common type of accident – the running down of railway staff or members of the public. Details of these were less rarely recorded[1] and so we know much more about the death of passengers than of railway staff; not until 1871 were railway companies obliged to inform the Board of Trade of deaths of their servants.[2] Nonetheless, we know that collateral deaths were numerous in the early days: in the six months between 1st July and 31st December 1849 the York, Newcastle & Berwick's fatalities included ten trespassers, three railway staff and three passengers getting into trains incautiously.[3]

The annual death toll of railway workers became a cause of national scandal in the mid-1800s as fatalities reached hundreds a year. Here is the list for six months on the Great Northern from January to June 1860 – including only the company's losses on the main line:

> 6th January: platelayer killed walking on line at Huntingdon
>
> 13th January: contractor killed getting into wagon at Retford
>
> 26th January: platelayer killed walking on line near Corby Glen
>
> 23rd April: derailed train at Hatfield killed platelayer at the lineside
>
> 27th April: number taker killed crossing line at Peterborough
>
> 23rd May: engine fitter standing on top of tender of moving train killed when he collided with bridge near Biggleswade

The companies continued to lose staff in large numbers, although not always on the East Coast line, of course; in 1890 the Great Northern lost 31, the North Eastern 17 and the North British – with a much less intensive service – a staggering 34. One of the most unusual must have been the driver who collapsed and died on the platform of Doncaster station in

August 1871 – of sunstroke.[4]

Building work and improvements to the line added to 'routine' fatalities. Various widening works conducted as traffic grew led to increased fatalities because trains were still running as the work continued, often with local labourers walking to and from the works along the line. The widening between Sandy and St. Neots in 1897 cost several lives, typically with a man run over by a ballast train as happened at Tempsford. A labourer run over at Great Paxton whilst walking along the track was reported as having been 'stone deaf'.[5]

In the new century things were not much better. A few months at Hitchin[6] saw a succession of accidents:

25th May 1906
B.Chalkley and G. Stevens, platelayers killed by 202 down express due Hitchin 7.54am near Cambridge Junction.
26th May 1906
Guard Pacey fell from brake near Cadwell working 748 'A' down goods. Left Hitchin 10.22pm. Was badly hurt and taken to Hitchin Hospital.
15th August 1906
Fireman knocked off engine of 373 down express, Langley Bridge, and killed.
25th August 1906
Wymondley Porter knocked down at Wymondley by engine. Guard Welch knocked down 11.00pm. Died 5.00am 26th.

Wartime conditions were especially dangerous due to reduced lighting and there was an unusually serious accident at Hett Mill, near Ferryhill, on 13th June 1940. Three platelayers were struck by a York to Newcastle train, with one of the victims being carried on the buffer beam of the locomotive for a quarter of a mile. All three died.[7] Even the provision of look-outs did not guarantee safety; after a death at Hornsey on 25th October 1964 it was found the look-out had

positioned himself where station buildings restricted the view of approaching trains to only 300 yards, leaving too little time for permanent way workers to get out of the way.

Railway staff were especially prone to sudden death if working in goods yards, at the trackside or even in railway sheds. There have been many hundreds of these, but a few examples will illustrate the problems. John Land, referred to in the contemporary press as a 'joiner' or perhaps a shunter, was killed on the York & North Midland at York in November 1845 when caught between the buffers of two wagons which "pressed against his hips".[8] H. Bulmer, a 'striker' at Thirsk, was killed between the ticket platform and some trucks in March 1874.[9] Often the death of railway workers received the barest notice:

"On Monday evening, William Anderson, 27 years of age, a goods guard on the North Eastern Railway, was killed at Gateshead."[10]

On 9th December 1879 a 19-year-old railwayman with only four months experience was crushed to death between the coupling hooks of two wagons, having stood between them with his back turned to the oncoming danger. Events such as this were almost routine and related to working practices of the time, many of which are not fully known today. Another young man to be killed was John Riddell, 17, at Dunbar on 7th April 1937. Riddell was helping a relaying gang by putting their tools back into a wagon which had been left in the dock siding at Dunbar, behind which ran a short siding used for shunting. Riddell took a short cut across this siding without looking and was crushed by the buffers of some vans that were being loose shunted. Six months later Charles Stoker, an experienced shunter at Dringhouses Up Yard in York, was killed when he fell over in stepping out of the way of a shunting engine.

It was quite common for men working alone to be found dead at some later stage. Fred Lockwood was the horse shunter at Ranskill station and in February 1926 was found dead with his foot trapped in the 'V' of a crossing. It appeared he had been walking alongside or in front of his horse pulling a wagon and after he got stuck it had run over his right leg. Safety guidance clearly set out men should not attach the horse to the hooks or couplings at the front of a van, but Lockwood had ignored this.

Members of the public could also be killed in goods yards. On 15th November 1853 a potato dealer was crushed between an engine and a carriage at King's Cross goods depot. There were also the ancillary workers, such as the postal messenger run over crossing the line at Ferryhill station on 22nd December 1851.

Workers' use of the railway as a footpath from one spot to another rendered them vulnerable too. Goulding Hunt, a GNR platelayer who lived in the railway gatehouse at Eaton, near Retford, set out in January 1874 along the railway one morning and was almost immediately run over by a goods train. He was found with both legs badly hurt

PLACING A FOG SIGNAL.

A perilous job depicted in the Illustrated London News *in 1844 – placing a fog signal in front of an oncoming train.* (Author's collection)

and taken to the Queen's Hotel in Retford. Dr. Pritchard was sent for, but he was away and so his assistant Gerald Miller attended. Miller decided Hunt should be sent by 'conveyance' to the hospital at Newark – 22 miles on unsurfaced roads, during which he died. The Retford Coroner was very unimpressed by this and lambasted Miller, "subjecting him to a long and very severe examination as to his antecedents, when he admitted that he had no medical qualification and no recognised medical education whatever". The Coroner thought that Miller had "embittered the last moments of a dying man through his culpable ignorance in attempting to have him conveyed to Newark".

Many were killed walking to and from work in this way, though some were patently unwise: on 14th June 1856 platelayer William Thompson was killed walking through Copenhagen Tunnel on his way home. A few months earlier, on 24th January, a platelayer was killed as he walked towards Huntingdon station – apparently after having drunk a large amount of alcohol.[11]

In 1900 an engine cleaner named Holmes who normally worked at King's Cross with a group of others was told to move to a new shed that had been built in Hornsey. Holmes and the others took a train there, without tickets, arriving at the station at 5.45am. They then set out across the tracks to the new shed, but Holmes was knocked down by an express and died the next day; his employers refused to pay compensation, saying that he had not been at work. His representatives brought a case against the Great Northern under the relatively new Workmen's Compensation Act of 1897, arguing that the company had directed him to Hornsey and was therefore responsible. The Judge agreed, taking the line that free train travel meant an effective contract and ordered compensation to be paid.[12] Incidentally, also in 1900 the Railway Employment (Prevention of Accidents) Act further helped to improve the situation. These in turn had replaced the less effective Employers Liability Act of 1880; the first GNR man to benefit from this was apparently John Pepper, driver of a snowplough train which was in a collision at Essendine on 19th January 1880.[13]

The death of railway workers whilst walking at the trackside has continued to be a problem up to more recent times. On the night of 7th January 1957 two men were killed close to Nineteen Mile Bridge, between Hatfield and Welwyn Garden City; they were experienced platelayers, walking back from having spent the day clearing up after the Welwyn Garden City collision that morning.[14] They were hit by the breakdown train, which was returning to Hatfield for water.[15]

Some railway staff deaths appear to have just been bad luck. At Selby in 1892 men were at work replacing the signals and had cut the wire stays when a locomotive came up and got entangled in the wires; this pulled down the semaphore signal which hit the three workmen, killing one of them.[16]. On 11th April 1910 a railwayman fell off the Ouse bridge at Huntingdon and drowned.

An unusual death was that of William Haigh,[17] a GNR carriage greaser, on 6th September 1855. The Queen was travelling north and, to avoid delays, a carriage greaser went along to provide en route attention to any hot axleboxes. The Queen had to change carriages at Darlington due to overheated axleboxes on four carriages including the royal saloon. As the Royal Train approached Darlington on the North Eastern, Haigh set out along the running boards to attend to a problem and was killed when he hit a wooden upright of the bridge across the River Skerne. The Queen awarded his widow an annual pension of £30 and the GNR directors made an allowance to his children of 2s a week until 1864.[18]

Living next to the line also made staff and their families vulnerable. On 15th February 1856 the wife and child of a platelayer were killed at Doncaster Decoy level crossing. The family lived in the gatehouse there and the child had run on to the line; mother ran to the rescue and both were hit by a train, the child dying immediately and the mother six days later. In 1860 the ten-year-old son of the station master at Sandy was knocked down and killed by an excursion train.[19]

Also at Doncaster, on the morning of 12th January 1892 the Great Northern Railway 0-6-0 locomotive No.180 returned from an overnight trip to Peterborough and went to the ash pit for attention. The duty of the driver and fireman was to see that the engine was placed into sidings or sheds before they left it. However, the driver, Edward Frankton, left at once in order to sign off duty, entrusting the locomotive to his fireman Joseph Bennett. It is thought that this was common practice although strictly in contravention of the rules. Bennett set the engine in motion tender first then got off to change the points so as to direct it to the sheds for cleaning.

The locomotive was in full gear and Bennett found that he could not remount the footplate as it gained speed. Several workmen observed it pass the driver who was on his way to the office. They estimated that the speed was in excess of 20mph.

The distance from the coal stage to the sheds was between 800 and 900 yards. The locomotive ran through the wooden doors of a yard alongside the sheds and into three wagons – the first loaded with fire bars, the second an empty coal wagon and the third loaded with sand. All were propelled into and demolished the 18in thick wall of the joiners' shop. The leading wagon mounted the debris and went forward through another wall into the coppersmiths' shop. The second wagon was driven halfway into the joiners' shop while the engine telescoped itself into the third wagon. A boiler filler jumped on to the engine and shut off steam.

Thomas Drury, Richard Kelly, James Atkins, George Richmond, Charles Maidens and J Curry were in the joiners' shop. James Atkins was seated with his back to the wagons, Drury and Kelly were on a joiner's bench facing the wall through which the wagons came while Richmond and Maidens were on one side of the shop near the door. Drury and Kelly were sent with considerable force into the coppersmith's shop. Drury died at the scene with head injuries. Kelly was found trapped under a wagon wheel. He died later in hospital. Atkins and Richmond were both seriously injured but survived after hospital treatment.

Richard Crundel and Samuel Temperton were in the coppersmiths' shop. Both survived although the latter was thrown into a trough of water and badly bruised.

Supt. Blake (Inspector of Weights and Measures) visited the scene and afterwards caused both driver and fireman to be apprehended on a warrant. Both were later charged with manslaughter at the West Riding Court and allowed bail, both in the sum of £25, with one surety each in a like sum.

A special sitting of West Riding Magistrates to hear the charges against the accused heard that Driver Frankton, who had been on the GNR for 35 years, had contravened Rule 310: he had left his engine while on duty. Fireman Bennett, who had two years' service, had no business to drive the engine. Both were committed for trial.

When the Coroner resumed the Inquest Driver Frankton repeated in substance his earlier statement that when he left the engine on the ash pit road he expected the fireman to put it away while he went to sign off duty. Fireman Bennett said that it had always been the custom since he had been on the railway for the driver to leave the engine. The Coroner summed up and asked the jury to arrive at a verdict upon the evidence heard in court. He pointed out that the fireman could hardly do less than he did when left with the engine.

The jury returned the following verdict: "The jury find that Richard Kelly met with his death by an accident caused by an uncontrolled engine dashing trucks through a wall into a workshop, where he was at the time. The said trucks were in an unprotected siding, and the jury think that the Company should provide proper stops, or catch points from the siding."

The Coroner stated "it is a verdict of accidental death with a rider. West Riding Magistrates will be asked to allow the charge of manslaughter against the driver and fireman to be withdrawn."

Trespassing incidents were especially common in the earlier years, on one occasion actually involving a railway engineer then working on building part of the Great Northern's system – a case which shows the impossibility of protecting people from harm when they flout all conventional safeguards. The case involved Richard Russell, an engineer from Bawtry who had worked abroad but had returned home to take a senior role in the building of the Doncaster to Gainsborough line in 1864. Russell wanted to get home from Doncaster to Bawtry but had missed the last passenger train, so instead he got into a coal train – which turned out not to be stopping until Retford. At that station Russell went to the goods yard and found that a 'special goods' was due to go back north, so he got into the guard's van. The guard objected and reported him to the station clerk, who ordered him out. A few minutes later he was ejected from the footplate of another train. After that he left the station and went to the nearby Queen's Hotel to order a 'conveyance', but lost patience waiting for it and set off on foot in the dead of night. He followed the road to a level crossing, when he started walking along the railway instead. Russell had got as far as Ranskill when he was run over and killed by the 'special goods' at about 11.10pm on 3rd December. His body was examined by his brother, the Bawtry surgeon.

However, trespassing cases did not usually receive such attention; more normally there was a brief note, such as to the effect that George Daniels had been killed trespassing on the line at Biggleswade in February 1856.

In the early years, drunks often ended up on the tracks with fatal results. Alcohol was almost a basic feature of the working man's diet with beer a cheaper choice than tea or coffee and much safer to drink than water; men who worked by physical labour – such as railway firemen – had few alternatives. Thomas Newland was run over and killed on the line near York on 6th September 1855. In March 1871 a platelayer found the leg of a man on the track near Gateshead, then a little further on another leg and finally the trunk. The remains were identified as those of a Scot, McLeod, and it was "supposed he had been present at the great foot race at the Gateshead Borough Gardens on Saturday, and probably, under the influence of drink, had lain himself on the line at night and had been run over".[20] However, even railwaymen were prone to drink and paid the consequences; in June 1865 Matthew Reynolds, a railway labourer, spent the evening "drinking freely" in Peterborough and disappeared on to the line at about 11.00pm. He was found the next day, "frightfully mutilated, the head being nearly severed from the body".[21]

There were also tragedies involving children. In August 1863 at a footpath crossing near Barnet one boy was killed and his brother escaped so closely that the locomotive "brushed his heel". The coroner commented that local people could not be bothered to use a bridge as it meant a deviation and urged the foot crossing to be replaced by its own bridge.[22] Just after Christmas 1875 two boys were killed on the North Eastern Railway at Gateshead; they had been playing on the line and stepped out of the way of a goods train, only to be run over by a fish train going the other way.[23]

Generally crossing accidents were connected with misuse by non-railway staff, but occasionally keepers made errors (as at Riccall). Crossing keepers were themselves occasional victims, most commonly when hurrying to set the gates after being surprised. On 24th May 1856 the gatekeeper or 'policeman' at Tallington, John Kirk, was run down by a pilot engine which he had not been expecting: he hurried out to open the gates for its path and was killed. In June 1928 the 10.10am King's Cross to Edinburgh killed crossing keeper John Hedes who was reported as trying to close the gates at Grove Road crossing near Retford.[24] Such accidents were more common with hand-controlled gates and thus commoner in the early days.

On more than a few occasions trains ran through crossing gates that had been left closed to rail traffic. This happened at South Muskham on 31st October 1960, when a new diesel train on a trial run went through the gates in fog and narrowly missed killing four council workmen. At the same crossing on 30th January 1967 a middle-aged woman was killed whilst talking with the crossing keeper. A mile along the line a man and his son were killed at North Muskham crossing and another boy pulled to safety by the crossing keeper – three serious incidents within a mile and within only seven years.

Other accidents involved passengers, like George Hanson who was run over at Retford GNR station whilst crossing between the staggered up and down platforms on 3rd October 1874. "Both his legs were cut off, the body being thrown a distance of six yards", it was reported.[25]

In the early days the occasional passenger died on the journey – most often when getting in or out at the wrong times. However, in November 1845 Burgman Wharton, a clerk of the Great North of England Railway at York, was killed whilst travelling near Copmanthorpe station. He was "supposed to

A brave attempt to convey a sense of a collision in fog, on this occasion at Hornsey. By 1882 a number of more sensationalist papers were appearing, and this is one of the few pictures to actually try to show an accident taking place with people being killed. (Author)

have fallen when incautiously climbing from his seat to the top of one of the carriages".[26] In December 1848 a new captain and mate were on their way to Eyemouth to take over a sloop, using the North British Railway from Edinburgh although there was a slight problem in that their train did not stop at the nearest station, Burnmouth. So they decided to leap out of the carriage at Flemington Bridge near Ayton – in complete darkness. The mate eventually crawled into Ayton station with a broken arm and a search party was sent out to find the captain – who was dead. It was believed that he had hit the wall of the rock cutting and died of a fractured skull.[27]

Some just behaved foolishly whilst drunk. In June 1862 a sailor joined a King's Cross to Manchester train in a state of some inebriation. Passing Potters Bar, he decided to climb out of the window and to dance on the roof. His head hit a bridge and was "shattered". It was reported that "the body fell across the roof of the carriage, the blood flowing down the windows and on to the steps".[28]

Passengers also fell out of trains and occasionally attempted suicide. If they were travelling alone in a compartment, it was not always possible to find out how they came to be dead at the lineside. How did Algernon Kingsford end up dead by the tracks inside Stoke Tunnel in September 1882? When the parts

of a dead man were found on the line at St. Neots in October 1885, no-one knew who he was although he had been seen near the line the previous day in an 'agitated' state.[29]

Others simply jumped out – and some survived, most famously the criminal Charlie Peace[30] albeit his train had just left the East Coast line and was heading to Sheffield near Kiveton Park. In September 1860 a man jumped out of a 'speeding' train (well, 30-40mph) near Tallington on a dark night and was presumed dead. Having bounced on the ballast and then plunged head first into a mound of gravel, he walked to Tallington station. "He appeared to be frenzied from the effects of liquor", it was reported.[31] In April 1862 another convict took his example from Peace and tried to jump out of a train in Peascliffe Tunnel near Grantham; like Peace, he was still handcuffed. As a result his skull was badly fractured and his arm trapped beneath the wheels so that "his left arm was completely ground to a jelly by the wheels of the train passing over it". An engine was sent to find him but he died at the Railway Inn. He had been on a 'ticket of leave' from a seven-year sentence of transportation for burglary.[32]

In the annals of the East Coast Main Line, one 'accident' that should not be omitted is the legendary 'accident that never happened.' This started with a letter from Dr. Waddington of Wakefield, printed in *The Times* on 27th March 1860 and then regurgitated in *The Guardian* the following day. Waddington, apparently writing from the safety of an hotel room in Charing Cross, reported how he had left Wakefield that morning by Great Northern only to be involved in a hideous accident approaching Doncaster. He was "suddenly alarmed by violent oscillation of the carriages", following which the engine, its tender and the first carriage left the rails, overturned and went down an embankment. Waddington reported that the driver leapt clear but the stoker had a bad head injury and eight passengers were trapped in a carriage crushed beneath the wreckage. "The shrieks of the passengers in the overturned carriage were fearful and for some time their extrication was impossible", he reported. Waddington said the tyre of the locomotive had "flown off" and "it is clear that the engine was not in a condition to ply between the stations of the Great Northern Railway." It was not expected that the stoker would live.

This report was followed the next day by a terse response from the Great Northern, saying that there had been no accident at all on its system that day and that there was no Dr. Waddington staying at the hotel in London. Then a real Dr. Edward Waddington of Wakefield wrote in to say that he had not been travelling by train that day. Someone, then, had played a dirty trick on the Great Northern and *The Times*… but who might it have been? However, the dirt did not stop there, for there was then correspondence in the *British Medical Journal*[33] condemning the real Waddington for claiming himself to be 'MD' despite not having attended university.

The story of East Coast disasters includes several trains being buried in bogs with men being dug out and a few narrow escapes from death by falling from a height or drowning. The accident at Carlton-on-Trent in August 1853 is thus not notable for the death toll, but for the ways in which passengers survived being immersed in water on a stormy night. One of the passengers recalled "in the midst of rushing water, the carriages were dashed to pieces in fearful confusion" as the engine plunged deep into a dyke filled with water. Edward Maitland recalled "in the midnight darkness and pouring rain, we were struggling to recover ourselves from what seemed a drowning fate, I groped about in the water and rescued my infant, and my son in the same way saved his little brother. The hand of God alone saved us from destruction in that awful night".[34]

Tunnels and viaducts were potentially the worst place for disaster though the worst tunnel disaster, at Welwyn, luckily involved goods trains.[35] There were narrow escapes from disaster on viaducts, including the turning over of a passenger carriage on the Newcastle High Level Bridge and near disaster on the viaduct over the River Idle at Bawtry such as in October 1853 when a passenger train narrowly avoided hitting a goods train where a broken wagon axle had caused derailment.

Most of the accidents in this book are operating accidents – in other words, the main cause of the accident lay in the train, the track or the signalling. The technology of these changed enormously over the course of more than 150 years of railway operation so an overview of these changes is helpful.

Railway signalling evolved from a simple system of trying to keep trains apart by an interval of time, to the use of signals to indicate aspects of safety and then to the concept of a block of space separating trains rather than time.

Until the late 1860s the NER mainly used rotating disc signals which showed a red face to oncoming trains if there was danger and no face (ie they were 'end on') if clear, with corresponding red and white lights at night.

The North British Railway at first used a system of flags and fixed boards for its signals – a white board for clear whilst a green flag or board meant caution to walking pace whilst red meant stop, albeit 'with reservations.'[36] In 1848 it experimented with a time interval signal that involved a ball being hoisted to the top of a tall post when a train passed, then gradually descending.

As far as signalling was concerned, the Great Northern gained some benefit in not immediately adopting practice already established elsewhere until comparatively late and it was able to instruct its officers to develop a signalling system in 1848.[37] The North Eastern's constituents operated without semaphores until about 1852[38] but began to install signals on its main lines from 1851.[39] Indeed, one historian of the GNR has said that it "profited from the experience of earlier railways, and from the start provided semaphore signals".[40] The semaphore signal had developed in place of the earliest signal – a man with a flag, initially operating on a 'time interval' system, which had had the intrinsic disadvantage of providing no protection against a train ahead which had broken down. This was eventually replaced by the 'block' system, by which a train could not enter a section unless a signalman ahead had confirmed that the preceding one had left; this system relied on a telegraph connection between signalmen.

In the early 1850s the drivers of the NBR had a rather relaxed approach to signals as their locomotive superintendent felt that a danger signal was advisory rather than compulsory. A driver who ignored a signal at Dunbar was found guilty of a breach of duty despite the defence by William Smith, the locomotive superintendent.[41] Smith himself was on the footplate when a light engine passed the red light being shown by a train starter at the east end of Edinburgh station in August 1853; Smith was reprimanded by his directors. This slack and dangerous manner of working was also the key factor in the fatal accident at Calton Tunnel in December 1854, covered in Chapter 8, and which led to a successful criminal prosecution.

The Great Northern started operating on the time interval system, with signals being put to danger for five minutes after a train had passed, then kept at caution for another eight minutes and eventually to clear after the set interval. The presumption that 'clear' was the normal position clearly increased risks.

The Great Northern also introduced fixed signals at stations – the origins of the 'home' signal. Trains had to stop if the arm was extended horizontally, to slow to caution if the arm was at 45° but if the arm dropped to vertical into the slotted post the signal could be passed at 'clear'. Problems with the signal sticking in the 'clear' position, especially in snow and ice, were to be fatal in years to come notably at Abbotts Ripton[42] in 1876 during a snow storm where other signals also failed in a 'clear' position. The slotted post, with the signal arm pivoted inside the slot, was also common on the North Eastern Railway.[43] Edward French of the GNR is said to have invented the centre-balanced 'somersault' arm as a replacement in 1877. However, the North Eastern's slotted post signals continued in use into the 1960s[44] but the NER was more adventurous in installing one of the first automatic signalling systems in Britain between Alne and Thirsk in 1905[45] and electro-pneumatic signalling at Newcastle in 1909.

As speeds increased in advance of braking power, signals needed to give a warning at a greater distance. To the 'home' signals were added additional caution signals at junctions and later 'caution' or 'distant' were signals developed to give advanced warning of the home signals. The NER's distant signals caused complaints amongst its engine drivers in 1873 as they were low down and sometimes did not work properly.[46] To start with, the Great Northern only had 'signalmen' working points and signals at junctions whereas the semaphores at a station were the work of lower grade staff[47] as they also were on the North British. Signals were accompanied by lights – at first white for clear, green for caution and red for danger. Initially these were illuminated by candles, later by oil. It took surprisingly long for the 'white' signal to be identified as a risk and then eliminated – into the late 1880s on main railway companies although from 1893 green was the standard 'proceed' indication; the GNR had begun adopting green from 1877 and at the same time began to add a ring to signals that applied to its goods lines – giving them also a purple light.

The 'absolute block' system became common, but there was also the 'permissive block' where a train was allowed to enter a block even though another was in front of it – commonly used for movements of goods trains and leading to several accidents. On the GN line and the North Eastern it was also common for goods trains to shunt at wayside stations and this was, of course, protected by the 'block' system; however, several accidents showed the risk of a train over-running the previous block section and so hitting a train shunting in the next block section – this is a feature of several accidents in this book such as at Arlesey

Holloway station looking north with GNR 2-2-2 No. 879 on an up train. On the right, under the up main distant signals, is a fogman's hut. No room for creature comforts in there!

(Allan Sibley)

Siding in 1876. The solution to this was 'blocking ahead' or 'blocking back' to create an extra space between the trains.[48]

On the earliest railways signals were controlled by a man adjacent to them, but more remote control gradually replaced this using rods or wires grouped together and operated from a signal box – especially for distant signals. The invention of signal control by wire is often attributed to Robert Skelden in 1847, who was at Hawick Junction on the North British at the time, and his company soon installed a system at Dunbar; this also enabled the development of the distant signal. However, there were limits to the distance at which a signal could be operated using these methods, hence sections between stations often had intermediate boxes though these were also associated with providing extra 'blocks' to increase the capacity of the line. An example of this was Wymondley, between Hitchin and Stevenage[49] whilst the block box at Peascliffe features in an accident in this book.

Effective block working replaced a 'time interval' between trains with a more secure 'space interval' but it could be improved by telegraph operation, first being effectively promoted in the pamphlet *Telegraphic Railways* of 1842 although previously considered by the Stockton & Darlington in 1832.[50] Telegraphs were installed along the North Eastern Railway from about 1846, but not at that stage used to control trains.[51] The telegraph ran from York to Berwick by 1847 and by 1854 was being used to send messages for train control.[52] In 1851 the Great Northern contracted with the Electric Telegraph Company to install the telegraph over its system. It was first set up through tunnels in the London area and extended to York by 1852.[53] This was the same year in which the electric bell and block telegraph were combined in a single invention to enable coded communication between signal boxes. However, the electric telegraph was not used for signalling at this stage except through the tunnels (there was a serious fear of collision in a tunnel) but from 1854 the GN gradually installed block telegraph working as far as Hitchin by 1856, with nineteen telegraph 'stations',[54] and at Peterborough and Doncaster; intervening sections, though, had no block telegraph. The introduction of the block system and the telegraph consolidated the importance of the signalman working from a signal box but some signals – such as shunting signals – were still worked separately and this contributed to the accident at Retford in 1869.

At the end of 1860 the GNR relaxed its block signalling system, partly as a result of heavy traffic joining from the Midland Railway at Hitchin. The places deemed most vulnerable – the London tunnels again – were to be controlled by a proper block system but for the rest as far north as Hitchin there was to be a mix of time and space intervals regulated by electric telegraph. Under this system, a following train could be allowed to enter the next section after the signalman had telegraphed ahead to the next box and also warned the driver – this was a type of 'permissive block' working and carried inherent risks apart from the fact the instructions were so confusing that Colonel Yolland referred to them as "not very intelligible" when investigating a collision at Colney Hatch (later New Southgate) in 1865. Yolland said that "as far as I can make out from these instructions, the block system is entirely given up…" Yolland was astonished that the 'ordinary rule' of at least a five-minute gap did not apply on the GNR, except perhaps where there was a tunnel. The main cause of the accident was in fact the error of a Midland Railway driver, but Yolland pointed out this driver knew very little about GNR regulations. Yolland was also upset about the means by which a train was 'cautioned' which did not require the train to be actually stopped at a signal first. Following this embarrassment, the GNR reverted to block working.[55] The accident in one of the Welwyn tunnels in 1866 led to extensions of and improvements to the block system and a return to the true absolute block system south of Hitchin.[56] The whole saga shows the way in which safety systems were an attempt to balance cost and risk, but also by the 1860s a powerful press could be as effective an influence for change as the Board of Trade's inspectors.

Nonetheless the GNR's improvements were still piecemeal. A special committee made visits to various places on the line in 1868, but only agreed to extensions in key places such as Peterborough and Grantham. Only after another accident at Retford in 1869 was more effort made and block working introduced over the whole line south of Peterborough in 1871.[57]

By 1872 the whole line to Doncaster was covered, with many additional wayside signal boxes having been provided. Almost immediately, though, the company discovered it had not allowed for enough capacity and built more boxes.

The North Eastern was similarly sporadic at improvements. Not until May 1871, following an accident at Thirsk, did it decide to fully install the absolute block system[58] and take the 'first steps' to introducing interlocking. A petition from its drivers in 1873 forced the NER to respond more energetically but work was not completed until 1878.

The telephone was not invented until 1875 but then quickly became a feature of the railway system with signal boxes soon being connected. The telephone was a development of the 'speaking' telegraph block instrument system that expanded on the GNR in the 1870s. However, as several accidents in this book illustrate, the first systems did not allow indiscriminate access to 'the line' and men needing to send urgent messages were prevented from doing so as others refused to 'give way.' A factor in the Abbotts Ripton disaster[59] was limited access to the speaking telegraph for the signalmen.

Initially signalmen controlled signals and points but it was physically possible to set one against the other. This problem was solved by interlocking – which meant that a point could not be set for a particular route without the corresponding signal having been pulled 'off' – and the Great Northern began introducing this from about 1866 with Hitchin being one of the first in 1867[60] although it was hardly in the vanguard of improvement in this respect. The North Eastern also began adopting the system from 1867 and it was generally in place by 1871, having been prioritised following the accidents at Thirsk and Brockley Whins.[61] However, neither was at the forefront since the first interlocking points and signals were at the East Retford Junction of the Manchester, Sheffield & Lincolnshire in 1852 – so the Great Northern would have been well aware of the possibilities.[62] Subsequently the railway inspectors placed considerable pressure on railway companies to adopt the system and most of the GNR main line was resignalled with interlocking in the mid-1870s.

An historian of GNR signalling summarises it as a conservative, perhaps parsimonious, company: "The GNR was very conservative in its approach to signalling and allocated its resources sparingly. Although it conformed to the Board of Trade's latest requirements, it never did more than was necessary and during the first decade of the 20th century it was completely unmoved by the vogue for power signalling embraced enthusiastically by a number of other railway companies."[63]

In the same book the GNR Engineer Richard Johnson was blamed for his opposition to interlocking which delayed the spread of it in the company's system until the 1870s.[64] Block signalling and interlocking effectively became a requirement of the Board of Trade following the passage of the Regulation of Railways Act, 1889.

In the event of a train breaking down or derailing, there were strict rules which applied. In the early days these were important because locomotives sometimes 'ran out of steam' between signal posts and had to wait to get steam up again. The guard was then required to walk back from the rear of the train to give hand signals to warn any oncoming train; later detonators could be placed on the track, the first of these appearing in about 1845.

Detonators were also very important in fog after they were invented in 1841. The North Eastern Railway positioned 'fog markers' about 200 yards from the signal box, which acted as a guide for the signalman when fog working needed to be introduced. At first detonators were placed on the track by railway employees such as platelayers, who often lived in tied houses near the line and could be called out at any hour. Later signal boxes were given equipment that allowed detonators to be placed on the track remotely.

Fog was a problem for the signalman, who might not be able to see where a train was standing. Another problem was that signalmen might sometimes forget altogether that they had a train waiting at a signal and the solution to both issues was track circuiting whereby a train standing at a particular place showed an indicator in the signal box. Many of the earliest accidents could have been prevented by this system but it did not become known in Britain until the early 1890s. At first known as 'insulated rails', the GNR began introducing the practice at Gas Works[65] Tunnel north of King's Cross in 1896[66] and at King's Cross itself from about 1900.

Signals depended on drivers seeing and reacting to them and the problem of how to reduce the risk of this taxed railway engineers for many years. Vincent Raven of the NER developed a mechanical system of cab warnings from about 1896 and an electrical one from 1905 which was installed between Newcastle and Durham.[67] Widespread use of the automatic train control (ATC) or automatic warning system (AWS) was delayed repeatedly, indeed abandoned by the LNER,[68] until the late 1950s after which magnets placed in the track interacted with indicators in the locomotive cab to give visual and audible warnings to the driver. After the Morpeth accident of 1969 they were also used to give advance warning of speed restrictions.

Track was generally wrought iron, with steel being introduced gradually. Steel rails were laid by the NER on the Newcastle High Level Bridge in 1862 but widespread use did not really accelerate until 1873.[69]

The other key operational factor in many accidents was the stopping of the train. Early trains had no real brakes at all but could be stopped by putting the engine into reverse. Later the tender would have a hand brake and trains also had a 'brake van' controlled by the guard – the driver could whistle for the brake to be put on. 'Distant' signals evolved to give advance warning and had to be placed at increasing distances as speeds advanced – only 600 yards or so to start with, up to 1,200 yards by the 1870s. These signals were amongst the first to be wire operated.

Passenger trains were gradually equipped with continuous brakes so that every carriage was braked, all being controlled through a vacuum system. The NER experimented with Westinghouse air brakes and in March 1874 ran trial trains between Newcastle and Berwick, but the slow adoption of continuous brakes contributed to the accident at Morpeth in March 1877 where damage would have been less had carriages been able to brake automatically once detached. Following discussions with the American Westinghouse, the GNR opted to try Smith's vacuum brake in April 1875. In June 1875 trials of various systems were conducted on the Midland Railway at

Newark, the GNR supplying a train with Smith's brake. The GNR became more enthusiastic after the Abbotts Ripton accident and by May 1877 reported that it had fitted vacuum brakes to all fast stock except that on Scottish services. In June 1877 some Scottish stock was equipped with the Smith vacuum brake. In June 1879 the North Eastern Railway held its own trials with Westinghouse brakes, which it adopted, except for the Scottish stock shared with the other companies. Typically, the Great Northern engaged in some obfuscation by claiming that its use of Smith's brake meant that it could be "self-acting in cases of accident"; this claim was soundly rebuffed by experts who reported that each carriage was not braked and 'sucking pumps' installed had never been used.[70] A report of 1878 acknowledged that the North Eastern and North British had both adopted the Westinghouse brake whereas the GN had gone for vacuum brakes[71] and this duality caused problems for some years with the GNR gradually adopting the automatic vacuum from the early 1880s.[72] Continuous brakes were required for all passenger trains after the Regulation of Railways Act, 1889. However, most goods trains did not have this until into the twentieth century, although the London & North Eastern introduced a 20-ton brake van for its fastest services in 1929 that became a standard for years to follow.

Some of the key figures in this story are the Government railway inspectors. As a result of the Railway Regulation Act of 1840, from 1842 any railway accident where a member of the public was injured had to be reported to the Board of Trade which could send an inspector to investigate although, in many early accidents, the wreckage and evidence was often cleared away before the inspector could examine it. Inspectors often used their reports to try to persuade the companies into making systemic improvements which were not actually required by law as Government was often reluctant to force requirements on companies. It took the Armagh accident of 1889 to overcome this reluctance and enforce block working with interlocking of signals and connections on all passenger lines, whilst passenger trains then had to have continuous automatic brakes. Inspectors also visited lines to approve their opening for passenger traffic.

As previously noted, for the first 70 years or so the East Coast line was operated by three companies – the Great Northern, North Eastern and North British. From 1923 these three were 'grouped' into one – the London & North Eastern Railway – and of course from 1948 these became part of the nationalised British Railways. At the end of the 1990s the story became more complex after privatisation, with the running and operating of trains being the preserve of firstly the Great North Eastern Railway and then a series of successors with varying fortunes. The track and equipment was operated and maintained separately, firstly by Railtrack with much of the work performed by its contractors. The resultant complications were a significant factor in the accidents at Hatfield in 2000 (see Chapter 4) and Potters Bar in 2002 (see Chapter 8) as well as a minor but significant derailment at King's Cross. Railtrack was later succeeded by Network Rail with much of the work then being handled 'in house.'

FOOTNOTES

1 Many early Board of Trade returns listed accidents by company but not their precise location
2 P W Kingsford, *Victorian Railwaymen*, p.47
3 *Appendix* to the *Report of the Commissioners of Railways*, 1849, p.303
4 *Penny Illustrated Paper*, 19 August 1871
5 John Slack, *The Secret Life of St Neots Station*, Ashbourne, 2010, p.88
6 Hitchin South signal box records, from Derek Talbot and Allan Sibley.
10 *Newcastle Courant*, 2 June 1871.
11 *The Secret Life of St Neots Station*, John Slack, Ashbourne, 2010, p.54
12 Adshead Elliott, *The Workmen's Compensation Acts*, London, p.23
13 J Wrottesley, *The Great Northern Railway Vol II*, London, 1979, p.129
14 See Chapter 2.
15 *The Times*, 8 January 1957.
16 *Northern Echo*, 8 August 1892
17 Some reports 'Haig'
18 A J Wrottesley, *Great Northern Railway*, London, 1981, vol.1, p.191-2
19 *Bedfordshire Mercury*, 16 May 1860.
20 *Newcastle Courant*, 13 March 1871
21 *The News Magazine*, 1865; this seems to have been an annual summary of the news by the headteacher of the local school.
22 *Penny Illustrated Paper*, 29 August 1863.
23 *Leicester Chronicle*, 1 January 1876
24 This is as it was reported at the time, but it seems surprising such a busy box had no gate 'wheel' or perhaps the press account assumed that these were manual gates.
25 *Manchester Guardian*, 6 October 1874.
26 *Newcastle Courant*, 6 November 1845.
27 *Manchester Guardian*, 1 January 1849
28 *Penny Illustrated Paper*, 12 April 1862
29 Slack, p.74.
30 Peace was a notorious master-burglar and murderer, who was being taken back to Sheffield where he had murdered a woman. He was later hanged at Leeds.
31 *The Times*, 26 September 1860.
32 *Penny Illustrated Paper*, 28 June 1862
33 *British Medical Journal*, 20 October 1860
34 *The Times*, 17 August 1853
35 See Chapter 8.
36 John Thomas, *The North British Railway*, volume 1, Newton Abbot, 1969, p.53
37 A J Wrottesley, *Great Northern Railway*, London, 1981, vol. 1, p.30
38 C J Allen, *North Eastern Railway*, Shepperton, 1966, p.212
39 W W Tomlinson, *North Eastern Railway*, Newcastle, 1915, p.532
40 Wrottesley, vol. 1, p.38
41 Thomas, volume 1, p. 72
42 See Chapter 7
43 An example of one can be seen on: ; accessed 11 November 2011.
44 Letter and notes from Michael Back, 20 May 2012. David Percival refers to one surviving at Haxby, between York and Scarborough, until the early 1980s.
45 Allen, p.225
46 Allen, p.223
47 Vanns, *An Illustrated History of Great Northern Signalling*, p.12
48 Several correspondents have queried the term 'blocking *back*' but on 7 January 1877 *The Observer* reported: 'The shunting at Arlesey ought not to have been allowed until the line had been – to use a technical term – 'blocked back' to Cadwell.
49 Wrottesley, vol. 1, p.124
50 Tomlinson, p.371
51 Allen, p.212
52 Tomlinson, p.533
53 Wrottesley, vol. 1, p.86
54 Report on the accident at Colney Hatch, 30 August 1865.
55 Wrottesley, volume 1, p.128
56 Vanns, p. 13
57 Vanns, p.14
58 C J Allen, *The North Eastern Railway*, Shepperton, 1964, p.146
59 See Chapter 7. The railway spelt its name as given but the local spelling was 'Abbots'.
60 Wrottesley, volume 1, p.175
61 Tomlinson, p.649
62 J Simmons and G Biddle, *Oxford Companion to Railway History*, Oxford, 1997, p.447
63 Michael Vanns, *An Illustrated History of Great Northern Railway Signalling*, Shepperton, 2000, p.5
64 Vanns, p.12
65 Purists may dispute the name being 'Gasworks' but it has been both; David Percival cites the 1960 Sectional Appendix, which spells it without a space five times and with one three times.
66 J Simmons and G Biddle, *Oxford Companion to British Railway History*, Oxford, 1997, p.523
67 *The Times*, 10 September 1913
68 Allen, p.225
69 Tomlinson, p.671
70 *The Times*, 3 August 1877.
71 *The Times*, 27 September 1878.
72 J Wrottesley, *The Great Northern Railway Vol II*, London, 1979, p.148

2

DRIVER ERROR

Missed Signals – Losing Control – Shunting Errors – Excessive Speed – The Effects of Alcohol

1. Missed Signals

In the early days trains fitted with only the most rudimentary systems of braking depended on the vigilance of their drivers to avoid accidents. Although signalling soon developed to reduce the risk, safety still depended on the driver seeing the actual signal and automatic warning systems with in-cab displays did not start to gain a foothold until the early twentieth century and then took 50 years to become adopted nationally.

In August 1873 a collision at Retford resulted in three fatalities – making it only a moderate disaster by the standards of the time although it attracted a great deal of press attention due to the unusual image of one train slicing through another at a crossing of two main railway lines. Though the cause of the accident was attributed to the driver of one of the trains, the arrangements at the crossing were heavily criticised and substantially altered thereafter. The arrangement at Retford requires some background explanation.

In 1846 Parliament had authorised two lines that crossed at Retford – the Great Northern from Grantham to Doncaster and the Manchester, Sheffield & Lincolnshire[1] from Sheffield to Grimsby. The deposited plans showed that the lines would be built on levels 9ft apart but the 'limits of deviation' allowed for the GNR to be built 5ft higher than on its plans so that it could cross the MSL on the level, though the latter was opened first by a few weeks in 1849 and so held 'right of way'. The crossing of the two was in the charge of an MSL signalman who controlled a home signal on the GNR line; the GNR signalman had to secure his permission for a train to cross. A curve from the GNR south of the flat crossing towards the west onto the MSLR line allowed the GNR to operate through trains from London to Sheffield, as well as to reverse its trains into Retford MSLR station until its own premises opened in 1852.[2] After this, passengers had to make their own way between the two stations.

In February 1854 a better arrangement was announced with temporary platforms and a booking office close to the crossing.[3] The MSLR station was closed and all passenger trains diverted to call at the GNR station just to the north of the crossing on 1st July 1859. This meant that trains from Sheffield took the new Ordsall or 'Whisker Hill' curve into the north end of the GNR station, after this was opened on the same day as the station.[4]

They then crossed the main GNR line and regained the MSLR line via a curve at the south end of the GN station. To make matters more complicated, a siding looped behind the GNR platform on the west side of the station and also crossed the MSLR Ordsall curve on the level. When Colonel Rich investigated the 1873 accident, he thought these other crossings were much more dangerous than the famous level crossing itself.[5]

This complicated arrangement was controlled by equally complex signalling. The MSLR part was relatively straightforward – it had a signal box at the flat crossing which controlled their line and the home signal for the GNR line. The GNR had its 'Tower' signal box which controlled its station and a flagman at the north end of the down platform who controlled the crossing over the west to north loop. The Tower cabin had a distant signal and a home signal for the up line, the latter in the station and only about 90 yards from the crossing. The crossing home signal had no accompanying distant signal; this was seen as unnecessary since all trains (except the 'Flying Scotchman'[6]) stopped at Retford – and even the 'Scotchman' only passed at 6mph. However, trains could pull into Retford station and be only 90yards away from another train going over the level crossing. If they wanted to go straight on they had to whistle twice, if round the curve to Gainsborough then thrice. If the Tower signalman wanted a route over the crossing, he had to sound a gong to draw the attention of the Crossing signalman – or send a message. Although Colonel Rich found that the Tower signalmen worked to rules, they were not printed or written down – he was concerned that if the signalmen died no-one would know what they were.

Nonetheless the busy station had been worked with only a few problems but none of them serious. On 28th February 1869 an up express collided at low speed with some goods wagons left on the up line whilst a down goods shunted to the sidings on the up side north of the station. On 24th August 1871 shunting had been taking place on the MSLR tracks when the rear wagon had fouled the crossing and been hit by a GNR train. On 1st January 1872 a Sheffield to Lincoln train had run through the siding at the back of the down platform and collided with empty stock on the south curve. A southbound GNR coal train had failed to stop in the station but the signalman had diverted it onto the north to east curve, where it had also collided with empty passenger stock. On another occasion a passenger train starting from the siding at the back of the down platform had been struck by an engine coming off the Ordsall curve.

On 23rd August 1873 a southbound fish train was arranged to run with a relief portion, driven by George Bryant. Under the rules this was expected to operate on the same arrangements as the original train, including stopping at Retford, although the driver still asked his guard whether they had anything to drop off there.

As he approached Retford, Bryant's fireman went out on the running plate – then a common practice – to oil the engine which had slowed to about 20mph. The signals could be seen well in advance – the distant and home signals controlled by the Tower for Retford station and the crossing home signal at danger beyond these. Charles Whitehead, the Tower signalman, had his distant set at 'all right' and the home signal set at 'caution'; this signal could not be set at 'all right' (although it could be at danger) and caution was the correct setting to permit the train into the platform so caution more or less meant the same as 'all right' – which was not meant to matter as all trains except the 'Scotchman' had to stop. The signal for the crossing could only show 'open' and 'closed' but had no distant signal to protect it as all trains were meant to stop in the station.

Except Bryant did not stop, but continued at something around 10-20mph through the station. His guard realised that they were going too fast and struggled to put his brake on, but Whitehead did not react. Crossing over in front of the fish train under clear signals was a thirteen-carriage excursion from Deepcar to Cleethorpes, with most of its passengers on a works outing for Greyson & Lowood. The fish train "dashed through the middle of the passenger train, completely cutting it in two."[7]

The fish train ran right through a carriage of the excursion train on the crossing, then its engine derailed and demolished much of the crossing signal box from which signalman Whelpton was lucky to escape, with "the bricks and other material being thrown about upon the unfortunate people". This box had been damaged in a collision only ten months before. Mr. and Mrs. Allott and their nephew, in one of the carriages, were all killed; Hannah Allott was found under the ruins of the signal box.

In the aftermath of the accident, many of the injured stayed on in Retford. Several agents for legal companies arrived, touting for business, and were made unwelcome. One of them was "publicly and ignominiously kicked out of the bar of one of the principal hotels" in the town.[8]

The Times quickly blamed the railway staff – "the accident, if it can be so called, for a due attention to the regulations would in all probability have averted the catastrophe". Colonel Rich, the Board of Trade inspector, had difficulty coping with several aspects of the accident when he investigated. His initial assumption was that Bryant had been drunk, telling those assembled that he had never known a driver risk his own life in such a way unless under the influence. Then he began his investigation by asking to see all the Acts and plans connected with the building of both lines and focussed on the 90 yard[9] space between the home signal and the crossing, which he considered inadequate. Rich soon began to hear stories about trains failing to stop quickly enough and fouling the level crossing. "I wish it to be distinctly understood that the arrangements do not seem to me to be satisfactory as regards this crossing" he observed on 6th September. He also disliked the Ordsall curve and the south curve from the station to the Gainsborough line built in 1862: "Colonel Rich thought these were much more dangerous than the crossing at which the accident occurred."[10] Before he had finished his inquiry he opined that the view of the Board of Trade was that the level crossing "must, if they had any power, be abolished".

That the railway companies suspected the signalling arrangement had contributed to the disaster was shown by their reaction. Before Rich had really made much progress with his investigation, they had devised plans to build a new signal box of 67 levers to control both lines at the crossing; it was also agreed that the station home signal would remain at danger unless the crossing signal was clear. However, the inquest recorded a verdict of manslaughter against Bryant, taking the view that the arrangements had not previously caused a fatal accident so it must have been due to the driver's lack of care. Bryant had been

censured for passing a distant signal eighteen months earlier. Rich's report was published in October and recommended a deviation or complete resignalling with interlocking.

The accident preyed on the mind of signalman Charles Whitehead at the Tower box, who had not previously been involved in any accident. He had had three choices when he realised disaster was imminent: to derail the fish train which would have risked killing its footplatemen, to have sent it round the curve and ensured a sidelong collision, or he could have let it carry straight on as it did. He effectively had to make a split second decision on which would be the 'least fatal' outcome. Whitehead was depressed by this and told a doctor that "when he saw the fish train rushing towards the passenger train he wished himself dead". He committed suicide that December.

Before leaving the subject of rail crossings, we should note that there was – and still is – a similar crossing at Newark, though without the other complexities that were a problem at Retford. Inspectors had wanted signals set to 'danger' but the Midland Railway had insisted that the normal setting should be 'clear' for its own trains as its line from Nottingham to Lincoln pre-dated the Great Northern.[11] However, the signals were provided by the GNR which also paid for the signalmen, although they were employees of the Midland.[12] The result was an accident on 4th October 1852 when a Great Northern express running an hour late "dashed through the middle of a goods train", hurling one of the goods trucks into the river. Both drivers had made frantic efforts to avert disaster – the GN's by putting his engine into reverse, the Midland's by trying to accelerate clear. No passenger was seriously hurt but all the carriages were damaged as they scraped through the goods train and the GN driver lost two teeth. The Midland driver was blamed initially as it was thought the signals were in the GN's favour, but terrible disaster was avoided here as it was the goods which was cut through. The signalman insisted that the signals had been set to danger against the Great Northern, but the GN's driver, stoker and guard all insisted they had seen clear signals. At this time signals were normally left at 'clear' or 'off'. Later it transpired that signals for the GN express had been changed from white for 'clear' to 'red' as the Midland's signalman gave priority to his own company's goods train. However, the Board of Trade held the Midland responsible.

Captain Wynne, the Board of Trade inspector, was very annoyed about this accident as his recommendations for making the crossing safer at the opening of the line had been ignored. He had recommended that "four distant signals should be maintained at the stop" – in other words, kept at danger, as he said was the common practice at many other junctions – and a crossing should be treated as a junction. But at Newark after the accident he found that "the signal at the crossing is so constructed that it can only stop one line; that is to say, when it is turned against one line, it necessarily opens the other..."[13]

The famous accident in the snow at Abbotts Ripton in 1876 occurred when a goods train was setting back into a siding to allow an express to pass and the latter ran through signals to hit it in the rear. On that occasion there were reasons for this happening but a very similar accident at Castle Hills Junction, the junction for the branch to Bedale north of Northallerton, on 4th October 1894 could not be explained by snow or – despite the conditions – fog.

The wreckage at Castle Hills Junction, Northallerton, in 1894 with the locomotives and Pullman carriage very evident.
(Author)

"marvellous escape" of the express train conductor. This man, Sanderson, was thrown out of his smashed van, "pitched over the carriage which followed it" and onto the platform of the Pullman carriage. Also fortunate was the guard of the mineral train who jumped from his moving train: "I heard a train coming a short distance off at high speed, I jumped off at the east side of the train, kept my feet, and my van had only moved forwards three or four yards when the collision occurred.'

The first vehicle behind the express locomotive was a van, then one carriage with few passengers and then the Pullman carriage *Iona,* behind that ordinary stock which suffered little damage and none was derailed. "So little were the coaches behind the Pullman affected that some sleeping children were not awakened."[14] However, two passengers were apparently so frightened that they "made off into a field, and when the special was made up to take the passengers south there was some difficulty in finding them."[15]

There were several features of the events before the accident that demonstrate how several problems can coalesce into a disaster. The first set of problems surrounded the 10.25pm Newcastle to Hull goods, which left Newcastle late and was 95 minutes late by the time it left Darlington. As there was no other refuge siding between Northallerton and Thirsk, it had to be shunted at Castle Hills Junction to avoid delaying the express – except the express was also running late, hence Darlington sent on the mineral train behind the goods and in advance of the express. The locomotive on this train was already running badly but at Darlington one van was detached and ten added – taking it over the loading limit; the shunter defended this by saying that most of the vans were only lightly loaded and the driver did not object, even though he was already having problems. The report condemned the adding of wagons as "highly improper". The problems got worse after Darlington with the train taking 52min instead of 32min to Castle Hills and, because the express was late, the mineral train was sent out behind the goods.

Charles Clack, driving the train engine of the express, had also been having problems and at Darlington had called for a pilot engine to be added on the front. Clack knew that it was still his responsibility to check for signals under rule 290, but as they pressed on at about 60mph he saw almost none of the signals at all: "I saw none of the Caunton signals, nor of the Danby Wiske, nor Wiske Moor signals, nor the Castle Hills up

One factor that certainly contributed was the practice – by this time hardly suitable for a main line with speeding expresses – of handling the mix of slow and fast trains by getting the slow trains to set back into sidings when a fast was approaching behind. In the small hours of 4th October 1894, with thick ground fog causing problems, the signalman at Castle Hills Junction had first one goods train, and then a following mineral train, to deal with in this way whilst anticipating the arrival of the 10.40pm Edinburgh to King's Cross.

Signalman John Almond shunted the first train, which was labouring with a heavy load and an engine that was steaming poorly, back into the long siding on the up side and instructed its driver to set back far enough so that he could put another train into the siding in front of it. This second train, a more lightly loaded train mainly carrying coke, had been held up by the preceding goods and arrived at Castle Hills only a few minutes later. It stopped and was slowly starting to set back when Almond was distracted by the "violent shaking of the block instrument"; this was because the signalman at Wiske Moor was trying to send an urgent message to say that the expected express had passed all his signals at danger and was on its way to Castle Hills Junction.

Within what seemed like seconds it was there, approaching at 60mph with apparent disregard of signals in the fog. The driver of the first goods train, realising the situation, blew sharp blasts on his whistle and the express seemed to slow – perhaps from 60 to 40mph, over the next 200 yards as it bore down on the shunting mineral train. The double-headed express ploughed into the mineral train at 3.06am, killing the driver of the leading engine and badly injuring the fireman – who was unconscious for several days and who could never recall the events preceding the accident. However, perhaps the most remarkable part of this accident is the fact that not a single passenger of the 130 or so was killed and the accident report was moved to refer to the

distant." He said this was due to a combination of the fog and steam beating back from the leading engine, driven by Adamson. They should have received a warning from fog signals at Wiske Moor, but the signalman there had no apparatus for placing detonators on the up line and said that he was unable to get across to it because of a down goods – though the inquiry was not convinced by this. Brakes had been applied, probably because the whistling of the goods in the siding at Castle Hills alerted Adamson to where he was, but had not been very effective in reducing the speed. Major-General Hutchinson's report suggested it was time to add extra relief lines for the mineral traffic but the real cause of this accident went with Adamson to the grave.

For some reason then both locomotive drivers missed all the Wiske Moor signals at danger. This might have been fog but the accident report still could not satisfactorily explain the "extraordinary fact" of Driver Adamson on the leading engine with 43 years' experience passing all the signals at danger and at speed. Although four of the signals were on "lofty" posts and might have been obscured by ground fog, the Wiske Moor advanced home signal was not and should have been easily visible. Adamson and his firemen both knew the route well, so should have been alert for the risks. The inquiry could only comment on their long working hours – they were both 9½ hours into a twelve-hour shift.

The next major incident occurred several years after the end of the Great War. When an up goods, loaded to 50 wagons, stopped on the up main through line at Retford station in the early morning of 13th February 1923, it did so as a result of a number of minor errors. In its load was a cattle wagon, marshalled somewhere in the middle, that was being sent to Kiveton Park, just a few miles away on the ex-GCR Sheffield line. Despite this proximity, the goods porter at Doncaster Decoy did not know where Kiveton Park was and so telegraphed Peterborough to tell them it would be detached there.

Its driver was aware he would need to stop at Retford, but failed to give the 'crow' whistle as he passed Ranskill box that would have led to him being diverted into the up goods loop between Canal and Babworth boxes. Instead he stopped on the through line where Retford station staff dealt with the unexpected problem efficiently; however, although they knew an up express was expected, they chose to split the train on the through line and only then thought to shunt it out of the way into the platform road.

Bearing down on it was 4-4-2 No.298/Z[16] with a train of sleeping cars and a few fish trucks, travelling at 'high speed'. As the goods was setting back, the express tore into its side, crushing the brake van and smashing sixteen wagons. The express engine overturned, probably as its carriages pushed the tender up over the footplate – killing the driver, fireman and a locomotive inspector. *The Times* reporter referred to the tender having been "thrown over" the engine. No passengers were killed. Wrecked goods wagons were strewn around, leaving a bizarre mixture of fish, sweets and farm produce.

Driver Jubb and Fireman Tubbs were experienced men whilst they were also with Acting Inspector Turner, who was travelling to test the coal. Did the extra person prove a distraction? Certainly a number of accidents on the line involved additional men on the footplate.

"The accident happened in thick fog at a spot where shunting is constantly taking place" commented *The Times*,[17] which seemed clear as to the causes. The press commentaries make several references to thick fog, but witnesses were inconsistent as to the extent of the fog at the time of the actual accident. The jury at the inquest decided the driver had overrun signals due to fog and requested fog signals be provided. The accident was never satisfactorily explained, though its cause was obvious to Col. Pringle: "failure of the enginemen of the express to observe and obey the danger position of signals was the direct cause of this lamentable accident". Why they did so went with them to the grave, though the Colonel felt "this case is typical of the class of accident preventable by automatic train control". The fog alone could not be blamed, as the train must then have been going too fast for the conditions. The geographically ignorant porter at Decoy also took some of the blame.

Pringle's investigation took account of the signalling arrangements at Retford North, Babworth and Canal, where the signals were closer together than he liked though arranged so that they linked with each other. Some thought it was misty, but not foggy enough to explain why three men ignored signals.[18] Pringle also noted that two signalmen had realised the danger and had tried to place detonators – but had not had the time; he suggested machines for doing this should be installed.

The great press interest in the fog at Retford perhaps reflected that it had also been seen as a significant contributory factor in an accident there only a few months before – on 16th November 1922. On that occasion a Great Central train from Manchester to Cleethorpes had been preparing to leave the up platform when it was hit in the rear by a Great Northern local passenger train. Ten passengers and the GN guard were hurt. Major Hall concluded that Signalman Talbot in the North box had become confused in the fog and thought he had received a 'train out of section' signal from Green in the South box – which Green denied. Both men should have known that a new rule of September 1922 required the out of section signal to be followed by a repetition of line clear one prior to any alteration of the block instrument to the line clear position – and this had not been sent.

During the years of the Second World War the main line saw very heavy traffic and some improvements were made to allow for this. For example, the additional goods or 'intermediate[19]' lines north of Potters Bar were authorised to be converted when necessary to allow their use by passenger trains although this only came into operation in January 1946. However, the layout was constricted because there were only two tracks through the station, so slow up trains had to cross to the up main line in order to call at the station, whilst the up slow line terminated in buffers just before the platform. The signalman at Potters Bar therefore had to often make decisions on whether to allow a train on the fast or slow lines to take precedence – and it was usually the former, of course.

On duty at Potters Bar box on the night of 10th February 1946 was T. Baines. Baines dealt with a Peterborough up local which ran from the slow to the fast line and had the late-running 9.32pm Hatfield to King's Cross approaching on the slow line and due to call at the station; but he also had the 5.00pm Bradford to King's Cross approaching further back on the fast line behind V2 No.4833. Part of his attention was also distracted by the approach from the south of the 9.45pm King's Cross to Edinburgh with another V2, No.4876.

Baines pulled off his inner and outer home signals to clear for the fast line and maintained at danger those for the slow line. However, he was shocked to see the local train run past the signals. Baines had seconds to make a decision, the sort of decision that no signalman wants to make – he had two trains and one track, but how could he cause the least damage and death? His greatest fear was that the slow train would run into the short siding and then onto the platform, killing the waiting passengers. Baines hastily reversed the up fast signals to danger and then tried to pull over the crossover from the up slow line to divert the train to the up main line.

Baines was seconds too late, changing the points under the first carriage of the local train. The N2 tank engine ran into the siding at the north end of the station and derailed, causing little damage, but the carriages derailed as the points changed between the bogies of the first carriage. The vehicles fouled both the up and down main lines.

The down Edinburgh express ran into the wreckage at about 40mph, derailing its locomotive and six of its crowded carriages. Seconds later – there was some confusion amongst witnesses over which train actually hit first – the Bradford train ran into the confusion having failed to stop at the hastily changed signals. Its fireman recalled seeing all the signals at clear, then spotting someone at the trackside waving a red lamp before the distant changed to caution and the inner home to danger. The Bradford train was almost brought to a stop before it was hit by the Edinburgh train's engine. A ganger thought the Bradford had stopped before the down train hit it. There was general confusion about the precise sequence of events.

The first three carriages of the local train were "almost completely demolished" and two soldiers in them were killed. The wooden bodies separated from the steel frames and were carried forwards by the locomotive of the down train. One of the frames was buckled into a 'U' shape around the front of the V2 and the buffer of one of the carriages punctured the locomotive's tender.

The locomotive on the up Bradford was struck a glancing blow by the down train engine and derailed, turning over. The down engine similarly turned on its side. In such a triple disaster, only the two soldiers died. It was generally considered that buckeye couplings saved many other lives.

In the dark, some of the railway staff had little idea what had happened. The fireman on the down train was bewildered and had no idea they had also hit an up express until he climbed out of his overturned engine and "we found the other engine the other side". He was one of those who thought the up train might have already been there when they derailed, whereas it arrived afterwards. Nonetheless he went to the signal box where Baines told him "It isn't you, you were all right."

The initial investigation seemed to go badly for Baines. The ganger reported going to the box and seeing the crossover 'pulled' while wreckage caused some of the signals to show clear when they should not have. Then Driver Stanley Trigg of the local arrived to give his evidence; he reported that the home signals had been showing a red for the up fast and a green for his own train and that he was "almost certain that the signal in the off position was the one applicable to the up slow line". His fireman, Dungate, backed him up by saying that the up slow distant had been 'on' but the outer home and inner home for the slow line were both 'off'.

This gave Lt. Col. Mount a bit of a problem – footplate crew and signalman were contradicting each other. To make matters worse for Baines, it was clear that he had altered his train register by a minute or two to make the sequence of events look better and had tried to get another signalman to do the same – though Colbert at Greenwood box refused to comply. However, there was widespread confusion about the precise sequence of

events, especially with the two expresses, so Baines's behaviour may be understood.

Mount decided that Trigg was responsible for having passed signals at danger, and thought that he might have confused the two sets of signals maybe having forgotten the changed use of the 'intermediate' line to passenger service.[20] Some considered Baines had made an error in changing the points beneath the train, but this was an understandable attempt to reduce disaster. Mount said that work in converting Potters Bar to two island platforms should be done as a matter of priority and commended Florence Halden, the woman guard of the local train, for meeting her duties in running up the track to warn the Bradford train.

Accidents also occurred in more recent times with the use of permissive working, where one train is permitted to enter a block section already occupied by a preceding train. This problem persisted into the early 1960s and on the East Coast line it was made more complex by the rules about the 'relief' lines; in fact these lines were known as 'goods' or 'slow' line according to the rules under which they were operated. So the down relief line between London and Peterborough, which was not continuous, had various sections of being either slow or goods; the difference was that a 'slow' line carried goods or passenger trains under absolute block rules, whereas a goods line could be used for goods trains operating under permissive block rules – unless a passenger train was diverted onto it, in which case permissive block working was not permitted. Permissive block working was useful on busy lines with goods traffic, as it enabled a series of goods trains to be drawn up out of the way of express passenger trains.

All this contributed to the multiple collision referred to as at Connington South 15th December 1961, although actually nearer to Wood Walton at milepost 66. The signalman at Connington South was having a busy evening, signalling first

an unfitted goods off the two-track section from Holme and onto the goods line beyond his box in very foggy conditions. This was followed by a fitted goods, hauled by a V2. Next through was 'Deltic' *Crepello* hauling an empty coaching stock train from Scotswood to Holloway and this was also signalled onto the goods line to make way for an express goods carrying meat from Aberdeen.

Perhaps not expecting to be sent onto the goods line, perhaps confused about permissive block working, and certainly going too fast in the conditions, Driver Jones ran his diesel locomotive into the rear of the fitted goods train in front of him. Wagons from this train were pushed over and fouled the up and down main lines. Within a couple of minutes, a northbound fast goods travelling at around 50mph behind an A3 Pacific struck one of the wagons a glancing blow and itself derailed on its side, taking 32 wagons with it. Several minutes later the fast goods from Aberdeen came up the main line and ploughed into the wreckage.

The signalman at Connington South was unaware of any problems until he received a call from Control at Peterborough – which had itself been alerted by a farmer who had heard the noise. Although the damage to stock was very considerable, this multiple pile-up resulted in not a single serious injury or fatality. Colonel McMullen blamed Jones but also commented that "permissive block working on goods lines is a legacy of the past". It was also considered that the lights from the diesel locomotive headcode panels reflected back off fog, making visibility more problematic.

Despite McMullen's comments in 1961, a system that was considered by some to be 'inherently dangerous' survived to be a factor in the fatal collision between Peterborough and Fletton Junction on 11th March 1968. This was the time when there was heavy traffic in flyash from coal-fired power stations for emptying into the old brick pits at Fletton. Late in the evening, a Drakelow to Fletton flyash train[21] should have arrived before the one from West Burton, but was in fact running behind it crewed by a driver, a trainee driver and a relief driver in the cab. The West Burton train pulled up at signals and the Drakelow was allowed to follow it under permissive block working[22] but the driver made an error of judgement and hit the back of the West Burton train.

Two of the flyash wagons were forced into the air and one came down on the cab of the following train's locomotive, killing two of the men and trapping relief driver Aubrey Dolman by the legs with a 20-ton wagon poised above him. The fire brigade was poorly prepared and had to resort to trying

Electric trains of the Newcastle suburban network collided at the city's Central station in 1951. (Author)

to cut him out with a hammer and cold chisel, during which operation they sustained Dolman with tea, sandwiches and a pipe of tobacco. Getting him out took ten hours and the fire brigade subsequently accepted that it needed better equipment.[23] Although permissive working clearly contributed to the accident, the Ministry of Transport inspector concluded that the second train should have been able to stop in the distance available given the visibility of the rear lights and the driver being aware of having a train in front of him.

Another mistake with permissive working killed a driver near Finsbury Park on 15th April 1971. An empty stock diesel multiple unit was signalled through Harringay West towards Finsbury Park on the up goods No.2 line. On entering the section Driver Holman's train was held for about a minute at a signal although rules on permissive working stipulated being 'brought nearly to a stand' and then cautioned. Holman then ran into the back of a car-transporter train standing ahead of him, blocking all the adjacent lines except the up fast. The first carriage of Holman's train was destroyed.

The car train was running very late and Driver Greensmith took charge of it at Harringay West at 16.25. At 17.58 he finally moved forwards, but only as far as Finsbury Park. At about 18.05 he spoke to the signalman by telephone and returned to his cab when his train was hit from behind – sufficiently hard to move it seven or eight yards.

The surviving guard on the diesel train, Cato, confirmed that they had been held by a signal for about a minute and he thought there had been no brake application at all. However, further evidence revealed that Holman had passed a signal at danger on four occasions, following which he had been confined to yard shunting duties for about a year. After restarting from the signal, he would not have seen the car train until 200 yards from its rear and was travelling at about 40mph. There was also the strong possibility that Holman had been misled by the stop at the signal and had not realised the section

ahead would still be occupied, there being no 'calling-on arm'. The regulations were amended so that a clear warning should be given.

Newcastle Central station has featured in many accidents over the years, but almost none of them have been fatal. Speeds in the station are slow due to its pronounced curve and the fact that almost all passenger services stop there – indeed, many terminate. A typical accident at Newcastle therefore includes an event such as that on 30th June 1977, when the 09.45 Newcastle to Newcastle via Benton failed to stop in time and hit the buffers at the end of the platform whilst still travelling at 4mph; 23 passengers and the guard were injured.

The eastern end of the station was especially busy with suburban services, particularly those running on the North Tyneside lines. These were electrified in 1904 and were organised in much the manner of a London commuter service: platforms had gates that could be closed when a train was due to depart, guards could signal readiness to depart to drivers using electronic push buttons on the platform pillars and there were similar links to the signal box. None of this proved sufficient to combat slack behaviour by railway staff and it was unable to prevent an electric train setting off against danger signals.

On 17th August 1951 Motorman R. Kindness was working a typical shift. He knew all the procedures well, having mainly driven electric trains around Newcastle since 1945. Having completed one working, he left his train at Newcastle Central and went to the room set aside for footplate staff to wait for his next turn, which was the 10.35 Newcastle to Newcastle via Wallsend. Kindness did not leave the staff room until 10.30am, then went to the toilet, before going up the platform to his train. It was a different unit to his previous one, so he had to walk along and write down all the numbers – though he did not record the number of the leading motor car as he thought he could do that later.

In Kindness's own account, he reached his cab at about the time the train was due to start and noted that signal 226, the starter, was at danger. He then said that he heard the ring of the guard's starting bell – rung from a bell-push on the platform to indicate that all was safe to start. Kindness later reported that, standing outside his cab, he saw the guard "walking away from the bell push with his green flag in his hand". He then got into his cab, checked that signal 226 was clear, then looked back to check the guard. The guard could not be seen, so Kindness assumed he had already got in and started the train. Within a few seconds he heard a lot of whistling and shouting so, thinking the train must have hit a barrow on the crossing or something, he braked. Just then, as his train emerged from behind a stationary locomotive with a couple of vans attached on an adjacent track, he saw another electric train coming into the station towards him in a conflicting movement. Kindness thought his own brake application had slowed his train to a stop by the time the other hit it – he had enough time to scramble across the cab to the far side and so escaped certain death. The driver of the in-coming train, Heir, was not so fortunate and

The aftermath of the accident at Welwyn Garden City in 1957, when A2/3 Pacific **Owen Tudor** *on the up 'Aberdonian' ran past signals in fog and collided with the rear of a local train.*

(Ben Brooksbank)

was killed. One passenger was killed outright and another died later; nineteen were taken to hospital.

The problem with the account of Kindness was that it tallied with almost nothing reported by other railway staff except in so far as he had been very late getting to his train.

Only Kindness himself claimed that his train had started from Platform 2 with signal 226 at clear and the evidence suggested the combined speed of the trains at the collision was 25mph – so few thought that he had brought his train to a standstill.

Both trains were eight-car electric units, built in 1937. The carriages were steel and the underframe of the outgoing train rode over that of the incoming one so that the front carriage of the arriving train was "converted to a mass of crumpled plate" and 35ft of its body side was torn off.

One possible excuse for Kindness was that he might have been unsighted, though of course he should not have proceeded without being sure of a signal. The electric units had retained their metal blackout screens to protect drivers from the sun's glare and also from stones that were thrown at the trains by vandals. Because of this, a driver at Platform 2 would have to lean forward to see signal 226. Similarly, it was not easy to see back to the guard's signal in the shade under the platform roof – this was why the guards also had buttons on a pillar that could be pushed to sound a bell and show an indicator. The station staff also had buttons to push when they were ready for a train

to start.

The incoming train was running about seven or eight minutes late. Signalman Blackburn at Newcastle No.1, who was liable to be accused if Kindness's account was correct, had identified that this would set up a possible conflicting move with the departing 10.35am and hesitated over what to do. He could have directed the incoming train to Platform 3, which would have avoided the conflicting movements, but decided in the end that this would cause problems for platform staff and so stuck to the original route. Blackburn was then astonished to see the 10.35am start to move out, so he immediately set all signals to danger and rushed to the steps of his box, blowing a whistle. He was 'emphatic' that signal 226 had been at danger the whole time. Inspector Richardson, who looked up when he heard the whistle, could only confirm that 226 was at danger at that time – as it would have to be if a train was being signalled in.

The guard on Kindness's train was F. Plenty, who reached the platform at 10.31am. He denied using the starting bell, but agreed he had shown the green flag – though this was not a sign for the driver to start if the signals did not permit it. He said that he knew signal 226 was at danger, so had sounded the bell that told the signal box the train was ready – not the one for the driver. Then he had jumped in and not seen the signal again. He was injured in the crash, with broken ribs.

Foreman Armstrong confirmed some of this story, being certain that the guard had pressed the bell that linked to the signal box. A Carriage and Wagon foreman, who had been a passenger on the outgoing train, was convinced there had been no brake application before the crash.

With this contrary evidence, Kindness was given a chance to respond by the investigating officer, Lt. Col. Wilson. The motorman insisted that the bell to start had been rung before he had even entered the driving cab, but that he never saw the green flag waved. He decided to retract his statement that his train had almost stopped before the collision. However, Wilson noted that "He could offer no satisfactory explanation for his arrival on the platform at the last minute after more than an hour with nothing to do."[24]

The only remaining possibility was a signal malfunction. Inspector Reid, of the Signal & Telegraph Department, thought there had been several occasions when the electro-pneumatic signals had wrongly cleared due to deterioration of the cabling – but the cabling of the relevant signals had been perfect.

Lt. Col. Wilson decided to ignore almost all that Kindness had told him. He was convinced that Blackburn had never cleared signal 226, even for a moment, because the interlocking would not have allowed him to change it back. Instead he blamed Kindness for having made mistakes "in a state of some confusion arising from his failure to arrive on the platform in good time to perform his necessary duties". He had started the train on the guard's signal but without checking the signals; moreover the guard had been distracted by late arriving passengers and could not be responsible for the driver's duties. However, the accident did lead to some discussion about whether guards should also check the signals before giving the 'right away' to the driver.

The accident at Welwyn Garden City on 7th January 1957 involved only one fatality but was unusual in two main respects. Firstly, the basic event of one fast-moving train running into the back of another moving more slowly was similar to the more disastrous accident which had occurred at almost the same spot two decades earlier; secondly, it is one of the few accidents where the investigating officer clearly felt that railwaymen colluded in a misguided attempt to protect one of their colleagues.

The morning rush 'hour' had been complicated by a succession of late-running trains that day. The Welwyn Garden City signalman, Betteridge, received 'train entering section' bell signals from Welwyn North at 7.01am for up express No.111, at 7.05am for up local 1565 and then at 7.10am for the up Aberdeen express No.113. No.111 was itself then checked through the station by the slow progress of a preceding train, so the signalman set the local train onto the up slow line so it could get into the platform road. He then notified Hatfield that he would offer it forwards on the fast line.

The 6.18am Baldock to King's Cross fast commuter train (No.1565) was pulling away from its stop on the up slow line at Welwyn Garden City at about 7.11am on a misty morning with dawn starting to break. The driver of L1 tank engine No.67741 was looking forward to making up some time after signal checks. Visibility was about 200 yards. As this train was fast to Finsbury Park and running eleven minutes late, the signalman was technically correct in deciding to transfer it to the up fast line in advance of the 7.10pm overnight train from Aberdeen. The signalman had accepted the express from his colleague at Welwyn North onto the up fast line and, with full interlocking, had all his signals set to danger. However, Betteridge now had the advantages of track circuiting and could watch the progress of the two trains; he realised that the express had travelled towards the points which linked the two lines much too quickly and appeared to be overrunning the signals. What could he do?

Betteridge was faced with a hard dilemma. He could quickly put his up starting signal back to danger, but he could not be sure whether this would confuse the driver of the up local train who might make an emergency stop. On the other hand, the express would hit the No.37 trailing crossover at speed and possibly derail with potentially many lives lost. So Betteridge, as late as he could, waited for track circuit BD to clear and then returned the crossover to its main line setting, reckoning that running one into the rear of the other would be the lesser of the possible disasters. Events proved him correct in this because the L1 tank engine had already got its train moving steadily.

The express hauled by A2/3 No.60520 *Owen Tudor* passed the up distant signal, then the outer and inner home signals all at full speed. It then ran over the emergency detonators placed by the signalman and past the red lamp held out by the signal lad without appearing to slacken pace at all. Driver Knapp had taken over the express at Peterborough. He was a New England man but had only taken this turn after the 'Top Link' driver assigned to it was late for work; it was his first run on an express to London for three weeks.

By this stage the local train had accelerated to about 30mph and this helped to prevent utter carnage when the express crashed into its rear at about 60mph and 1,000 yards beyond the station. The fireman on the express, Tyers, said "All of a sudden I saw a red light, and we were into this train. Everything happened in such a short time that all I could do was to put my feet on the board and prepare myself." Driver Thurston on the tank engine felt "a push forwards and a draw back". Nonetheless, the train was broken into three sections with its two rear carriages overturned and the rearmost largely wrecked; one passenger, a former RAF pilot, was killed and about 25 taken to hospital. Its guard, who would have been killed, survived the accident as he had gone forwards to check a door handle. The front buffer of *Owen Tudor* was forced under the headstock of the rear local train carriage, destroying its bogie. The engine turned on its side so that its left side was partly buried in ballast. A feature of this accident is that the buckeye couplings and steel-bodied carriages proved highly successful, with almost no injuries in the express train at all. Only the brake second at the rear of the local train, which bore the brunt of the collision, was wooden bodied.

Passengers on the express train quickly made their way to the front. There they found driver Cecil Knapp: "We found the driver in the steam-filled cab, stiff with shock. He was in a state of numbed rigidity, and we had to bend his arms. We pulled him out and put him in a carriage to wait for a doctor."[25]

Knapp was suffering from shock and was taken to hospital; he was unable to give evidence for several weeks. He said that there had been a belt of fog at the viaduct but he had seen "all green lights" at the bracket where the up main outer distant was positioned. Knapp said he had then missed seeing the outer home signal due to smoke and steam and when he had come into sight of the local train's tail light had at first assumed it was on the slow line. Knapp said he did not see the starting signal or the lamp from the signal box, nor did he hear any detonators. His apparent readiness to continue at speed despite not having seen a home signal he explained by saying he had been given a 'clear' by the distant. He acted with surprise when told he had passed signals at danger.

Knapp's fireman, Tyers, denied seeing any signals after Welwyn North, and also said he had not heard any detonators. He said that the smoke and steam had been drifting alongside his side of the boiler and the weather had been 'pretty thick.'

In the inquiry, attention focussed on up main outer distant signal No.31 which was new in September 1956. This was fitted on a bracket below the Welwyn North home signal and seems to have been unpopular with some of the drivers. Some called it the 'accelerator signal' whilst signals of this type were also known as 'hurry up distants' and there had been complaints about the intended function of this one.

Another unsatisfactory feature of this accident was that Automatic Train Control could have prevented it. The ATC system was already installed on the track from London to Grantham, but not fitted to the locomotive involved. Lt. Col. Wilson noted this in his first report, which was followed by a coroner's inquiry blaming the fatality on the negligence of Cecil Knapp.

The inquiry had concluded when there were reports of another incident on 8th March 1957. This again involved train No.113, this time behind class A2/3 No.60514 *Chamossaire* which also had no ATC and which passed the up main inner home signal at danger in daylight and at about 30mph. Its driver, Fowler – who was also of New England shed – said that the main outer distant signal had been showing clear and he had then been shocked to find the inner home at danger – having missed the outer home due to smoke drifting across from a coal train. After stopping close to the station, the fireman, Kingswood, went to report to the signalman and made the comment "We have not forgotten Driver Knapp". The signalman, Dolby, was surprised to hear that the distant had been showing clear as he was confident about the interlocking. Kingswood later commented that Dolby had been 'sceptical' when they had spoken. An express train faced with unexpected home signals at danger would have made an emergency stop, yet the guard on 8th March thought that the stop had been just as if they were calling at a station.

Fowler backed up his incident with reports of at least six other alleged incidents with the same distant signal, so Lt. Col. Wilson was forced to reopen his inquiry. One of the drivers he named, Crisp, denied any knowledge but Wilson identified there had been a problem on 14th March 1956 when a lineside fire affected the cables. A goods driver, Lupton, said that he had been suddenly diverted to the up goods line despite the up main distant showing clear – three times in a week, but what he said conflicted with the records in the train register. Evidence of a complaint made by Driver Rolt of King's Cross about a problem with the distant in October 1956 was also unclear. Wilson concluded that four of the six stories were unfounded and the other two uncertain.

One rumour which circulated was that the distant signal had suffered malicious interference, but Dolby told Lt. Col. Wilson that he had not heard any such rumours. In his final report, Wilson lay all the blame with Knapp and – to an extent – Tyers. Of Knapp he said "His general outlook did not strike me as particularly alert or receptive". He plainly suspected that the engine crews had tried to protect Knapp by creating doubts about the distant signal and reported "I am not altogether convinced of the honesty of the evidence of Driver Fowler" whilst also noting that Lupton "became confused" when cross-examined so he had "no confidence" in his evidence whilst his guard, Houghton, was "plainly untruthful".

Nonetheless, the problematic signal cluster was replaced by a multi-aspect colour light and junction indicator within a few months.

There were, of course, many hundreds of minor collisions caused by driver error that attracted no attention as passengers were not injured, though disruption could be considerable. Although neither was fatal, A1 4-6-2 No.60123, named *H. A. Ivatt* in 1950, was involved in two rear-end collisions. The first was when it was almost new on 25th October 1949 when it ran into the rear of a slow goods whilst diverted off the East Coast Main Line via Lincoln and running under permissive block rules. On this occasion it turned on its side and slid down the embankment. On 7th September 1962 it was again involved in a rear-end collision at Offord when working a down goods to Leeds. The driver overran the Offord up home signal and collided with the rear of a stationary goods; the guard of the stationary train heard it coming just in time and leapt to safety – though he was injured by a piece of debris. A wagon from the stationary goods brought down a telegraph pole and cut all block, telephone, signal and track circuit repeaters to both north and south. Chaos duly occurred, made worse by a slight accident to the New England crane.[26] No.60123 was deemed not worthy of repair and was scrapped.

2. Losing Control

Surprisingly few serious accidents appear to have been caused because a driver lost control of the train, even in the early years before basic safety mechanisms reduced the likelihood even further. Most such incidents were minor, as with the collision at Edinburgh on 11th May 1850. A locomotive that had been attached to the carriages ready for the next express to London was found to be defective, so a porter was sent to the engine sheds to get a replacement. However, the North British Railway had been in dispute with its drivers and had sacked most of them. A mechanic from the sheds was deployed to drive the locomotive to the station, with the porter as his fireman. Pulling into the platform, the 'driver' mistakenly put on steam rather than slowing the locomotive down, whilst the porter turned the tender brake the wrong way. They smashed into the waiting stock, but fortunately there were two vans at the front so no passengers suffered serious consequences. The Board of Trade asked the NBR for details of its roster of drivers, finding that of 42, 21 were 'mechanics' of whom only three had previous driving experience.

There are few known instances of errors occurring when

drivers went the wrong way! However, an error made at Newhailes Junction, just east of Edinburgh, on 1st January 1941 led to a goods train being routed from Newhailes on the main line along the branch to Musselburgh despite the driver having no route knowledge and it ran away out of his control on the steeply graded branch line. With 550 tons of train, the driver, John Hunter, was unable to control it.

Quite how the train came to go down to Musselburgh has never been clearly established. Its driver should have been aware from the signals that it was routed wrongly and the Newhailes signalman tried to warn him with a red lamp and whistle, but Hunter later said the distant signal was clear but he did not see the Newhailes home signals.[27] Hunter and his fireman were both Tweedmouth men and had no knowledge of the branch line, nor did the guard – who tried to control the train by applying his brake but without success. Hunter did not know he was routed onto the branch until he reached the points but after that the weight of the train was too heavy for the train's brake power to hold.

Emergency bell signals were sent up the branch and the signalman at Musselburgh phoned his station, seconds before the train arrived. To prevent a collision it was diverted into a siding but ran straight through the buffers and entirely demolished the station bookstall, killing nineteen-year-old Ella Krause. The engine then ploughed into the station offices, damaging them and the station master's house above – the station master was in bed. Its bathroom collapsed as wagons piled up behind. Although sources say that charges of manslaughter were considered against the driver and fireman, it is unclear why the train was signalled onto the branch and why its driver failed to realise this from the signals.[28]

The deaths of two passengers on the 6.00pm King's Cross–Leeds/Bradford on 4th February 1945 was the result of one of the most unusual accidents in East Coast Main Line history. The King's Cross signalmen saw A4 Pacific No.2512 depart into the Gasworks Tunnel with seventeen carriages behind, albeit rather slowly. In fact one railwaymen said that it made such a slow start that "some passengers had little difficulty in joining the train an appreciative time after it had begun to move". However, the express eventually disappeared down the short 51-yard decline at the start of the tunnel, after which it would have to climb steadily at 1 in 105. The signalman changed the points behind it ready for the next working.

The signalman watched the track circuits for the tunnel on the signal box diagram slowly clear – they were as little as 50yd long in some cases, but then was astonished to see a circuit behind the train revert back to blocked – and then another. He realised that the train was somehow rolling back into King's Cross, where it would head back into No.10 Platform line where the stock of the 7.00pm to Aberdeen was already filling with passengers. Thinking quickly as the rear carriage did indeed emerge back out of the tunnel, he switched the points to run into an empty road – but was fractionally too slow. The rear carriage derailed and a first class compartment was crushed against a steel signal stanchion, killing the two passengers. Soon afterwards, the driver rang the box to ask for banking assistance out of the tunnel, unaware of what had happened.

So how did an express train come to stall in the tunnel and

then run back again without its crew noticing? Several minor factors, not serious on their own, contributed to this accident but also human error – or perhaps human confusion – played the key role. The ascent out of Gasworks Tunnel had a reputation of testing all but the best drivers, made worse in this case by new rails and new tyres on the locomotive. The tunnel was also damp and a preceding 0-6-2T with empty stock had also slipped to a stand – in fact in the previous six months there had been nine cases of trains slipping to a stop. Because of this, trains with sixteen or more carriages were, since December 1943, meant to be banked out of the station by the engine which had brought the carriages in – but in the case of the 6.00pm, they had been reversed in. Driver Catmore had also noticed problems with the A4's sanding equipment and, in the tunnel, this failed to work – probably because damp sand clogged both sets of gear.

However, the crucial factor was that driver, fireman and at least one guard failed to notice the train starting to run backwards. Several factors contributed to this, but there were lights on the sidewalls at least part way through the southern end of the tunnel. The very slow speed of the train and the engine's fierce battle to make progress had made conditions in the tunnel almost intolerable for its footplate crew – who had pulled down a steel shutter at their rear to keep some of the fumes out.[29] When it slithered to a stop, the fireman was almost totally overcome by the poisonous atmosphere. Although there were suspicions the driver had accidentally put his engine into reverse, it is most likely that their failure to engage any brakes meant that it slowly started slipping backwards and they did not notice this.

Also criticised was Guard Smith, who also failed to notice what was happening – and he was in the part of the train which had lights on the tunnel wall. Major Wilson, who investigated, had tests done on the A4 that confirmed the sanding problems but he was clearly unimpressed with Catmore's driving skills or level of alertness. He recommended continuous lights through the tunnel, but was dissuaded from radically altering King's Cross signalling on the chance of a repeat event!

One of the two killed was Cecil Kimber, who had been managing director of MG and "a brilliant designer, works organiser and motivator".[30] He was responsible for the "distinctive character" of the MG Midget and had led the setting-up of the famous Abingdon works.

3. Shunting errors

Interlocked catch points were not a feature of sidings on the Great Northern in the early 1870s, but the down siding at Biggleswade was protected by a 'chock block' which was placed into position by a porter, apparently to prevent wagons being blown down the siding onto the main line.

Carelessness whilst shunting a train backwards off the main line also caused the accident at Biggleswade on 22nd August 1871, which was reported to have led to the death of a Mr Palmer of Boston who, in ill health already, died later. A returning excursion from London to Lincoln and Doncaster was running late so, with the 'Scotch Express' behind, it was decided to shunt it at Biggleswade rather than Sandy. 115 yards south of the signal box was the down siding, points to which were controlled by a ground lever in the care of a foreman porter at the station. To prevent wagons being knocked on to the main line, or being "blown onto it", the siding was also equipped with a stop block made of wood and iron; this was six inches high and two feet long and normally placed across the west rail. A porter going off duty correctly put the chock block back into position across the line – but no-one remembered to check if it was still there when a down Lincoln and Doncaster excursion was similarly reversed into the siding a little later that night.

The station master supervised operations and the foreman porter, Jonathan Crow, waved his lamp to indicate it was safe for the excursion to reverse into the siding. The train, with twenty vehicles attached, then moved backwards but the rear van hit the stop block and derailed, taking other vehicles with it. The result was that four carriages were derailed, with some minor telescoping; two of the 400 passengers reported injury and there was a greater impact on one passenger, "Mr. Palmer of Boston who had, it appears, been previously in bad health, and who has died since the accident, in consequence of the shock to his system…"

In the aftermath of the accident, various members of the station staff blamed each other. When a similar move had occurred with another train an hour earlier, the station master had reminded Crow about the stop block and the foreman porter had moved it out of the way. For the second shunt, the station master had not reminded him again and Crow had not looked – because he had not returned the block to its place. However, another porter, Taylor, had put it back before he went off duty. This occasioned further argument about whether the station master had told Taylor to do this or not. Captain Tyler wisely decided not to try to sort out who was the problem, observing that provision of safety points would solve these problems. He also noted that passengers had complained they could not get out of the carriages since both sides had been locked.

At St. Neots on 13th January 1900 a single passenger, John Jennings – who happened to be an off-duty goods guard travelling as a passenger, was killed due to a poorly executed shunting manoeuvre with a passenger train. The 8.38pm stopping train from King's Cross had reached St.Neots 25 minutes late in the care of a relief driver, Walter Selwood, after detaching and attaching various vehicles at Hatfield, Hitchin and Arlesey. There was not time to send it on to Huntingdon before an express was due so its driver, who was on his second run with this train, was told to draw forwards and then back into the down siding – which was in fact the remains of the old down line from before the recent quadrupling and which Selwood may have thought was still the down slow line. The guard, Lodge, was also unfamiliar with the arrangement.

However, Selwood completely misjudged the reverse so that his train carried the buffers completely away and some of its vehicles telescoped, killing John Jennings[31], while the third carriage ended up where the iron buffers had been. He had had no idea of the length of the siding – 215 yards – or the length of his train, which was 167 yards. Jennings's head was crushed and the artery in his throat cut.[32]

The driver argued that he had been misled about the length of his train – saying that the number taker at King's Cross had been vague, no-one had told him about a van added at Hitchin and he had thought there were 'ten on' not thirteen. Nonetheless, the siding was 40 yards longer than his train. Another factor was a short rising gradient at the start of the siding, with the rest of it falling away at 1 in 300. Although the driver took the brunt of the blame, his guard was also culpable for not informing him of the changes to the loading and no-one at St.Neots had supervised the shunting. Selwood should have reversed cautiously and halted as soon as he was clear of the points, but instead had continued reversing in the assumption that the guard would signal him when to stop. The whole matter reflected poorly on the GNR.

The disaster at Darlington late in the evening of 27th June 1928 was one of the worst ever on the East Coast Main Line. 25 were killed or fatally injured and 45 seriously injured; the death toll included fourteen – of which thirteen were women and one man, all from Hetton-le-Hole, and all part of a Mothers' Union group returning from a day's outing at Scarborough.[33] Although the accident was caused by driver error due to lack of understanding of the signalling arrangements, the majority of the deaths were caused by telescoping of the coaching stock as one carriage over-rode another.

That evening Driver R. J. Bell[34] and Fireman McCormack were in charge of an up parcels train which carried passengers as far as Darlington, where it was to detach some vehicles and attach others. Bell mainly worked as a fireman but as a passed fireman he did two or three days' driving each week, mainly around Blaydon and Heaton at Newcastle. Bell had not signed the Road Book, but later said that he would have done so if asked. This evening he was signalled into Platform 1 to stop and then to shunt; although he had once stopped at Platform 1, he had never shunted there.

The arrangement at Darlington was (and still is) that the main lines pass to the east of the station, which is effectively on a loop to which the entry was controlled by the North and South Junction signal boxes. Once inside the station, movements were controlled by a small box known as East Platform,[35] which acted as an intermediate box and was only 415 yards from Darlington South Junction. Bell was signalled to the south end of the Platform 1 road, beyond the scissors crossing in its middle, so that another train could pull in behind his. Alongside him and to his left was the Up Duplicate line, on which the vans he had to attach had been positioned, and beyond that was the up siding.

Shunter Morland told Bell that they had first to move forwards in order to then set back into the duplicate line to collect the vans, a movement forwards which was controlled by a complex arrangement of 'calling on' signals. Bell's engine was still coupled to some vans and he ran forwards a good way to be clear of the points to the duplicate line – perhaps excessively so as it seems possible that even at this stage he got close enough to the main line to technically be foul of it. However, he then set back and collected the vans on the duplicate line.

It was now necessary to reverse the manoeuvre but with the extra vans coupled on. The small arm of signal No.8 was cleared, which Bell thought meant he was able to move on to the main line, not realising that he also needed clearance by signals 18 or 14. Forwards went Bell with Morland in the van at the end. As they moved ahead, perhaps at about 7mph, Morland saw all the signals for South Junction at danger and realised they were going too far and fast forwards towards the main line. In his own account, he put on the brake in the van and the train seemed to check so, fearing that it would 'divide', he then released it again. However, the train did not stop and as they passed the signal at danger he put the brake back on.

One of the two signalmen on duty at South Junction, Walls, assumed the parcels train would stop at his signal No.18 – but it did not. Meanwhile he had accepted a returning excursion from Scarborough to Newcastle which was accelerating after a signal check and approaching at about 45mph. Both signalmen were alarmed by a strange clicking noise that came from the signalling frame, but reacted quickly – throwing all the signals to danger and pulling the detonator levers. What they had heard was a sound caused by locomotive No.2369, driven by Bell, forcing its way through points set for the main line.

On the approaching excursion, Driver McNulty suddenly saw the headlights of an engine emerge in front of him, but had too little time to react. He reached for the brakes, but within seconds a head-on collision had resulted. Bell's engine was already on the main line with the first few of his vans, but he had braked almost to a stop and seen the approaching train. He had time to release his brake to lessen the impact before McNulty's 4-4-2 No.2164 hit him. The impact drove Bell's engine 185ft back along the line and destroyed the first four vans whilst its others were knocked back along the No.1 Platform line. No.2164 ran nearly 200ft before turning over onto its side, but the real disaster lay behind it. Both McNulty and his fireman survived – the former being found wandering around Darlington station in a dazed condition.

The first carriage of the excursion escaped relatively unscathed but the underframe of the third carriage over-rode the frame of the second so that nearly half of the body and roof of the second carriage "forced its way inside the third coach". The rear 5½ compartments of carriage two and the first half of carriage three were telescoped together so that seats were overlayered and the passengers trapped between. Nearly all the deaths were in the second coach as the third was not nearly so full.

One witness said that there "a silence of perceptible duration followed the crash. Then the air was filled all at once with shrieks and moans and cries for help". One of the first eye-witness reports was that "there were distressing scenes. Women passengers lay groaning, unable to free themselves from heavy pieces of wreckage. A horrible sight, one of many, was that of a man's body on the top of one of the telescoped carriages". It took many hours to release some of those trapped during which fire was a constant fear – though only the first class carriage had gas lights. A Mr. H. Francis was waiting to be rescued and watched as a rescuer cut a hole in the roof above him; unfortunately the man then dropped his lamp through the hole and Francis watched in terror as the naked flame spluttered close to him – but out of his reach – "fearing every moment that it might set the carriage on fire" – until finally going out. The death toll climbed over the next few days and it was soon clear that this was the worst British railway accident for thirteen

years, with particular attention being given to the fate of the Hetton-le-Hole Mothers' Union.

Bell's mistake was plainly the result of his not knowing the signals and perhaps less surprisingly McCormack, his fireman, also claimed not to have known the signals – though he had often fired on the route since he had been promoted fireman in 1921 and passed his driver's exams six months earlier.[36]. Colonel Pringle thought that Bell should have realised he knew too little about the shunting arrangements at Darlington and should have asked for assistance. Morland had also made a mistake, in releasing the brake before he was certain the train was going to stop. Colonel Pringle was also unhappy about the signalling arrangements which he thought "open to criticism".

The following year the complex arrangement at Darlington again influenced the causes of a fatal accident on 9th March 1929, although the immediate reason was failure of a driver to follow the provisions of the rule book whilst shunting across the main line.

The 1928 Darlington disaster occurred at the south end of the station, but the 1929 collision was half a mile north, at the crossovers between the main line and the loop into the station. The down platform line was adjacent to the down intermediate line and two down sidings. Access from these was controlled by North box's signal 137, alongside which was an electronic 'plunger' so that the shunter could communicate with the signalman – who could not see the sidings from his position on the down or west side. The points and signals here were, of course, interlocked. At the north end of the station, a complex set of connections gave access not only to the station lines but also to the engine sheds on the east or up side of the line.

Signalman Martindale was on duty in the North box[37] with two assistants on the evening of 9th March 1929. He accepted light engine No.2019 on the down mainline to return to the engine shed at Darlington, first checking it to a stop at the down outer home signal before then allowing it forwards. He was also aware that he had No.274, which had left some vans in one of the down sidings alongside the intermediate road, also needing to return to the shed. He was also awaiting the up Newcastle to York express, which needed to cross over from the up line to enter the station which was on the down side. Martindale refused to accept the up express from Parkgate[38] box as No.2019 had already been given the road and so it was held awaiting clear signals.

He had previously cleared No.274 to come out of the siding and shunter Teasdale maintained that he had pressed the bell plunger to confirm that the engine was moving off. Driver Charlton took it out past signal 137 but it was held at signals, standing on the main line, for at least a minute – and maybe as much as five. Charlton knew that the Rule 55 laid down that any driver held in such a way should immediately send his fireman to the signal box, but he later admitted standing for at least a minute before commenting "I hope the signalman has not forgotten us."

Martindale could not see where No.274 actually was, so he put back to danger signal 137 which controlled egress from the siding and sent his assistant Oliver out to check the location of the engine – the correct procedure. To make the check Oliver had to walk across four tracks and look along the down lines.

He thought he saw the dim red light of No.274 still in the down sidings and reported back to Martindale that it had not yet moved and so was safe behind signal 137.

The Newcastle to York train was then routed to cross from the up main, across the down main line, and into the platform – but in doing so it came into sideways collision at the south end of the diamond crossing with No.274 which was actually standing on the down main line despite what Oliver thought he had seen. Although the passenger train was only travelling at 10mph, the impact was sufficient to force the light engine back 50 yards across both the up and down main lines. The engine of the passenger train, C7 4-4-2 No.2205, turned over onto its right side. The fireman on the light engine and the front guard of the passenger train were killed.

Lt. Col. Anderson concluded that the main responsibility lay with Driver Charlton, who had stood on the main line for up to five minutes and failed to carry out Rule 55 (b) which required immediate sending of the fireman to the signal box. There was also criticism of Oliver, who had relayed false information to Martindale – though Anderson considered the margin of error made a mistake highly likely, Oliver plainly should have taken more care. However, the accident did highlight the advantages of track circuiting which would have allowed the signalman to see where everything was without leaving his box at all.

Drivers also had to work passenger trains with 'slip carriages' which were detached from the rear of speeding trains to serve intermediate stations. A rare accident involving a slip carriage occurred at Werrington Junction in 1887 which was caused by driver error.[39] A slip carriage at the rear of an express became detached too early and the train driver's attention was drawn to this by a gang of platelayers, who waved a red flag. The driver braked to a stop too hastily – at which point the slip carriage ran into the back of the train. Several were injured.

4. Excessive Speed

In the early days there were many accidents, often relatively minor, because speed was excessive given the level of protection the rudimentary signalling system could offer. Drivers sometimes showed a lack of caution which directly led to deaths of passengers, not helped by the lack of speedometers or efficient brakes.

One of the earliest accidents on the GNR was at Hatfield on 21st September 1850, the line there having opened on 7th August. Sources vary as to whether this was fatal, though the driver and a fireman were variously reported as seriously injured and unable to answer questions. The acting station master at Hatfield, Unwin, faced a busy evening when the GNR's first attempt to run a cattle train led to disaster. This train was scheduled to run from Firsby in east Lincolnshire, which it left 3hrs 40mins late after the station master there delayed its departure waiting for extra cattle to arrive – against express orders. The train made slow progress although three engines were put on to haul 40 wagons; despite this, none of the station masters along the line made a decision to shunt it as it was considered an important train for the company.

At Hatfield, Unwin knew that the cattle train was being followed by the up Parliamentary train,[40] running late after picking up crowds from the races at Doncaster, and also an express from York. He decided to shunt the cattle train on arrival across to the down line but he knew that there would also be a down stopping train shortly. Unwin's options were limited – the siding was too short to take the whole train since it already contained ten or so coal wagons, whilst he worried about letting the cattle train stand on the line and block a level crossing.

Unwin set the 'station light' to red but he knew visibility of the station from the south was affected by the curve, so he sent a porter along the line with a danger signal. The porter had gone about 700 yards when the down passenger train came steaming past "at a furious rate"; although he waved the signal furiously, no-one on the train seemed to notice. In fact neither the driver, fireman nor two guards saw anything until the station signal came into view about 400 yards more up the line. The train was estimated to be travelling at 40mph and had little chance of stopping – indeed, it would certainly have run right through the station anyway. It ran straight into the engines of the cattle train, badly damaging the first and turning the second right over. Damage was estimated at £2,000, but the worst injuries were to Carter, the down train's driver.

Captain Wynne's investigation for the Board of Trade was initially critical of Unwin but the down train's fireman squarely blamed his driver, whilst saying that he had not noticed anything as he was firing. Unwin complained that he had put out the correct signals, but the driver ignored them. Wynne did argue that the cattle train should have been placed "below instead of above the station, beyond the level crossing". Wynne was also much exercised about the late running of the cattle train as being the "initial cause" of the accident and said that "the man most to blame was undoubtedly the station master at Firsby". However, the real cause was Carter's driving and it was significant that there was much evidence of his excessive speed: he was running at up to 40mph when the timetable only required 24mph and he had also overshot the previous station. Wynne also complained about the use of a main line for a siding.

When an accident can occur in a smoke-filled tunnel with a train running at 12mph, it hardly seems appropriate to ascribe the incident to excessive speed by the driver. Indeed several of the hazards of the early railways were shown by the minor collision in Stoke Tunnel on 14th December 1853. A northbound goods was being followed by two trains of coal empties, but the driver of the middle train thought it likely that the goods might stop at Great Ponton so slowed as he entered the tunnel. The tunnel was filled with smoke from the train in front, so he slowed to walking pace – and was hit in the rear by the third train, also running blind in two lots of smoke, and 'estimated' with suspicious accuracy as having been travelling at 12mph. The guard of the middle train was badly injured and a number of trucks wrecked. Although the obvious cause was the speed of the third train, it was plain that the GNR's systems were inadequate for a busy railway.

After the Stoke accident, the GNR installed signalmen with 'magnetic signals' at the ends of their tunnels and introduced a system to prevent more than one train being in a tunnel at a time[41]– which still failed to prevent the accident at Welwyn a few years later. However, systems introduced did prevent any accident resulting from the partial collapse of Stoke Tunnel in 1855.

Although it has remained the case that it is always railway 'accidents' that are investigated, as the 1800s progressed it was increasingly understood that most disasters had essentially human causes. Brakes could be improved and signalling became increasingly sophisticated, but they were all essentially methods for reducing the risk of human error – just as staff training and rule books were. 'Accidents' on the Great Northern in particular were increasingly seen as the result of bad management. By 1876, following the Abbotts Ripton accident, *The Times* was already clear that such things could not be seen as accidents and went into full campaigning mode after the Arlesey Siding[42] disaster of 23rd December 1876. When the coroner's jury largely ignored what Captain Tyler had told them by blaming the dead driver, it called its verdict "inexplicable". The editorial continued: "It turns out…after full inquiry, that the case is but one more illustration of the almost uniform lesson of Railway 'Accidents', so called. It proves that, strictly speaking, there was nothing whatever accidental in the matter."

The newspaper's view was that the practices of the Great Northern were slack, their signalling regulations inadequate, the pressure on drivers to go fast excessive and the brake power of their trains lamentable. Pointing at the company's managers, it observed "On them rests the whole blame of the accident which, in point of fact, was no accident at all."

The facts of the accident were relatively simple. An up goods train arrived from Peterborough at Arlesey Siding and needed to access the sidings on the down side. Despite the fact that the first portion of the down Manchester express was expected in five minutes or so, signalman William Graves set the points so that it could shunt across the down main line into the siding. The points and signals had been fully interlocked only two years earlier, so Graves was confident that the manoeuvre would be protected. However, as the goods shunted across two wagons of sand[43] and one of coprolites from the total of 25 became derailed. As permanent way staff struggled to rerail them, a porter came running to the signal box. Graves was about to send a warning signal to the box to the south, Cadwell, but then received the 'train on line' indication, so he told the porter to run up the line with a red flag whilst also putting his own flags out.

However, no accident should have occurred, because Graves's distant and home signals were between the approaching express and the stricken goods – and both had to be at danger because of the interlocking. The distant signal was 898 yards from the points and the home signal 283 yards.

As the men struggled with the derailed trucks, "the distant roar of an approaching express train made all present only think of self preservation". Mrs. Walters, the station master's wife, saw its fireman jump from the footplate and then its driver, Pepper, "and fall with terrific force upon his head in her garden". Her husband recalled seeing the driver "between the engine and the ground". A porter recalled the fireman step off the bottom step from the footplate: "I saw him topple over two or three times head foremost". Pepper was found against a post by Stephen Didsbury, an engine driver from the coprolite works.[44] The 2.45pm Manchester express came charging through the signals and ploughed straight through the goods, scattering the working platelayers who were lucky to escape with their lives. The engine appeared to 'jump' the trucks, but left its bogie behind on which one of the carriages ended up, still attached to the tender. The locomotive "became embedded in ballast some distance further on". Meanwhile "the carriages in the front part of the train became entangled with the trucks in a confused heap". Six carriages were reported with their bodies smashed and with frames resting on top of goods trucks to an apparent height of twenty feet.

"For a moment all was hushed and terror pervaded the minds of all present. But presently there arose from underneath the ruined carriages the cries of the wounded and imprisoned passengers."

The bodies of the driver and fireman were found 100 yards before the accident; the driver Pepper was seen to be moving his lips, but he died without ever speaking. Three lady passengers were killed and all the bodies were laid out in the stables at the Lamb Inn. There were some miraculous escapes, including a man who was hurled through the roof of a carriage and landed in a sandbank. John Fowler, an engineer at the nearby brickworks, used jacks and saws to remove people from beneath the wreckage as heavy snow started to fall.[45] A railway policeman, who had been a passenger in the train, went to the signal box to keep passengers out; the signalman was faced with a phalanx of angry and shocked people, some wanting to telegraph relatives and others keen to blame him for the disaster.

The emotional stress was too much for the station master, Walters, who was reported as "so affected by the accident that he temporarily lost his reason and had to be removed".[46] Presumably this breakdown came after the main events, for Walters was generally praised for his prompt actions in getting platelayers to help with the rerailing. He sent messages for help to Hitchin and Peterborough while Mrs. Walters opened her doors to all.

After such accidents, attention was normally focussed on the signalling. It was very quickly established that Graves's signals had indeed been at danger, so witnesses were sought who could confirm anything about the express and its driver in the moments before the collision. Its second guard, William Thacker, heard the driver whistle for brakes but could only confirm the home signal had been at danger.

Graves confirmed the weather had been reasonable and that the train was visible a mile and a half away. He also commented on its speed, as did several eyewitnesses and indeed railway staff who were on board. Most thought the speed beyond Hitchin had risen to 60mph – the fastest speed generally ever reached. A GNR policeman on board thought it had been travelling "very rapidly". Guard Simeon Woodhouse thought the express was going at this speed when he saw the distant signal at danger, but reaction had been too slow – "The train did not pull up as it ought to have done. He did not feel the steam shutting off."

There was disagreement as to exactly when the driver had whistled for the brakes – although the engine was fitted with vacuum brakes, there was no continuous brake on the train and Pepper had needed his guards to respond. Woodhouse thought

Pepper had whistled on passing the distant signal but other witnesses, including those at the lineside and at least one who was not interviewed by Captain Tyler of the Board of Trade, thought that the whistling came before this. Didsbury, the driver at the coprolite works, thought Pepper had whistled for brakes 150 yards before the distant signal – although Pepper ought to have seen it much before this.

Captain Tyler attended the inquest and read out most of his accident report to the coroner and his jury. Tyler was critical that Graves had not 'blocked back' to Cadwell during the shunting. By this he meant that not only the Arlesey Siding block signals should have been set to danger, but those of the preceding block post as well, but GNR regulations at that time did not require this extra precaution. He thought that the decision to shunt the goods when the express was expected was a poor one.

Tyler then noted that the express was heavily laden with fifteen carriages and that the collision occurred 283 yards beyond the home signal at which it should have stopped. He accepted that the driver might have been incautious, but considered there were factors influencing this because the train had lost time in climbing out of London on 'greasy' rails: "There is a considerable pressure on the engine-drivers of these fast trains to maintain punctuality…" However, he then went on to try to explain why Pepper, an experienced driver with many commendations, had been unable to stop – and he focussed on the simple fact that the space between signals was shorter than the train's ability to stop. He noted that the same problem occurred at Abbotts Ripton, where the fatal over-run of the home signal had only been 68 yards.[47] The GNR's locomotive engineer agreed that the train would have needed 1,200 yards to pull up, which it might have been able to do if Pepper had reacted to the distant signal earlier than he did. A witness discovered by the Amalgamated Society of Railway Servants thought that Pepper had whistled for brakes 300 yards before the distant signal. In a telling detail, Tyler commented on how the second portion of the Manchester express – running only five minutes behind the first – failed to stop at Cadwell's danger signals and overran the home signal as well.

In conclusion, Tyler thought that "want of caution" was part of the explanation but "to a much greater degree" it was due to the failure of regulations to insist on 'blocking back' and the lack of brake power on the express. He reported that "unless the telegraph instruments are made use of to block back for the protection of shunting trains, the so-called block system becomes in this respect a delusion and a snare".[48]

Although Tyler read out his report pretty well word for word and spelt out his conclusions very clearly, the coroner's jury ignored his emphasis. It exonerated Walters and Graves, but identified Pepper's "want of caution" as the prime cause and said deaths were due to his neglect. As a secondary factor, it blamed inefficient use of the GNR's block system. This verdict provoked a furious editorial from *The Times*.

In the aftermath, the Great Northern held a routine meeting of shareholders in a sombre atmosphere. The press report included a comment that "every one present must feel convinced that both the Abbotts Ripton accident and the Arlesey accident were attributable to defective brake power".[49]

The high speed derailment at Goswick on 26th October 1947 (Chapter 10) was one of the most destructive accidents in the LNER period but is also notable for having occurred in the exact same place as the fatal goods train derailment in 1908.

On that Sunday, work was being carried out renewing three underbridges beneath the main line between Goswick and Beal; all trains needed to be diverted on the loop or 'intermediate'[50] line just beyond Goswick station. The work had been postponed from the 19th October to the 26th, a fact which had been printed up in the North Eastern area weekly notices but which had not been passed on in time to make it into the separate printed version of the Scottish area notices. Signalman T. White reported for duty that morning and bolted the facing point lock of the points, then put collars on the lever so that he could not mistakenly set the points to the main line.

White, with lengthman McIntyre in the box to assist as flagman, accepted a succession of five up goods trains; in each case he kept his home signal for the intermediate line to danger until the train had nearly stopped, then cleared it to take the 'intermediate' line through the sharply diverging points.

At 12.45pm White accepted into his section the first up express of the day which he then saw approaching under the bridge to the north of the station. He noticed that the engine, A3 Class No.66 *Merry Hampton,* was blowing off steam through its safety valves, so assumed that the driver had slackened off having seen the distant signal at caution and that he was coasting under the bridge. In his first accounts of what happened next, White said that he had cleared the up home signal when the train was about 200 yards from it since he had assumed that it was slowing – though he later changed his story to 360 yards. This should have been a fairly safe assumption, as the express had already received a warning from the up distant signal being at caution.

However, as the express drew nearer to the signal box, White realised that it was still 'steaming' and was going far too fast. "Good God, he will not pull up" White shouted to McIntyre. He rushed to put the up home back to danger and ordered the flagman, who was having his lunch, to put out the flag. After the accident, driver and signalman disagreed about the signals and the driver claimed the up main to intermediate signal had been 'lowered' when he saw it – but his speed would still have been excessive.

The express passed the signal box at about 60mph, unchecked by White's hastily planted detonators, and tore into the points and reverse curve that had so destroyed the goods train 39 years earlier and which were not safe for more than 20mph. The engine passed through the reverse curve, but came to grief as the track straightened. "When the train left the track, the engine plunged over on its side and buried itself in a nine foot culvert" reported the *Manchester Guardian,* "three coaches were telescoped, and one was smashed to pieces, only the roof remaining intact." Four of the carriages cleared the deep culvert and landed in the field. White watched with horror – "What seemed to take up my whole attention was the coaches, one after the other, just being crushed up and the glass dropping down."[51] Of the fifteen carriages, eight ended up in the ditch or the field but one – part of a triple articulated set – slid 70 yards up the line to foul all the lines except the down independent line.

First on the scene to help were Sunday worshippers from Windmill Hill chapel, and some of the dead were later carried to the chapel. One witness said "When I arrived I saw a dreadful scene of destruction. Most of the casualties had injuries to the head, back and limbs. Their spirit was splendid."[52] One of the injured to be rescued was the express's fireman, who was trapped with his feet in the firebox and was rescued badly burnt by a group of soldiers. A golf clubhouse was used as a casualty centre.

One of the unusual features about this accident was the time taken to locate and identify all the victims. As usual, there was also confusion as to how many people had actually been on the train. A day after the disaster, three dining car staff and two businessmen were still being reported as 'missing'; two days afterwards it was said that 24 deaths had been confirmed and the two businessmen were still missing, believed buried in the ditch. By 30th November, deaths had reached 28 and the two men had been found buried after 60 hours of searching. The death toll included 27 of the 420 passengers on board, plus one dining car attendant. The injured included a naval rating who had been illicitly travelling on the footplate of the locomotive.

Station master Danskin of Goswick rushed to the signal box and was there less than twenty minutes after the accident. He confirmed that the up distant lever was locked and its repeater was at caution – so the train should have slowed. A special train was laid on from Tweedmouth carrying a group of doctors.

In the aftermath, attention focussed on White and the express driver, Begbie. Both Begbie and his fireman, Baird, were badly injured and were unable to give evidence until 5th February 1948.

A lot of interest focussed on who the third person on the footplate had been and whether he contributed to the disaster. This man was T. Redden, a naval stoker whose brother was a railway fireman and who aspired to join the railways as soon as he could get out of the Navy. He had had no authority to be on the footplate, but had dressed in his brother's overalls and Begbie had sneaked him through a rear entrance at Haymarket sheds to avoid passing the foreman's office. The debate was over whether Redden had distracted Begbie; Begbie, Baird and Redden all later disagreed as to who had been standing where on the footplate in the crucial moments. Baird claimed not to have known that Redden had no authority to be on the footplate.

Of greater significance, perhaps, was the question of whether Begbie had known of the bridge works on the main lines between Goswick and Beal. The driver maintained that he had studied all the notices, but told the inquiry that he had not seen the late notice for Goswick–Beal which had been posted up the previous morning. His fireman, Baird, did not look at the notices at all – his duties did not require this. At Waverley, Begbie looked at the Scottish Area printed notice which included a reference to the postponed works at Goswick–Beal. From his hospital bed he said that he vaguely recalled a reference to Goswick in the notices but on 5th February, to the inquest, he admitted that this was not true. The guard, Blaikie, also did not see any notice about the change of date of the bridge works.

Although this evidence seemed to suggest dereliction of duty by Begbie, the Scottish Area arrangements had been shambolic.

Whereas the North Eastern Area had had time to print the amended notice, this information missed the Scottish printed notices. Instead the information was telegraphed to Haymarket where, as staff were going off duty, it was not typed up but written out in pencil and put up "with no conspicuous heading". To make matters worse, the lighting at the guards' depot was so poor that reading notices was difficult.

The possibility of distraction by a third person and the confusion over the notices should not have led to a disaster because, White said, the train should have been checked by his signals – starting with the distant signal. Begbie's initial statements in hospital did not quite match what he told the inquiry – his first version was that he did not see the distant, saw the home at clear when close to it and then that the starting signals were at danger. Begbie's account to the inquiry was that he had not seen the distant signal as it was obscured by smoke in the south easterly wind; he claimed that he had shut off steam but had not applied the brake as he had seen the home signal at clear. He claimed the home signal was still at clear when he passed it but then "the starting signal was thrown to danger in his face". Baird said he had not seen the distant as he was firing and he thought that Begbie shut the regulator just before reaching the home signal. Blaikie, the guard, and a ticket inspector were confident that there had been no brake application before the train came to its sudden halt. The investigating officer concluded about Begbie that "he gave no satisfactory explanation for his failure to observe the starting signals until he was passing the Home".

The only way out for Begbie would have been if White could be proved to have erred in his handling of the signals. However, the official report largely sided with White: "We were impressed by White's evidence and we consider that his frank statements should be accepted, but his replacement of the Home may only have been just before the engine passed it, and we think Begbie is entitled to the benefit of the doubt as to whether the replacement was reasonably visible to him."[53]

An inquest at Alnwick in January 1948 found that death was caused by the negligence of the driver and fireman but also claimed there had been an error by the signalman. The Coroner made clear that the negligence was not criminal.

The official inquiry found the accident's causes were the failure of Begbie to see the official notice and his failure to take appropriate action at the signals. Having not seen the distant signal, he should have assumed it was at caution and applied the brakes; although the home signal may have shown clear, he should have noticed the up starters beyond it – and the starter for the main line was locked at danger. The inquiry report noted that "statements of the engine crew [were] at various times conflicting and unsatisfactory". Although the main fault lay with Begbie, French and Wilson, the reporting officers, criticised the display of traffic notices at Edinburgh and improvements were made immediately; they also said the accident would have been avoided with Automatic Train Control.

The introduction of diesel locomotives did not coincide with the full revolution in railway working that might have been imagined and unfitted freight trains continued for some years afterwards. Although rather undisciplined working practices may have contributed to the freight train accident at Hatfield

The 1969 derailment at Morpeth showed the advances made by having steel-bodied carriages; despite widespread damage, the body sheets remained largely intact.

(Ken Hoole Collection)

on 23rd March 1968, it was excessive speed that was the main cause. Driver Kilford and his 'fireman' Smith took over a down freight from Temple Mills headed by No.D5622 at Finsbury Park which, in the early hours of the morning, was scheduled to make stops at Potters Bar and Hatfield. The load consisted of 28 wagons and was the equivalent, under the system then being used, of 62 'basic wagon loads' in weight although the guard, Martin, and the man who had driven from Temple Mills seem to have given lower figures.

The nature of the train was significant. Rules permitted a weight of 50 'basic wagon loads' running loose coupled, but with more than this the guard should have ensured that the first two wagons were vacuum fitted and connected to the locomotive's brake pipe. In fact the first wagon was vacuum fitted, but it was not connected, and Martin had made no attempt to provide the 'fitted head' which the rules required. However, later tests showed that the train would still have been able to stop despite this – has it been driven at judicious speed.

Kilford was signalled into the down goods at Hatfield and the points were set to take him onto a spur line which terminated in buffers just short of a bridge abutment. Kilford seems to have allowed excessive speed to build up down the 1 in 200 into Hatfield and as he approached the signals and points he started to sound his horn in desperation, with sparks flying from the locomotive brakes. The Hatfield No.3 signalman, who had gone out to get some coal, made a frantic effort to get back into his box and change the points away from the siding but he was too late. No.D5622 ploughed through the buffers and into the bridge abutment, killing the two men in its cab. The crushed speedometer was found stuck at 29mph.

When Driver Byers signed on at Gateshead for his evening shift on 6th May 1969 he was worried about a warning notice he received for losing time on a previous run. Putting thoughts

aside, he readied himself to take over the 19.40 King's Cross to Aberdeen overnight express from Newcastle station. In the cab of No.D9011 heading north, he seemed to drive well for a time and obeyed the relevant restrictions but approaching Morpeth he "relaxed his customary concentration and…allowed his mind to be distracted".[54] He told the inquiry "I am afraid I began reliving [the warning notice] and I neglected my duty."[55]

South of Morpeth station was the notorious curve, which took the line from northbound to eastbound, before reversing back again the other side of the station. A speed restriction of 40mph was imposed on trains round this curve, but Byers approached it at 80mph or even slightly higher, just after half past one in the morning. His secondman, Graham, had not been concerned earlier in the journey, but as the signs of Morpeth approached he realised speed was too high; at first he hesitated to intervene, then he started up across the cab. As Graham described it: "I was that shocked and amazed that the speed did not slow down that I got it in my mind that I would have to do something. Why I did not shout to the driver I cannot tell. I tried to get up but was thrown down. We were on the curve then."[56]

Suddenly realising the danger of the situations and coming to his sense, Byers had braked sharply, throwing Graham over, but the first vehicle of the train derailed and took the others with it.

A woman passenger said later that "the inspector was just checking our tickets when suddenly sparks began to fly. Then it was pandemonium. The next thing I remember was the inspector being pinned to the ground".

By the time Byers's engine drew to a stop in Morpeth station, 500 yards further up the line, his train had virtually disappeared. All that remained attached to the 'Deltic' was the underframe and pieces of the body from the van that had been the first vehicle of the train.

Behind it, the locomotive had left a trail of destruction. The scattered carriages had severed the signal cables and it was up to the train crew to protect the line. The train guard took some action but forgot to protect the rear of the train with detonators, which was unprotected by any working signals to the south. A following Freightliner train, approaching under extreme caution because of the complete failure of the signals, only just stopped in time to avert a double disaster; later reports indicated that it was Driver Byers who had run down the line to give the warning.[57]

The first vehicle, M81300, contained largely parcels for Dundee and Aberdeen, but others contained sleeping passengers. The first sleeping car left its bogies 250 yards behind and ended up partly on the foundations of the old signal box, which stopped it from careering into a house and the highway. The fortunate houseowner had been campaigning to get rid of the old signal box – "It was a real eyesore but last

A graphic night-time scene following the accident at Darlington in 1928. This shows the impact on railway infrastructure such as signals. (Ken Hoole Collection)

night it saved us."[58] The third, fourth and fifth carriages also suffered serious damage. The sixth carriage was penetrated by an old rail which passed through all six compartments and a similar fate befell the seventh. A young doctor who was a passenger worked tirelessly to help the injured despite his own wounds. Only six fatalities, including the ticket inspector, in such a high speed disaster reflected the strength of modern rolling stock.

Initial interest centred on the sharp bend, but it did not at that time have any great notoriety: "There has been little evidence that the bend has been particularly dangerous in the past" *The Times* reported, "the last accident there was at least sixty years ago." Despite the horror of the situation, the investigating officer, Col. Robertson, was moved by Byers's position. At one point in the process he was reported as having told Byers "You have told me in a frank, forthright and admirable way what you did." He retained this view – "I was much impressed by Driver Byers," he wrote in his report "he struck me as a very good type of driver and a careful and conscientious man."[59]

5. The effects of alcohol

Cases where accidents have been caused on the East Coast Main Line by a driver being drunk have been very rare, although in 1852 the down mail train from York collided with a light engine near Gateshead which was stationary; the light engine was running from South Shields to Newcastle in the care of two men who were drunk and who allowed the fire to go out! Luckily the collision was not fatal and the passengers spotted one of the light engine's crew who was so drunk that he could not talk.[60]

On 22nd October 1910 Fireman James Lough, an experienced man stationed at Tweedmouth, went to see the locomotive superintendent there, Francis Collinson. Lough had been out on goods duties several times with Driver Peter Connolly, but now he asked Collinson to change his duties as he was worried that Connolly was taking liquor as he smelt of drink and was not entirely sober on duty.

Collinson must have known Connolly well for he had been a driver for twelve years and he spoke to the driver informally. Connolly explained that he had taken some brandy to steady himself after a bout of diarrhoea and so Collinson dismissed Lough's doubts and refused his request. Having told the driver that it was his fireman who had complained, he sent the two men back to work together. In doing so, he sent Lough to his death for Connolly's drinking seems to have been the main reason behind the crash at Darlington on 15th November 1910 that killed them both.

Collinson should not have been so dismissive of Lough's complaints, for the stories about Connolly's drinking were already well known in Tweedmouth. On 19th April 1909 the station master, Horsley, had reported his concerns about the driver to Collinson and on 11th May that year there was a slight collision involving Connolly's locomotive; stories that this was caused by his drinking circulated, but Collinson found that Connolly was merely "excitable" because of the accident and he was exonerated.

Horsley's view of Connolly was entirely different, but he had no authority over the locomotive men. Later he told the inquiry that Connolly "was not at all times a sober man. I have seen him on duty when he was not sober, and I have also seen him off duty when he was not sober". Apart from the incident on 11th May 1909, when Horsley thought Connolly was "not sober", he had seen him in the locomotive shed on 19th April "worse for liquor" though he was unsure if the driver was on duty. However, Horsley only reported the 11th May incident to Collinson as "it was not much use unless I could get the local officials to support me".

However, James Davidson, a locomotive foreman at Tweedmouth and junior to Collinson, also had his concerns. He had seen Connolly "under the influence" on 19th April 1909. He had also seen Connolly "suffering from the after effects of liquor" and on 29th October 1910 – days before the accident – the driver had been missing from his engine when he was due to take the goods out. Ten days earlier Connolly had woken up all his neighbours by making a row in the street. After the 29th October incident he spoke to Horsley – significantly not in the chain of command – and the station master had told him to report it to Collinson. Davidson told the superintendent that he had "great doubts as to the man's general character" and he had also spoken to Connolly, who had said that "he was impelled by a power which he could not resist". Although shed foreman

Robert Stork had no suspicions about Connolly, another foreman had seen him "staggering up the street" at 11.00 in the morning. Yet Collinson did nothing of consequence and therefore consigned the unfortunate Lough to a sudden and blameless death along with Connolly.

Collinson's decision not to refer the concerns about Connolly anywhere meant that on the night of 14th November 1910 the errant driver was again teamed with Lough to crew the 10.45pm Newcastle to Leeds express goods. This was a heavily loaded train that they had run before. This time they had a locomotive fitted with both Westinghouse and vacuum brakes which operated on the locomotive and its tender, but with no continuous brakes on the train. The guard on the train was Thomas Garnett, but he knew nothing about Connolly's condition that night as he told the later inquiry that he had "no communion at all" with his driver. However, Garnett thought Connolly a "careful man".

The train ran well through the night, being checked by signals at Lamesley and Birtley but responding to both. Signals were clear after Durham and the train built up speed, seemingly going faster as they neared Darlington and travelling at an estimated 35mph. The train was booked to average 26mph between Durham and Darlington but in fact averaged 37mph from Ferryhill to Darlington. Garnett at least was alert and, looking ahead, saw that the Darlington North signals were at danger – yet speed did not slacken. "I did not think we had travelled any faster than that during the whole journey" he said. Speed did not slacken and the goods steamed past the distant and then outer home signals, so Garnett put on the handbrake in his van – to little effect as it continued past the home signal. "It did not appear to me that the train checked speed at all…" he said. At this point the line was "perfectly straight" with a slight falling gradient and it was a "clear moonlit night." The succession of signals was plainly visible.

William Kirk was on duty at the Darlington North box. He had previously passed the Parkgate to Hull goods to South on the main line and knew that it had stopped further down the line where it was to take on water and detach thirteen wagons. South refused to accept the Leeds goods on the main line so Kirk hesitated before offering it to South on the 'independent' relief line. South accepted it at caution, but Kirk did not have time to change the points and signals before the Leeds goods was upon him. He realised it was approaching far too fast and managed to place an emergency detonator on the line in front of it; despite the danger signals, Kirk thought "the train did not appear to have checked speed in the least until it reached the detonator". However, he was able to confirm that guard Garnett had indeed put his own brake on.

The guard of the stationary Hull goods got out of his van and walked along the train to uncouple. He stepped back and watched as the driver moved forwards and perhaps later reflected on how narrow his own escape from death had been – if he had been in his van, or still doing the uncoupling, he would have had no chance. Instead he watched in terror as the Leeds goods, still doing perhaps 30-40mph, ploughed into the back of his train. Its locomotive was thrown over on its side, the brake van and five wagons of the Hull train were smashed to pieces and some of the Hull wagons were propelled half a mile along the line by the impact. Two wagon examiners were working alongside the Hull train and heard the detonator; when asked if he saw the crash, Fred Kay explained that he had had more important priorities – "I at once made off as fast as I could. I did not see the collision actually occur as I was looking the way I was running."

It was reported that Connolly was found "pinned between the engine and the tender and quite dead". The unfortunate Lough was thrown clear, but also died.

In the aftermath, Assistant Divisional Locomotive Superintendent Edward Thompson[61] examined the wreckage. He found the regulator shut and the gearing in reverse; there were skid marks on the wheels indicating an emergency attempt to stop the train only shortly before the collision.

Lt. Col. von Donop investigated the accident and initially heard reports that Connolly was sober on the night of the accident – and he heard from Francis Collinson the story of the brandy and diarrhoea. However, as the inquiry progressed the other evidence from men at Tweedmouth, questioned by the North Eastern Railway after Collinson's evidence, gradually emerged including the telling evidence from James Davidson about all the neighbours being woken as well as seeing him drunk on duty on 19th April the year before. Faced with such reports, von Donop recalled Collinson who was forced to admit that Horsley, Lough and Davidson had all spoken to him about Connolly being a drinker.

Von Donop was left with plenty of evidence that Connolly had a drink problem, but none that he had been drunk that night – indeed, two witnesses said he had not been. Yet his train had ploughed onward to disaster with no attempt to check it until the very last moments so the inspector had to settle for a theory that Connolly had been "practically asleep" due to the effects of his drinking on previous days. Von Donop flailed at any drinking by locomotive men – "Drunkenness, even off duty, is an unpardonable offence in the case of a man carrying out such responsible duties as an engine driver, and no man who is ever known to be on any occasion the worse for liquor should be allowed to take charge of an engine."[62] Von Donop said the locomotive staff at Tweedmouth were "very much to blame" for not taking action, but he could not prove that anything other than drowsiness was to blame that fatal night.

This was an unsatisfactory conclusion in some ways, for it does not explain why Lough – who would have had at least some idea of their speed and location – did not himself act earlier.

Another high speed derailment at Morpeth occurred on 24th June 1984 at 00.40 to the Aberdeen to King's Cross overnight express. Approaching Morpeth into the curve from the north to west at 85mph, it left the track and turned over, damaging two houses and cutting the cables to the signals. 35 people were taken to hospital. Driver Allan was charged under the Regulation of Railways Act and the Offences against the Person Act of 1861, though he was only tried on the latter charge. Blood samples showed alcohol and Allan admitted having drunk two pints of Tennants' Lager at Edinburgh. The defence argued that Allan had been overcome by a bout of "incapacitating" coughing, but he had no medical records of this. Lt. Col. A. G. Townshend-Rose, who investigated the accident reported "I must say I am strongly inclined to the possibility that he fell fully or nearly asleep…" This accident had a lasting impact on all British railway staff with a total ban on alcohol, reinforced by the Transport and Works Act of 1992, being introduced for all grades, including office staff who were in charge of nothing more dangerous than a typewriter.

FOOTNOTES

1   Authorised as the Sheffield & Lincolnshire Junction Railway.
2   George Dow, *The Great Central*, Vol. 1, Shepperton, 1985, p.132
3   *The Times*, 4 February 1854
4   Wrottesley, Vol. 1, p.121
5   *The Observer*, 7 September 1873.
6   This spelling was commonly used in the press at the time. Several of my correspondents have queried it and suggested the 'Flying Scotsman' name, but the train was introduced in June 1862 as the 'Special Scotch Express' and according to *The Times* of 25 January 1872 'popularly known as the Flying Scotchman.' The official report on the Abbotts Ripton disaster of 1876 uses the term 'Scotch' 37 times, 'Scotchman' twice and 'Scots' or 'Scottish' not at all! B Gwynne, *The Flying Scotsman* (2011), reports that the name gradually evolved from 'Scotch Express' to 'Flying Scotchman' and later 'Flying Scotsman' – though in the early 1880s the name was most commonly used for a racehorse and perhaps that had an influence. *The Penny Illustrated Paper* referred to the 'Flying Scotchman' in August 1880 as a generic term for any Edinburgh express, it would appear. In 1892 a pen that ran as smoothly as an 'express train' was called the 'Flying Scotsman' too. By 1900 press references were favouring the 'Flying Scotsman' form. Wrottesley, Vol. 1, pps 150-2, discusses the name and refers to the 'Flying Scotsman' name as being used in 1893. So, we must stick to the version as most commonly used at the time of an incident.
7   *The Times*, 25 August 1873.
8   *The Times*, 30 August 1873
9   Some sources say 80yds.
10 *The Times*, 7 September 1873.
11 J Wrottesley, *The Great Northern Railway*, Vol.1, London, 1979, p.200.
12 *The Times*, 16 October 1852
13 Report to the Board of Trade, 23 November 1852
14 *The Times*, 6 October 1894.
15 *The Times*, 5 October 1894.
16 This is as it appeared in the accident report but so far as is known the GNR never applied suffixes to the running numbers of the Atlantics.
17 *The Times*, 14 February 1923.
18 Michael Back also points out that there were irregularities in the block working: the express should not have been accepted by Babworth from Canal, as Retford North should not have given 'train out of section' to Babworth with the train in the station still within his clearance point. However, Colonel Pringle placed the blame on Driver Jubb.
19 This term is now largely out of use, but appears to have been a common designation in the early twentieth century.
20 Michael Back reports that it had changed from up goods to up slow (therefore passed for passenger) in 1926 so this seems a little surprising.
21 Michael Back, who worked at Toton Yard in this period, reports that there was an intensive daily service of up to four trains with a revenue of £500 per train.
22 *Hansard*, 13 March 1968
23 E Baker, *History of Firefighting in Cambridgeshire*, p.108
24 Accident Report, paragraph 18.
25 *The Times*, 8 January 1957
26 With thanks to Allan Sibley, Colin Garton and Ian Pusey.
27 *The Scotsman*, 7 March 1941
28 http://www.edinphoto.org.uk/1_edin_t/1_edinburgh_transport_railways_accidents_musselburgh_1941.htm
    Accessed 16 September 2011. This site includes extracts from *The Scotsman*, 7 March 1941 and the *Berwick Advertiser*, 9 January 1941.
29 These had replaced the glazing in the windows at the rear of the cab during wartime.
30 *Dictionary of National Biography*
31 Jennings was a GNR goods guard, travelling unofficially in the guard's compartment.
32 Slack, p.94
33 A new reredos and chancel panelling were erected at their parish church as a memorial.
34 He may have been a Passed Fireman rather than an actual Driver, hence his occasional forays at the controls.
35 There was also a West Platform signal box on the down side.
36 McCormack was 'passed' to drive in the immediate Newcastle area, so perhaps had not the route knowledge for this section.
37 According to the accident report, this was one of the most modern boxes on the line and only five years old. Three signalmen and a booking lad were on duty with Martindale in charge.
38 Here is an example of inconsistency – the accident report mentions this box twice, once as 'Park Gate' and once as 'Parkgate'. It was 878 yards north of North box.
39 *The Times*, 15 February 1887, identifies the working only as the 'north express'.
40 A train offering the cheapest fares as stipulated by an Act of Parliament of 1844 on at least one train per day.
41 *The Times*, 14 April 1854
42 Arlesey Siding was renamed Three Counties and was not the same site as Arlesey's current station.
43 Some reports say one of coprolites and a guard's van.
44 Coprolites were dug for use as fertiliser and were believed to be the fossilised dung of prehistoric beasts.
45 Although Arlesey is often seen as 'an accident in the snow', it was not snowing at the time of the accident.
46 *The Times*, 25 December 1876
47 This is a little misleading, as the train driver thought he was running under clear signals.
48 *The Observer*, 7 January 1877
49 *The Times*, 19 February 1877.
50 Several sources call the loop lines either 'intermediate' or 'independent'; in the diagrams of the official report, 'independent' is used, which was a common term on former NER lines.
51 *Manchester Guardian*, 1 November 1947
52 *Manchester Guardian*, 27 October 1947.
53 Accident Report, paragraph 32.
54 Accident Report.
55 *Manchester Guardian*, 21 May 1969.
56 *Manchester Guardian*, 21 May 1969.
57 *The Times*, 21 May 1969.
58 *The Times*, 8 May 1969.
59 Accident Report, paragraph 70.
60 *Manchester Guardian*, 26 May 1852
61 This was of course the same Edward Thompson who became Chief Mechanical Engineer of the LNER from 1941 to 1946.
62 Accident Report, p.31

3

SIGNALMEN'S FAILURES

In the early decades, technical apparatus was such that there was little to prevent disaster if a signalman's concentration was poor. Gradually, though, simple mechanisms such as interlocking frames and the interlocking of points and signals reduced the risks substantially but as successive accidents discussed below (such as Three Counties) showed, it was still possible to make errors. All the more frustration, then, when accidents still happened even though the means to prevent them had been available.

Interlocking could not have prevented the accident at Welwyn Junction in 1869. This long-forgotten station was opened on 1st March 1858 when the branch line to Hertford from Welwyn was opened. Welwyn Junction station closed to passengers on 1st September 1860[1] on the same day as another branch was opened to Luton and Dunstable; after that trains from Hertford and Luton ran to Hatfield station where there were bay platforms. This put too much local traffic on the main line, so in March 1869 an 'independent' line for Dunstable and Luton was added on the down or western side of the main line between Hatfield and Welwyn Junction.[2] Locking apparatus was installed at Welwyn Junction signal box in December 1867[3].

It was therefore shortly after the opening of the first 'independent' line on the down side when, on the night of 24th October 1869, the stopping train for Peterborough left Hatfield with thirteen vehicles in tow whilst a train for Luton ran just behind it on the parallel line, though there were some press allegations of running 'side by side' implying racing which the Luton driver denied at the inquest. The Peterborough train passed the Welwyn Junction 'signal hut' at upwards of 20mph; this was 32 yards south of the points. Most of the train passed across the points for the Hertford branch line, but then disaster struck. The guard's van at the rear instead "ran up the Hertford branch" and also two wheels of the coach in front. The couplings in the train broke and the last two carriages in the front portion of the train derailed. One of the carriages suffered a broken spring. Part of the train stopped 120 yards north of Welwyn Junction. Two of the horse boxes "ran a short distance by the side of the line, without doing or incurring any injury". However, other carriages were scattered all around – two landed on their sides on the Hertford branch and one on a manure siding to the east of the Hertford line with its frame and body split apart. An eye witness reported them "thrown into inextricable confusion".

A passenger on the train described how "the carriage… suddenly leaped off the rails with a quick swerve to the right, tottered for some seconds on the side wheels only, and then tore through the stones and metals with a succession of violent shocks".[4] After it stopped, the correspondent clambered out and "a few yards back lay something white and, coming up to it, I saw the body of a woman crouching on the rails. I felt her hand, piteously stretched out, but she was quite dead".

The driver of the Luton train stopped on the curve of his own line and ran back to give assistance whilst the station master, George Stothard, ran up from Welwyn station[5] to find a woman "lying dead outside the line of rails, her head and body fearfully mangled". Nearby a man was found dead beneath the wreckage whilst a young man was rescued with his leg crushed; he died later after an amputation. Two of the dead were a farm manager and his wife.

Witnesses could not explain what had happened. The guard, James Hitchis, had noticed an "oscillation" and then his van "got upon the Hertford branch line, but he could not tell how it got there". Ten minutes after the accident he examined the points and found them set for the Peterborough line. He became very confused about the signals and the points and changed his story four times in front of the coroner. The driver, though, was quite convinced the points were set for Peterborough when he had looked at them – even though it was dark at the time.

What could have caused this disaster? Welwyn Junction was well equipped by the standards of the times, with signals and points interlocked. When the signals for the down main line were lowered, the points were locked in position for the Peterborough line. However, the habitual practice on the Great Northern, which might otherwise have seemed desirable, was that the signals at a junction should be returned to danger straight after the passage of the engine and tender[6] – and this, of course, then disabled the interlocking. If the signals were returned to danger as the train was still passing, it was technically possible to alter the points under its wheels. There was a little damage to the points that had not been there earlier in the day, according to the permanent way foreman.

Lt. Col. Rich disliked the practice of putting the signals back to danger so quickly. "The practice is a most dangerous one, as the signalman… is almost certain at some point or another to make the mistake of moving the point lever when he should not do so." Rich ascertained that signalman Williamson telegraphed back "line clear" to Hatfield before the Peterborough train could have fully passed and perhaps then set the points for the Hertford train that was to follow it.

The signalman, George Williamson, was an unhelpful witness. He spoke of fire coming from the wheels of one of the carriages before the train reached the points and denied having changed the points under the train or changing them back again after the accident. The guard of the Hertford train, following no more than four minutes behind, thought the points were 'open' by half an inch.

Rich was also unimpressed by GNR rule No.70 which said that a train should reduce speed to 10-12mph when approaching a junction. This was routinely ignored by express trains and, as Rich pointed out, the timetable required them to ignore the rule. The rule "is never observed by any of the drivers of the express

The collision at Manor House, between Thirsk and Northallerton, on 2nd November 1892 combined a number of features to strike fear into the late Victorian public: "No element of horror was lacking in the awful accident" the *Manchester Guardian* reported.[7] The precise elements that caused such a reaction seem to have included the sudden destruction of a sleeping carriage in the middle of the night – with victims sent from sleep into eternity without knowing – and the trapping of other victims under the wreckage as fire broke out. However, the accident became one of the most famous ever on the East Coast Main Line because of the tragic situation of James Holmes, the signalman who was the main cause of the disaster.

Manor House signal box was a simple block post with only seven working levers near to Otterington, whose station master was its supervisor. Although small, it was a busy box handling over 90 trains a day, usually with the signalmen taking it in turns to work twelve-hour shifts as was then normal across the system.

The overnight Edinburgh to King's Cross train ran, as it often did, in two portions that night – though the first the signalmen would know of this was the two lamps hung on the rear of the first train to indicate a second train would follow. Normally the two expresses ran with about twenty minutes between them, but a decision was taken at Northallerton North Junction to fit a Middlesbrough to Starbeck goods in between the two – starting a few minutes behind the first train and about twenty minutes ahead of the second.

Eden, the signalman at Otterington, passed trains on to Manor House in accordance with the NER block regulations. Holmes first accepted the leading express, then set his signals to danger behind it. He then accepted the following goods train, but did not clear his signals – "I must have been overpowered by sleep" he said. "My mind became confused, nothing seemed perfectly clear."[8] He forgot to record anything in his train register book. The goods steamed up to his signals and stopped, at which point Holmes seems to have lost awareness of its existence. When Eden asked him to 'be ready' for the express he awoke in a confused state – he had forgotten about the stationary goods train and so accepted the express. He later said that he had not noticed the light of the goods train standing close to his box due to the thick fog.

The Middlesbrough goods, driven by Joseph Barnes, was held at the Manor House home signal for several minutes until it was cleared by Holmes – for the second express. It was just restarting, and had accelerated to about 6mph, when the express ploughed into its rear at a couple of minutes after 4.00am. "The collision was one of great violence and the result was most disastrous" Major Marindin wrote in his report. The body of the third vehicle, a Pullman carriage, "shot off" the bogie

main line trains" so he considered it should be dispensed with. However, as the evidence of the permanent way foreman proved, many GNR employees could not read and so had to have the rule book read out to them in any case.

The negligence of Williamson rendered the GNR liable for damages, which it tried to fight off. Nonetheless, it lost two cases including one on behalf of the three children named Walden of the couple killed; they received £170. The company was liable for the negligence of one of its servants, who it should not have employed if he were not capable.

The death of John Eisten from a crushed leg after the accident at Thirsk on 9th May 1869 could easily have been prevented if the North Eastern Railway had installed interlocking apparatus which would have cost it only £6 or £7 in the estimation of Captain Tyler. The signalman or 'pointsman' there, William Warriner, signalled a goods train into the loop siding so that a following passenger could overtake it. Though he set all the signals, he forgot to change the points behind the goods so that the express ploughed into its rear – but because the driver was alert, at a reduced speed of 20mph. Tyler investigated and attended the inquest, reporting that the signalman admitted "an act of forgetfulness." There was talk that he had been fined for causing a collision between an empty stock train and a goods train previously but had a good record over fourteen years. The jury returned a verdict of accidental death through non-criminal neglect, but criticised the parsimonious railway company as well.

frames, a sleeping carriage was buried beneath several others and there was telescoping of other carriages. Three passengers in one of the telescoping forward carriages were able to escape because one of them had the presence of mind to shout to raise their legs – so they were not then trapped when the seats all squashed forwards. Roland Ewart, driver of the express, was thrown into a field and the fireman into a hedge; Major Marindin thought both "had a most wonderful escape". Others were less fortunate – "One of the most shocking sights was that of a woman who had been thrown by the collision under the engine, and was literally burned to death." Yet damage to the goods train was relatively light, although its guard died, and was "found close to the line dreadfully mangled".[9] Dignitaries in the Pullman, including Lord Tweeddale, the Marquis of Huntly and General Lambton, were unharmed.

George Bean, a guard on the express, was at first pinned against the carriage wall by barrels of fish, but extricated himself and went straight to the signal box. The signalman, Holmes, told him "I have a dead child in the house. Had I been relieved as I asked this would not have occurred."

Nine passengers who died were all in the leading third class sleeping carriage, with the guard of the goods train also killed. Fire broke out about between 45 minutes and one hour after the accident and spread through the goods wagons and part of the passenger train wreck. Although there was believed to be water mains nearby, no-one knew where a hydrant was and the fire took hold very quickly. At one point it was realised that a child was trapped under the wreckage, with fire burning above, and the child's cries were found to be coming from below the trapped body of a dead woman. The fire killed some dogs in a van from Aberdeen before the child was rescued, with feet and legs badly burnt; Lottie Hamilton, aged two, died on the way to Thirsk. Two of the women passengers' bodies were so badly burnt that they could not be identified, only pieces of bone and some personal effects being left; there was substantial debate as to whether they had been burned alive. It was reported that the scabbard of a sword was all that was left of a young Black Watch officer.

In the aftermath there was much criticism of the railway staff. The fit and able railwaymen seemed to scatter in all directions to signal boxes and stations to summon help, with the result that there was virtually no-one on the scene rendering assistance for nearly an hour. At the inquest, a juror pointed out that there was a hydrant only 273 yards from the fire but no-one had realised.

Holmes had clearly broken several rules – hardly surprising, since he admitted to being asleep. For example, he did not follow Rule 2 which required him to send ahead 'Call Attention' as the first indication to the next signal box, nor did he acknowledge messages received by telegraphing them back.

However this was not a simple story of an unreliable signalman whose neglect scarred scores of lives. Holmes did contribute to the situation, but it was widely believed he should never have been at work at all. As a young married man of 22 or 23, he had come under extraordinary pressures. He had had 30th October off and had got up at about 9.00am on 31st. Although his usual practice was to have some sleep during the day before going on night duty, he instead worked in his orchard "pulling apples for the market". He then walked to work and was on duty from 6.00pm until 6.00am.

He walked back home (the investigating officer was later critical about signalmen living so far from their workplace) and got home about 7.15am – but the delay was partly due to his practice of meeting up for the walk home with the signalman from Avenue Junction box. When he arrived his wife told him that their little girl, 'Our Rosy', was not well, but he went to bed at about 8.00am. Near mid-day, his wife woke him to say that Rosy had had a fit and he went to get the doctor; this involved walking back to Otterington station, getting a goods train and going to Northallerton. The doctor was out on his rounds, so he left a message and walked back to Otterington – about 4½ miles. He got home about 2.00pm but the child had died.

Mrs. Holmes said she could not bear to be alone in the house with the body of the child overnight, so Holmes went to Otterington station to telegraph for his mother to come. He told the station master, Kirby, that he was not fit for duty and Kirby agreed to telegraph the inspector, Pick, for a relief signalman. Kirby sent a message that he needed a relief as Holmes's child had died, but crucially did not include any reference to the signalman's own stated view that he was unfit for work. Kirby defended himself, arguing that "He was distressed about his child, but I did not think he looked unfit for duty." Pick was not in the office and an assistant refused the request as there were no reliefs available – all having been drafted elsewhere due to a flood incident. Pick had 283 signalmen and seventeen relief staff under his control.

Holmes walked back to the station at about 6.00pm and was told that no relief was available, but he arranged with his 'mate' who was still on duty to cover for him until 8.00pm. Although he said he was "in bad fettle," he did not repeat his view that he was unfit after the relief request had been refused. In Holmes's words, "I said I would then go on duty although I was not fit for it." Kirby therefore did not take up the possibility of 'switching out' Manor House box. Holmes then went home, then back to the station to meet his mother, who unfortunately arrived on a later train, then walked to Manor House box. Altogether he had walked about fifteen miles and had little to eat or drink all day, having only slept for about four hours in the previous day and a half.

The signalman at Otterington, Henry Eden, was visited by Holmes at about 7.30pm before he went to his own box. He asked Eden to wire him if his mother arrived on the next passenger train and said "Harry, I am about done to start duty. I have never been off my legs since twelve o' clock. I have had to walk from Northallerton to Otterington and back." Eden later observed "When he was in my cabin he looked tired and upset", though he was able to wire over the message when Holmes's mother arrived at 8.58pm. Holmes finally got to his own box at 8.00pm, so his 'mate' had done a fourteen-hour shift.

Holmes was not the only signalman working long or irregular hours. Henry Eden was working a shift from 7.15pm to 7.25am due to problems getting a relief signalman. On the preceding Sunday he had started work at midnight and worked through to 1.25pm on Monday although he should have been relieved at 6.00am. Although he played only an indirect role in the accident, he did not notice that Holmes had not sent back the 'Line Clear' after the goods train until it got to the point where he offered the second express.

Holmes was well supported by his trade union, who perhaps advised him to be interviewed by the press. This resulted in sympathetic coverage of how "he rested his head upon his hand and frequently gave way to tears".

The inquest was held at Thirsk and recorded a verdict of culpable negligence against Holmes, though also criticising the relief arrangements and the behaviour of Kirby and Barnes, the goods driver. Holmes was bailed to appear before York Assizes on a charge of manslaughter, which he did in early December before a largely sympathetic crowd. He and his family spent some of the intervening period in the Sussex home of Henry Farmer-Atkinson MP.

Key evidence came from Pick, who said that he thought a child dead was sufficient reason to send a relief – except by the time he got the message it was 6.00pm and too late. This left Kirby to wriggle, which he did by saying Holmes could have refused to work as unfit and that the signalman had changed his self-evaluation to being merely "in bad fettle". No witnesses were called for the defence and Holmes was found guilty of manslaughter, but then the Judge decided only to have him "bound over in the sum of £50 to come up for judgement if called".[10] The ruling was greeted with "prolonged cheering" in the court. The Times reported "a tremendous outburst of applause which was with difficulty suppressed".

Marindin went as far as he could to exonerating Holmes in his official report; he said, of the facts of the case, that "if they cannot be accepted as a sufficient excuse for his subsequent failure to perform his duty… [they] go a very long way towards accounting for it". The circumstances that caused Holmes to fall asleep were contributed to by the signalman himself, Kirby and the staff of Pick's office. Major Marindin's report, published after Holmes's trial, found that he had been "manifestly unfit for duty" which was an indictment of the management. Holmes should not have been working on secondary employment when he should have been sleeping, but he had also not pressed his view that he was unfit. There was much criticism of Kirby, who could have switched out Manor House box although this would have been highly unusual – "in extreme circumstances" Pick called it. However, Marindin thought Kirby made a "grave error of judgement" in not telling Pick that Holmes was unfit to work. Barnes, the driver of the goods train, made no effort to alert the signalman whilst waiting at the signal and Ewart, the express driver, thought it was sufficiently foggy to require a fireman to be sent to the signal box if a train was held at signals as Rule 275a required:

> "In case of detention at a home or starting signal the engine-driver must sound his whistle, and if still detained the guard or fireman must go to the signal-box and remind the signalman of the position of the train or engine, and remain there until the signalman can give permission to go forward. In foggy weather or during falling snow the guard or fireman must, immediately upon the train or engine coming to a stand, proceed to the signal-box.
>
> "The duty must be performed by the guard or fireman in accordance with the following instructions: In the case of

a goods train with only one guard, when stopped at the home signal, by the fireman."[11]

Eden also made errors that caused time to be lost and Marindin noted that his record book was "very badly kept".

Marindin also reached some wider conclusions. He thought the fatalities were largely caused by marshalling light carriages between the engine and the much heavier Pullman coach, which rode forwards and crushed the occupants. He thought signalling could be readily improved by making it impossible for the 'forwarding' signalman to offer 'Be Ready' before he had received back 'Line Clear' or 'Train out of section' from the preceding train. And he thought that a shift of ten hours was quite long enough for a main line signalman and that night shifts should be shorter.

By the late 1890s the Great Northern had made much progress in improving the safety of its line. Interlocking of signals and points had been introduced and the quadrupling of parts of the route was helping to separate slow goods traffic from faster passenger trains. This helped to reduce the practice of shunting trains back into sidings to let faster ones pass, a factor in the accidents at Abbotts Ripton and other places. However, fringe practices continued to cause problems that could easily become dangerous if compounded by lax signalling work.

A practice which endured despite criticism was permissive block working. Whereas the safety of the 'absolute block' was ensured by permitting only one train in a block section at a time, permissive block allowed one goods to follow another into a block section providing it had been checked on entry by the signalman. By the late 1890s Lt. Col. Yorke of the Board of Trade considered this dangerous as well as a misnomer – there was no 'block' in permissive block. The accident at Three Counties[12] confirmed his views.

On 31st January 1899 an engineers' ballast train was working on the down main line on the four track section north of Cambridge Junction at Hitchin to deposit some of its ballast. Having done its work, it moved forwards past Cadwell signal box and onto the relatively new additional down goods line. Driver James Norton continued down to Three Counties where he stopped, planning to shunt his train into a siding and run round to take it back to Cambridge Junction with all the track men who were relaxing in the brake vans at the front and rear of the train.

Also heading north from Cambridge Junction was Driver Henry Howitt with a special goods train consisting principally of manure wagons. Whereas absolute block working applied to the main line, permissive block applied to the goods line so Howitt was checked at Cadwell box and told "One in, just in front", but was permitted to continue on. Fog was just starting to build up in the area and Cadwell's fogmen came on a few minutes later.

What happened next was the source of considerable dispute. At Three Counties, signalman Henry Gatward claimed that the ballast train halted near his box, he put the distant and home signals to danger behind it (they were interlocked) and waited while Driver Norton of the ballast train moved his engine forwards of the points in readiness to run round. In Gatward's version, he had just changed the points and the disc signal when

Howitt's manure train ploughed into the back of the ballast train. One of the men in it just had time to shout "Oh pray, look here's an engine!" before the van was demolished. "It was turned completely over and the body smashed to pieces."

The brunt of the collision was taken by the brake van at the rear of the ballast train. Unfortunately there were seven railway labourers relaxing inside it; all were injured and one, Charles Silsby, was killed. Howitt's engine was derailed and turned on its side. Some of the debris spread onto the down main line on which a train was due, but further disaster was averted when this managed to stop.

At first sight this was the usual permissive block problem of the following train approaching too fast and being unable to stop, but Henry Howitt, his fireman Mayes and his guard George Adams all gave convincing evidence that the Three Counties distant signal had been 'off'. Indeed, Howitt and the fireman had both been so surprised by this that they had commented on it before putting on steam in the assumption that the ballast train had been shunted out of the way rather quickly.

Both Howitt and the fireman had also thought that the home signal had been 'off', so had had little time to stop their train before it hit the rear of the ballast, shunting the wagons forwards at speed since the locomotive had already run forwards.

Either Howitt or Gatward had to be responsible for the accident and it was Lt. Col. Yorke's job to decide on what had happened. Though he did not write in his report that he thought Gatward a liar, Yorke's evidence plainly pointed to this. Yorke set out his most telling evidence at the end of his conclusion – the ballast wagons had been pushed forwards on impact and only brought under control because Norton had skilfully moved forwards and allowed them to slowly catch up with his locomotive. However, according to Gatward he had changed the points to the siding after putting the down goods line signals to danger – in which case the wagons would have burst through points set against them. Yet there was no damage to the points. Plainly Gatward's account was wrong – he had not set the points, so if he had put the signals to danger before the accident (and even this was doubtful) he must have done so only seconds before the impact.

The town of Welwyn has, through the occurrence of a tragedy there, came to give its name to a signalling practice intended to prevent similar disasters known as 'Welwyn Control'. One summary of this is: "A control applied in Absolute Block areas preventing the Signaller from accepting a second train until the first has occupied and cleared the berth track circuit for the Home Signal."[13]

The accident at Welwyn Garden City on 15th June 1935 was one of a small number of very serious accidents that affected the London & North Eastern Railway in the 1920s and 1930s, taking place at about 11.27pm on a stretch of line that was one of the most modern and best-equipped on the whole railway. Fourteen people died, including a railway guard, a twelve-year-old girl and two babies. It attracted great attention at the time, especially as the circumstances seemed to recall the worst of the Victorian era yet it happened in a modern station with the best technology: "This railway accident is likely to be regarded as one of the most remarkable that have happened in this country. That in these days of modern signalling an express train should run into the rear of another express train seems unaccountable."[14]

Three trains played a direct role in the disaster but, as will be seen, a number of others contributed to the situation. The three trains were all late evening departures from King's Cross, starting with the 10.45pm down, train No.825, which passed through Welwyn Garden City at about 11.20pm at about 60mph. This was followed by train 825A down to Newcastle, with additional passenger accommodation to supplement its predecessor, running as the 10.53pm with Driver Morris and Guard J. McIntosh. This train passed Hatfield at about 65mph but, approaching Welwyn, was checked by first its distant signal at caution and then by the very late clearance of the home signal. The third train was the 10.58pm express parcels to Leeds, train 826, which Charles Barnes drove this night with K3 No.4009 at the front rather than the usual but less powerful Atlantic. One of the signalmen called this train 'the News' which suggests it carried papers.

When the home signal cleared, the speed of train 825A was down to about 15 or 20mph as the driver had allowed it to "roll until the starting signal came into view". Meanwhile train 826 had made very good progress with its powerful engine at the front and, after Wood Green, had run under clear signals. Barnes ran at or around 70mph. Approaching Welwyn under a clear distant signal, its driver was astonished to see that the home signal was at danger and had little time to brake when he saw the rear light of the passenger train a few hundred yards in front of him. Driver and fireman both stated that they had managed to put the brakes on, but other railwaymen travelling as passengers held contrary opinions. The Leeds train ploughed into the rear of train 825A, which by this time had recovered to about 20-25mph, close to Welwyn Garden City signal box.

Fortunately most of the carriages in the stricken train were modern designs with steel underframes, but the body of the rear carriage was completely shattered. Its frame was found "embracing the front end of the engine of train 826" in Lt. Col. Mount's ill-judged phrase. *The Times* described the scene: "…the steel bogie of the coach was twisted out of recognition, a tangled mass in the form of a double S which wound itself round the locomotive on both sides". However, the engine was so little damaged that it moved away under its own steam, at least as far as Welwyn North. The second to last carriage lost both its bogies in the shock, but its couplings held firm and so it continued to bump along the track with about 30 people in it. Five of the carriages in 825A were gas lit, but the two fires that started seem not have been gas-related. In one carriage the floor gave way and a man fell through to the track. Of the 40 or so passengers, almost all were killed or injured. Damage to train 826 was relatively light, except for its wooden-bodied vans, and the story was reported of one passenger who went to sleep at King's Cross and woke up at 6.00am the next day oblivious of any accident and with only a bitten lip.

George Gale, guard on the Leeds train, described his experience after clambering out onto the track: "The scene I witnessed was too terrible to describe. Moans and screams were coming from the shattered train, and bodies seemed to be lying all over the line. People were running up and down shouting, and for a moment nobody seemed to know what to do. Very quickly the rescue work began. Mutilated bodies were dragged

familiar with and normally at least twelve trains an hour.

The close running of the three trains between Hatfield No.3 and Welwyn was a significant factor. At Hatfield, Signalman Crowe sent trains 825 and 825A to Welwyn about four minutes apart after receiving 'train out of section' and he then received a second 'train out of section' message at 11.23pm from Howes at Welwyn and so offered him the third train, 826. On reflection, Crowe was surprised to have received 'train out of section' so quickly and very unusually rang Howes to check that he meant that 825A was out of section. To understand how unusual this was it is necessary to realise that Crowe later said he only rang Welwyn about once a year! Howes reassured him that the train had indeed cleared the section but Crowe did not seek to confirm this by naming 825A specifically. After the accident and an 'obstruction danger' bell signal from Welwyn, the two signalmen spoke again and Crowe thought Howes said train 826 had run into 825 – not 825A. However, Howes rang his colleague at Welwyn North, who reported that he had said "The News has run into the second portion of 825... Oh, it's terrible."

Howes had had a busy evening since starting his shift at 10.00pm. In his first 85 minutes, he handled 21 trains on his own including doing all the signalling and the 'booking' of them – and this was late at night. His colleague on the earlier shift, Birch, was even busier and had dealt with as many as 21 in an hour.

Howes's version of the sequence of events said that he was distracted by a phone call about a missing parcel at about 11.22pm, so that when Crowe rang to ask about the 'train out of section' he had thought of train 825 not 825A. In fact Howes implied that it was the phone call at a busy time that explained his slowness in clearing the signals for 825A. As the train occupied the track circuits he put the distant back to caution and then the home signal to danger – which accounted for how 826 passed the distant at clear only to sight the home at danger. Howes thought that less than a minute passed between accepting 825A from Crowe and then the phone call to check on 'train out of section' – and because of this he assumed the call to refer to the preceding 825. He was also dealing with up trains, which were passing at 11.23pm (up goods 787) and 11.25pm, and clearly lost track of all the movements. "The only way I can account for the accident is that I did not know anything about 826" he said, denying ever accepting 826, though Lt. Col. Mount thought it likely he had become confused about the up and down trains and sent the bell signals for the wrong trains and on the wrong block instruments. With eleven block bells, this seemed possible with a signalman perhaps not suited to such intensive work. Another possibility was that Howes noticed his down main line block instrument still showed 'train entered section' and he then assumed he had forgotten to send 'out of section' for what was in reality the previous train.

Much attention therefore focussed on the character and abilities of F. Howes, the 43-year-old Welwyn signalman. Howes had enjoyed a steady if unspectacular career, apparently

from the wreckage and laid alongside the track waiting for stretcher bearers to arrive. At first the rescue work was hampered by the darkness. Heartrending screams and groans added to the horror."[15]

Some passengers were in shock, with one man standing amidst the wreckage simply asking anyone who came by what the latest score was in the Test Match. At the nearby Cherry Tree Hotel, a dance was taking place but this was interrupted by an announcement; the male dancers all left their women to go and help. Later, the inquiry was held in the same hotel ballroom.

The King and Queen sent a message of condolence to the chairman of the LNER whilst the fourteen coffins were each loaded into separate luggage vans and taken to King's Cross, from where they were attached to trains to the appropriate destination.

The scene of this accident was one of the best-equipped parts of the LNER main line. The station and completely new signalling had only opened nine years earlier, in 1926. The main lines through it were operated by a single signal box using three-position needle block instruments. There was a small amount of track circuiting covering trains standing at the down home signals, which were connected with the block instruments at Hatfield No.3 box in the rear. Whereas the signalman at Welwyn controlled both up and down lines, Hatfield had separate boxes for each; Welwyn was graded as a 'Class 1' box – the highest level apart from Special 'A' and 'B' boxes. It certainly required competence, with eleven block bells to be leaving Retford Signalling School with a good impression, progressing from the quiet country station (Class 4) of Navenby (1912-21) to Class 3 Kirton (1921-32), a nine-month stay at Class 2 Ranskill on the main line and then Doncaster 'A'[16] before moving to Welwyn shortly before the accident – this was his first Class 1 posting. A retired District Superintendent later recalled him from his days at Kirton – "I did not think he was a very brilliant signalman" – and was surprised that he had been promoted to a Class 1 box, commenting that "since the new method of dealing with promotion men have got to higher positions than one would expect". Indeed, the seniority system had produced two or three rapid promotions for Howes, each yielding 5s a week extra.

In moving to a new box, Howes had to familiarise himself with its conditions by working with another signalman until he was ready to be 'examined' and 'passed out' as fit to work it on his own. Birch, with whom he worked, perhaps condemned Howes by faint praise when he told the inquiry that "he seemed to understand the duties fairly well. The work in this district seemed different to him from the work he had been doing, but he appeared to be grasping it all right". Although he had worked in a busy box at Doncaster, he had not had to signal both up and down lines there.

Howes took five weeks before he felt confident enough, having never encountered track circuiting before. He was then examined by the local inspector, Hook, on 11th May – five weeks before the disaster. Again he was condemned, this time by implications: "Howes is the first signalman in my experience to have taken five weeks to learn a signal box… He did not strike me as one of the brightest men… I had to drag everything out of him as he was not at all forthcoming."

Only a week after passing his exam, Howes had got into serious trouble. On 18th May he had lowered an outer home signal too early and a train had overrun the inner home at danger. The signalman and the train's driver had then attempted to 'hush up' the event and he then refused to contribute to the station master's report. The result was a summons to King's Cross on 4th June for disciplinary discussions. A meeting on 13th June had decided on a severe reprimand and a letter confirming this was sent to Howes at the box; he received it when he went on shift at 10.00pm on the fatal night.

Birch was there when Howes opened the letter, but could not tell if Howes was upset. "I should imagine it is difficult to see when Howes is upset, as he is of a quiet and retiring disposition." An LNER rule stated that signalmen should not receive disciplinary letters at the start of a shift, but it was argued that this was only confirming what Howes already knew, whereas he thought the case had been finished after his trip to London.

Lt. Col. Mount concluded that the disaster was caused by "improper entry into the section by 826 when it was still occupied by 825A" and resulting from "a lapse of the most serious nature" by Howes. Although he could not pin down the exact sequence of events, he saw that Howes was the wrong man for the job: "I doubt also whether he has the power and habit of thought, so essential in such a responsible position." Mount thought that Hook had been wrong to sign off Howes in the face of his own doubts and noted that Hook had never failed any man; "I think the facts show that in the end he was really

deceived as to Howes' suitability for the post." The Coroner's verdict was "accidental death owing to a temporary lapse of memory and error of judgement" by Howes.

Although Welwyn Garden City had a modern signalling system, its operation had revealed some serious weaknesses and exposed human limitations. With such an intensive train service, only full track circuiting would have kept Howes secure on his knowledge of every train. The equipment was too easy to confuse, it was ridiculous for a busy signalman to handle calls about lost parcels and there was then no-one to help him 'book' the trains. Mount also thought the 'seniority' system of placing signalmen had its flaws and lamented the closure of the Retford Signalling School. The resulting 'Welwyn Control' was, though, one attempt to prevent such things happening again and the term 'Welwyn releases' is also used to this day for a manual device used in absolute block working to ensure the signaller acts consciously.

The complex of junctions and sidings around Doncaster had been due for resignalling by 1940, but the war had intervened and work did not start until 1946. South of the station, signals were gradually being replaced by colour lights when signalman James McKone took up duty at Balby Junction on a hot day in August 1947.

It was not an especially busy afternoon for a Saturday, though the 1.10pm from King's Cross to Leeds was running late as McKone saw it go past his box, only to be stopped at the down main home signal of Bridge Junction box a couple of hundred yards away – in fact the last carriage was barely 177 yards from his box windows and he could have seen six other carriages had he cared to look. The Bridge Junction signalman reported that it stood there for two minutes as he offered it three times to the box in advance, South Yorkshire Junction. It then had some difficulty restarting.

McKone later said that his normal practice was then to reverse the points to lie for the down goods line so that any following train could be accepted 'clear' under the block regulations. On this day the 1.25pm from King's Cross to Leeds was close behind its late-running predecessor. In actual fact McKone did not turn it onto the goods line over which it was not authorised to run anyway, perhaps because this would have required ten lever movements on a sweltering day; possibly he was confused by signalling re-arrangements. Instead, he accepted the second train and lowered his signals irregularly without obtaining the 'line clear' from Bridge Junction box. Its driver, Foster, was anticipating being put into Platform 8 at Doncaster so had reduced his speed and in his evidence thought that he was down to about 30mph though his fireman thought 40mph. Due to the curve, his fireman was first to spot the train ahead and shouted; Foster put the brakes on but did not have enough time to reverse his engine.

The V2 locomotive No.936 ploughed into the back of the other Leeds train, demolishing the rear three carriages and overturning a fourth: "No-one could understand how anyone in the four coaches destroyed had escaped, and it can only be assumed that they were thrown clear through windows wide open in the heat of the day… As the coaches were split open passengers fell through the floors and were trapped against the rails, struck by torn pieces of wood and metal, and pinned under

The serious collision at Balby Junction, Doncaster, in 1947 occurred on a hot August day and was caused by a signalman's error, though life-expired equipment was also a factor.
(Peter Tuffrey)

bogie wheels."[17] The V2 came to a rest some 90 yards after the point of impact, parts of a carriage frame wrapped around it.

Eighteen people died and 118 were injured or suffered shock, the wooden-bodied carriages giving little protection despite the steel underframes with both trains full and standing. The injured included Foster.

McKone's immediate response was confusion. The first that Signalman Taylor at Bridge Junction box knew was when he received an 'obstruction danger' bell signal from McKone. He was never offered the following 1.25pm train and when the men spoke on the phone McKone told him that carriages from the 1.10pm were obstructing the line. Taylor asked whether anything had hit the 1.10pm and was categorical that McKone told him "No".

McKone accepted responsibility and made this very clear at the inquest, but his story of what had happened as told to the inquiry was confused, although the most likely explanation was that he had forgotten his normal routine of reversing the facing points to lie to the down goods. He did not look along the line

to see the rear of the 1.10pm before he accepted the 1.25pm and was then distracted by a phone call. After it he cleared four signals at once, which account was disputed by Foster later. He told the inquiry that his first thought had been that the 1.25pm had derailed, which contradicted the impression he had given to Taylor. No-one could be found who had rung McKone, but it was an unsatisfactory though widespread feature of the system that telephone bells rang in five boxes on an 'omnibus line' even though the call would be for only one of them.

The inquiring officers were sceptical about McKone's tale of having forgotten his usual practice of changing the points to the down goods line. It was concluded that he had "proved himself no longer fit to hold such a responsible position as that of a main line signalman", albeit after 21 years' service, including seven at Balby Junction.

Within three weeks the LNER had replaced the signals with a colour light home signal and additional track circuiting, after which the inspecting officers felt no need to make further recommendations.

FOOTNOTES

[1]   1 October 1860 according to Wrottesley, Vol 2, p.126.
[2]   Some accounts say new independent lines came into use in December 1868 and the junctions were removed at this site in January 1869, but the accident report plainly refers to the signals and points for the Hertford line at Welwyn Junction. In 1876 another independent single line was provided on the eastern or up side for the Hertford branch.
[3]   Wrottesley, Vol 2, p.127
[4]   *The Times*, 27 October 1869.
[5]   Now known as Welwyn North.
[6]   Accident report, 13 November 1869
[7]   *Manchester Guardian*, 3 November 1892
[8]   *Penny Illustrated Paper*, 12 November 1892; this source also clearly states that

Holmes had been asleep.
[9]   *Manchester Guardian*, 3 November 1892.
[10]   *The Times*, 6 December 1892.
[11]   Quotation taken from the accident report.
[12]   This station was very close to Arlesey, and indeed was known as 'Arlesey Siding' for the first three months after its opening on 1 April 1886.
[13]   I Ellis, *Ellis' British Railway Engineering Encyclopaedia*, 2006, p. 423
[14]   *The Times*, 17 June 1935
[15]   *The Times*, 17 June 1935.
[16]   Doncaster 'A' might sound like a more important box than Welwyn, but Michael Back notes that it only covered the up lines.
[17]   *Manchester Guardian*, 11 August 1947.

4

OFF THE TRACK

Derailments were most often due to faulty maintenance work on the track or to technical failure of the rails, which was common in the early days but made a spectacular return with the Hatfield disaster in 2000. Track also failed due to heat, as described in Chapter 7. Though it might be assumed that derailments caused by poor work practices would have been eliminated by better safety routines, it has never been possible to end risk entirely. This was illustrated both in the serious derailment at Potters Bar in 2002 (see Chapter 8) and in an accident where there were no casualties but nonetheless also serious implications at King's Cross on 16th September 2003. Overnight engineering work by the contractor, Jarvis, failed to resolve problems with a cast crossing and ran over time; a plain rail was put in as a temporary measure, but a departing train was then signalled over a route that did not exist! After the derailment, Jarvis announced that it was pulling out of railway contract work[1] but as Jarvis-Fastline continued to do some work until going into administration in March 2010.

In the early days of the railways there was often uncertainty as to exactly what caused a derailment. After the 3rd March 1849 derailment at Morden Carrs, six miles north of Darlington, Capt. George Wynne surmised that excessive speed, a tendency of the Stephenson-built locomotive to "rock and pitch" and the "flexible line" laid across the bog all contributed.

A lightly loaded mail train, with only three first class carriages, was heading south from Durham; on board were two judges fresh from finishing the Assizes at Durham – Mr. Justice Coleridge and Mr. Baron Alderson.[2] Travelling at about 50mph, the locomotive derailed, throwing out Fireman John Hardy and Driver John Love, both of whom died. The coupling to the carriages snapped and they diverged to the west side but the engine and its tender tore up both lines. The engine seems to have rolled over before ending up in the bog on the east side, up to its wheels in the soggy ground and facing the opposite direction from which it had started. Its chimney had been broken off and was largely buried in the peat and it was concluded that the locomotive had rolled over at least once – so the breaking of the couplings had averted a major disaster. The two judges "alighted and minutely examined the scene of the disaster".

Captain Wynne was sent to investigate, but the inquest had started before he could contribute and, somewhat piqued, he noted that "On my arrival at Darlington I found the inquest over, and that the jury had recorded a verdict of accidental death. The proceedings were very short, and of the witnesses examined none were able to form a conjecture as to the cause of the accident." One can feel his annoyance at the tomfoolery of amateurs. Wynne took notes from the inquest where Thomas Harrison, the resident engineer, said that in his view the

derailment had been caused by suddenly putting on steam round the curve. Confusingly, the train's guard described the railway at this point as "nearly level and quite straight". However, Wynne was also interested in the construction of the line, which had been laid across a peat bog initially on cross-sleepers. However, three years earlier it had sunk in places and so had been rebuilt with 60ft piles sunk into the peat; nonetheless, he noted that "the rails yield considerably under the weight of a passing engine".

After the accident Wynne's office engaged in some correspondence with the York, Newcastle & Berwick Railway about speed restrictions. The YNB was evasive – having issued printed orders of a 25mph speed limit after the accident, it hoped to avoid questions referring to before it. After several letters, it admitted there had been no written instructions as such, though they had told the drivers to slow down across the Carrs.

Poor trackwork

As we have already seen, the sharp curve south of Morpeth station has a particular infamy in East Coast Main Line history as a spot where speeding trains come to grief. Speed was suspected as the main cause when the so-called up 'Flying Scotchman'[3] overnight train from Edinburgh derailed there on 25th March 1877. "In a moment the front part of the train was a wreck, and was heaped up in one mass of ruin" *The Times* report said. A day after the accident little was known, but this did not stop insinuation: "The cause of the accident is unknown, but there is a curve just after leaving Morpeth station which may have something to do with it."[4]

Attention therefore focussed on driver Enoch Shipley, who was suspected of having brought NER No.901 to grief, taking the lives of five passengers with it. The engine had clearly derailed first, crossing over the down line and damaging the Wansbeck branch; it ended up ploughed into the ground with sleepers and rails festooning its front. Comments quickly surfaced about trains rounding the "pretty strong curve" at "high rates of speed" and Shipley was said to have passed the station at full speed on a dark and misty night.

All the damage was cleared away by 5pm the next day and Captain Tyler was not happy to find most of the evidence gone by the time he could arrive from London. Damaged rails had mostly disappeared and broken chairs vanished, but by digging in the ballast he was able to find some broken nuts and other items of interest. He concluded that the leading wheels of the engine had mounted the off side rail of the curve and by the time the inquest opened there was speculation that the track had been damaged before the derailment.

Shipley was still too ill to travel, but his case was not helped by his fireman, Thomas Wiley, who had said that "the company ought to be ashamed of themselves to make us run round the

The devastation north of Berwick in 1880; at least two cranes have arrived to recover the wrecks, whilst onlookers have strayed onto railway property! (Author's Collection)

ACCIDENT NEAR BERWICK: VIEW LOOKING TOWARDS BURNMOUTH.

curve at such a speed" and who admitted that he had been "afraid" on several occasions at that location. Having listened to Tyler, the inquest jury came to the conclusion that the derailment was caused by a detached fishplate although it still recommended lower speeds whilst Tyler felt that an improved line would be helpful.

Defective work by platelayers was even more in evidence in the accident at Marshall Meadows, just north of Berwick, on 10th August 1880. This accident was witnessed by local resident Annie Arnot, who was standing on an overbridge watching the express pass at about 11.10pm. The impact was such that she lapsed into repetition: "Then there was a sound as if something had exploded, and I could tell no more because of the steam. As soon as the train stopped whistling the sound of the explosion came and I saw the steam fly… I then knew the train was off the line from the crash I heard."

The engine left the track, parted from its tender and crossed the tracks heading up the bank. The guard's van followed and ended in two pieces, the wheels and frame on top of the tender and its body twenty yards up the bank. The driver, Thompson, was killed instantly – "his remains presented a terrible appearance".[5] His fireman died soon after at Berwick Infirmary and another guard, who was travelling as a passenger, was also killed.

The surviving guard, George Hodson, gave a detailed account of the events also immediately afterwards. He was knocked out initially by the impact, but when he came to: "…found that the whole of the train was off the line, splintered, shattered and regularly huddled up. Some carriages were on top of the others, and one or two quite suspended in the air, so that one could walk under them. The lamps and windows were all broken, and the axletrees had come from underneath. He heard no screaming, but saw the passengers with their heads out of the windows, looking very pale, and some with blood-stained faces, calling him to unlock the doors. When all were got out he walked toward the engine, which was standing across the up line, turned completely round. The driver and fireman were lying on the bank, the life seeming to have been completely knocked out of them by one fearful blow. The fireman was not then quite dead, but died a moment afterwards. The guard (Pearce) was lying quite still on the bank..."[6]

For the time, this was a high speed derailment – with the train perhaps having been travelling at 60mph. The three dead were all railwaymen and they were all buried at Gateshead. At the time there was still concern about 'racing' on the two routes to Scotland and within a day a survivor had written to the press to say that the rails were out of line and the track not properly "riveted". By this time it was already known that a gang had been replacing sleepers on the line just before the accident.

A passenger on the train was North British Railway Locomotive Inspector Henry McGechen, who got out and looked at the track. "There was only one spike in each chair of the outside rail" he later told the inquest. One of those who testified about the trackwork was PC W. Moore, the first policeman on the scene, who by chance had previously spent eight months as a platelayer with the North Eastern Railway. "Those spikes I saw appeared to have been drawn" he said "and I would expect that would be preparatory to the sleeper being removed."[7]

Others who arrived later that night also looked in detail for the cause of the derailment. William Teasdale[8], NER Permanent Way Inspector, had no hesitation in identifying weaknesses of another company and found a rail length which "was too wide to the extent of an inch and three quarters".[9]

Teasdale reported to the inquest that he had examined the track 40 yards back from the rear of the train and that was where it was out of gauge. He found "a good many chairs with only one spike" and "some sleepers loose at the end". John Weallows reported seeing chairs without spikes and flange marks on the sleepers.

Colonel Yolland took rather longer to arrive and by the time he had done so the North British had removed the crashed stock and repaired the line – destroying all the evidence. Yolland was scathing about this later.

Grant Renton was the foreman platelayer or 'surfaceman' whose gang of four men had been working at Marshall Meadows. His initial reaction was to blame the train for being 'out of gauge' – a brave argument given it had already travelled from Edinburgh! He said that they had showed the warning green flag to warn that the track was partially spiked but that trains often ignored it – and this one had been doing 60mph.

The green flag became central to the inquiry. Apart from the fact that it was dark, there was no 'surfaceman' attending it and there was a lack of wind – it was unlikely a train driver travelling at 60mph would notice it and another driver testified to not having seen it. However, Turnbull, the train guard, said he did see it.

The coroner became involved in a detailed investigation into railway trackwork practice. He was told that it was common practice to put one spike into a chair and then let a train pass over "to get a better gauge"; the coroner found this extraordinary – "And the safety of the passengers is endangered so that you may get a better gauge?" he asked. Evidence was produced to show the flag was "faded green" (though it is hard to see what difference this would have made) and that the driver of the train received no advance warning of any trackwork. Amidst loud cheers, the coroner's jury returned a verdict of 'accidental death' though the case underlines the maxim that there is no accident without cause.

One of the strange features of this accident was the lack of damage to the locomotive and stock despite the three fatalities. A few days after the accident the engine was at Tweedmouth, waiting to be steamed. At the end of August it was reported that the locomotive and carriages were all at the East Coast Joint Stock company's sheds at Doncaster, where all marvelled at the lack of damage to the locomotive in particular.

Colonel Yolland delivered his verdict in mid-September. He concluded that "the foreman of the gang of platelayers is greatly to be blamed for having omitted to place a single spike in at least three of the chairs of the new sleepers" as well as having put in only one spike over a distance of more than nine rail lengths. However, Yolland was keen to ensure that blame did not attach to one man. He referred to the ignorance of Mr. Carswell, the North British engineer, who did not keep a close watch on his own tracks and was unaware of the 'single spike' practice; he also blamed the company itself which he complained had only equipped about six or seven miles of the line between Edinburgh and Berwick with absolute block signalling – which he considered essential for high speed running. And high speed, he thought, was the case – the poor trackwork would not have mattered had it not been for the "excessive" speed and lack of adequate warning. A green flag, which may or may not have been waving in a breeze, was insufficient warning for a train travelling at nearly 60mph – especially when not accompanied by a track worker.

This was the only fatal accident in the Berwick area, although on 11th December 1891 there were two serious incidents during snow. In the first a goods train shunting at Berwick station was literally sliced through by a Scots express in the middle of the night – without fatalities – and later in the day a goods guard was run over and seriously injured at Marshall Meadows.

After the accident at St. Neots in November 1895 (see later in this chapter), the Great Northern began to relay a lot of its main line to cope with heavier express engines. Although Major Marindin suggested 90lb rail,[10] most of the work was done with 85lb rails. The programme was a major inconvenience for the company and was done rather hastily, leading to fatal results at Little Bytham.

The 5.30pm up Leeds express on 7th March 1896 was travelling at about 60-70mph down the famous Stoke Bank through pouring rain when it reached a piece of newly relaid track (using 85lb rail) north of Little Bytham station. The track here had been relaid five days before, subjected to a 30mph limit with flagmen to enforce this until about eight hours earlier. However, the GNR practice was not to fully ballast the line until a few days later, so the combined effects of heavy rain and a 90-ton engine and tender combination, caused the track to subside and spread on one side as the train passed over it. The last two carriages derailed, the first hitting a bridge parapet and the final carriage going through the parapet, down 30ft onto the road and then partly up the bank on the far side, killing at least two passengers. Although the vacuum brakes had come on, it took the rest of the train nearly 1,000 yards to stop on the greasy rails. The train "had skidded down the line…like a skater going over ice, the sparks flying up and making it appear as if the train was on fire".[11] The penultimate carriage of the front portion, still attached to the train but minus its roof and most of its body so that "it looked… like a goods truck", remained attached and travelled this distance with one passenger still sitting in the wreckage. The guard was knocked out, but came round and carried an injured woman half a mile to the station.

Richard Johnson, the GNR's engineer, thought that the track had probably been put out of line by the heavy coal train that preceded the express, following a heavy storm. Major Marindin

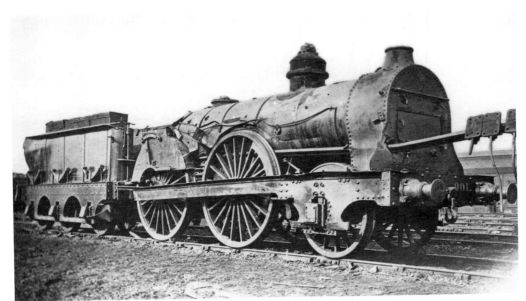

North Eastern No.901 was badly damaged in the derailment at Morpeth in 1877, where five died. It was followed by a number of wild claims and rumours.
(Ken Hoole Collection)

The cause of the New Southgate derailment was the excess of speed on poorly maintained track, but Driver Bill Hoole's career survived intact so that he retained his 'legendary' status.
(Ben Brooksbank)

criticised the lack of proper ballast especially outside the sleeper ends and a lack of depth, but also felt that having brakes on only half the wheels of the coaching stock was insufficient. The weight of the engine on the relaid track, and after heavy rain, had caused one side to move; this version of the famous Stirling 'Singles' had a high axle-loading of about 19 tons. Before this accident, no-one on the GNR seems to have had any concern about running full speed expresses over unballasted track for two or three days. Marindin also investigated the debate over whether the vacuum brake had worked, concluding that the lengthy stopping time was due to only half the wheels being braked. He recommended that all wheels should be braked if possible.

It might be argued that a derailment caused by poor maintenance of the track should be considered as dereliction of duty by those responsible, but in the case of the derailment at New Southgate on 17th July 1948 the problem was caused by a small error of judgement. In another railway grade, such as shunter, or at a different location this might not have led to a fatal accident. For Ganger Flitney it meant the death of a railway colleague was his responsibility on the eve of his retirement after a successful working life.

It was six o'clock in the morning when the 7.50pm Edinburgh to King's Cross entered Barnet Tunnel behind Class A2/1 No.60508 *Duke of Rothesay*. At the controls was Bill Hoole, one of the most famous of the 'Top Link' drivers, and he had allowed his locomotive to drift up to – and over – the speed limit of 60mph. The line into London had been authorised for 90mph before the war but track renewals and drainage work had slipped during hostilities so a lower limit had been imposed. Hoole's statement that he had shut off steam and was coasting was contradicted by the signalman at Hadley Wood. The average speed from Hatfield to Cemetery was 77.3mph and perhaps as high as 81mph from Potters Bar to the point of the final derailment.[12] As the report noted, "there was no margin of safety even at the moderately high speed of 70mph" but Hoole's error was not judged to be the fatal one – and he had an excuse. Lt. Col. Wilson concluded that "Driver Hoole was probably exceeding the authorised speed, but he was not assisted by an indicator on the footplate" since speed indicators had been removed during the war.[13] Such a let-off was not available for the man who looked after the track.

The 605-yard tunnel was notoriously damp and in its middle the trailing bogie wheels on the locomotive derailed just after a 'humped' joint. A driver of a down parcels train saw the express appear out of the tunnel with sparks coming from the engine's bogie and small pieces of metal showered on the northbound train as the chairs were broken up. Emerging from the tunnel, the locomotive's leading bogie then derailed nearly 700 yards along the line at a 'V' crossing just beyond Cemetery signal box. The leading wheels ran to the left and the trailing wheels twisted to the right so that the bogie was askew the up line. After this, Hoole said "the debris began to fly". The wheels ripped up the track and so the rest of the train derailed behind. *Duke of Rothesay* separated from its train and "heeled over gradually" to the right, killing Fireman Young who was on that side of the footplate although Hoole escaped with only a slight injury. The leading carriage also turned over, but there were no other serious injuries to passengers or crew. This result was seen as another success for the buckeye couplings.

Attention focussed on the track, which had been completely relaid through the tunnel in 1936 and again re-railed in 1944. This mile length of the four track main line was the responsibility of Ganger Flitney, who was nearly 65 and had served the railway for 44 years. It was a simple task to trace the damage to the rails back along the line and they stopped close to a joint in the tunnel which appeared raised into a hump that, with lighting, was visible to the naked eye. The track rose at 1 in 132 to this point and then fell at 1 in 80 straight after. This was at a point where there was a continuous drip of water.

This joint had been lifted and packed on 11th July by Flitney himself, the two sleepers either side of the joint being packed more substantially than the others with limestone chippings whilst traffic continued on the line. These two sleepers were closer together than others, being less than 18in apart. Flitney had expected the soft ground to yield beneath the pressure of passing trains, but had overcompensated for this at the joint and over successive days the 'hump' had become more pronounced and was ¾in when examined. After the accident a 15mph speed limit was imposed. Flitney's sub-ganger, Stevens, disagreed with his view that this joint had not been problematic and said that it required lifting "fairly often" due to the wet. Flitney also failed to notice that the cross-level was irregular and claimed to have checked it on 11th July.

Permanent Way Inspector Compton had supervised Flitney's work and inspected the line. He did not think the raised joint sufficient to derail the train and defended the ganger's work to the inquiry. His supervisor, Mowl, started by telling Mount that the joint was a "trifle stiff" but not dangerous, but gradually shifted his views to conclude that it was "undesirable" and should have been immediately corrected. No-one else, though, had complained of a rough ride.

Wilson concluded that the combination of the irregular cross-level with the rise and fall over the joint contributed to rapidly changing weight distribution on the bogie. "Speed in excess of the authorised limit appears to have contributed" he thought, noting that Hoole was "running faster than usual." Flitney's failure to check with the superelevation gauge was a serious omission, however, but Compton and Mowl were also criticised.

Broken Rails

A railway accident involving a high speed derailment and several deaths at Hatfield led to a trenchantly sober editorial in *The Times:* "…a railway accident which, for singularity of origin and consequences, has few parallels in the catalogue of such disasters… the source of fatal mischief may lurk beneath the smoothest and most satisfactory surface…"

This opinion could, even allowing for the slightly archaic language, have been written about the Hatfield derailment of 2000 when 'gauge corner cracking' became briefly the subject of national debate – and rather extended speed restrictions on the nation's railways. But this was not 2000, it was 1860, yet the two accidents at Hatfield occurred in much the same way and very close to each other.

The accident of 23rd April 1860, like its successor, required some forensic technical work and led to fears over railway safety. The 1860 editor noted that "a source of risk which, up to the present time, has been productive of little mischief" had led to the destruction of a passenger train. The fault lay in the materials. "We have hitherto been accustomed to regard wood and iron as tolerably safe, if managers and men would but use them properly, and we can ill afford to lose so agreeable a ground of confidence."[14] The impact in 1860, though, proved rather more short-lived than in 2000.

The train involved was the 10.00am King's Cross to Manchester and Leeds, which approached Hatfield as a group of platelayers was working on the down track. They were clearing ballast away from the rails near a set of points in preparation for 'paying up' part of the permanent way that had 'slightly subsided'. The men knew that an up coal train was also approaching, so they stepped aside into a siding on the down side.

Driver James Barefoot was heading north at about 50mph and had no reason to slow for the track work. As his engine reached the crossing beneath the station footbridge, he said that the engine "oscillated" before steadying itself. He later referred to this as if the rail had "sunk". The guard's bell, which was connected by a rope along the train, rang but then the rope snapped. The guard, Joseph Moorhouse, also felt some "oscillating" at the footbridge and put the brakes on when he saw some wheels off the track on the west side.

As the train passed in front of the platelayers over the points, the fifth carriage derailed, "dragging with it the remainder of the train in the most frightful confusion". As the train reached the next set of points, some of the wheels of the derailed carriages were wrenched off. Barefoot did not immediately realise what disaster had occurred, but after the rope snapped he looked around and put the engine into reverse in a desperate effort to slow it. He saw some of the carriages "jumping up". Moorhouse felt the Bradford carriage "go over". Some of the carriages came into contact with the passing coal train and diverted back across onto the down platform, bringing down part of the roof. The fifth carriage fell apart, with pieces dragged 200 yards on the side; its wheels were partly forced through the floor. The sixth carriage collided with a water crane and turned over, but the front part of the train continued forwards for 703 yards. The coal train was also damaged and coal blocked the line.

Barefoot's engine and tender had been disconnected from the first van of the train and he realised the unbraked carriages might catch up and collide with him, so he put on steam rather than slowing.

The train had 50 passengers and "it was somewhat marvellous how many escaped with their lives".[15] The one passenger killed was Francis Pym, a son of a former Great Northern director, whose body was found across the up line at a distance from the carriages – reports variously claimed the distance as between 15 and 35 yards. Pym had been travelling in the middle first class compartment of the fifth vehicle and may have been thrown out whilst trying to escape; he was then run over. A passenger in the next compartment had only a minor hand injury.

There was a second person killed, George Venables, one of the platelayers, who was hit by a piece of broken rail three feet long.

Barefoot went back along the track and saw Pym dying. He also found a broken rail at the crossing. There he met Thomas Williams, a GNR Inspector, who had been a passenger on the train. Williams immediately suspected an error by the platelayers so he ordered the station master to take their names.

The Coroner therefore centred his initial attention on these men, starting with John Ward, the foreman. Ward explained they had brought up new rails to be fitted but said they had only removed the ballast down to sleeper level and had not taken out any keys. Ward said the crossing had been perfectly safe for the express although one rail had lost part of its 'flange'. It is an interesting comment on practice at the time that Ward's gang were to replace a rail between express trains. Nonetheless the damage to track was at this point – the check rail had gone, the 'way rail' been torn out and four chairs were broken.

Attention shifted to the rail that had broken. It was found that this rail had a flaw – a very fine 18 inch crack – from its centre to the bottom at a point where part of the 'flange' had been 'abraided'. The Great Northern was using 'double sided' rails so when this rail had become worn and flattened on its top, it had simply been turned over – though part of the 'flange' needed to be removed to make it fit into the chair. George Morris, a foreman platelayer, reported that he had turned the rail several months earlier and he had broken off part of the top flange. Despite this evidence, the chief engineer said that "the longitudinal flaw was of no importance".

The family of Pym brought in an expert engineer of their own, William Pole, to give evidence. He argued that the ease with which Morris had broken off part of the rail showed its weakness and that there were two areas of weakness. He thought "the germ of a crack" had existed at the top of the rail before it was turned and then had grown worse in its unsupported position at the bottom.

The jury's verdict was unusually lengthy. After recording a verdict of accidental death, it noted: "…they think that the rail, in consequence of its being cracked, and of the flange of the rail having been partially knocked off, was unsafe, but that the crack was not visible, and was not known to the company or their servants, and that the ballast had not been removed sufficiently to affect the safety of the line, but they nevertheless think that the platelayers should have had instructions to signal to every train, especially express trains, while the points and crossings were under repair."

Yolland largely agreed with Pole's interpretation but also noted that it took three quarters of a mile to stop the train – arguing strongly for continuous brakes. John Ward was therefore exonerated after what must have been a very stressful period for him.

In November 1895 the great excitement over the 'railway race to Aberdeen' was perhaps just past its zenith, but the GNR was still proud that it had introduced new engines on its main expresses such as the 11.30pm down sleeper express to Scottish destinations. Laden to nine vehicles, the train had only 27 passengers on its fateful night, 9th-10th November.

The train left King's Cross at 11.30pm behind Stirling Single No.1006 and half an hour into the new day it was already well on its journey. 40 yards south of St. Neots station, opposite the South signal box, a rail broke beneath the train whilst it was travelling at 50mph or more and derailed its middle carriages, some of which collided with coal wagons in the siding opposite the North signal box despite the good working of the vacuum brakes. The effect of the first carriage's collision with the coal trucks was to drive its floor halfway through the body of the following carriage. A Miss Louisa O'Hara was killed when she was thrown out of a sleeping car, her head hitting a coal wagon, and Mr. Corrie, a flax merchant, died soon afterwards. The Countess of Rosslyn was injured as was a relative of the Duke of Portland, Mr. Frederick Cavendish Bentinck, who was thrown into a coal truck "and deposited in a quantity of coal dust, by which he was covered", suffering "a broken rib and severe shock".

Sir Henry Oakley of the Great Northern was very quick – if not too hasty – to defend his company. He told the press that there had been a "clean and sharp" break, blaming poor manufacture of a "brittle" rail. However, the press also reported an unnamed GNR official who told them the rail had broken beneath the engine – one of the GNR's new, heavier Stirling Singles.

Major Marindin investigated, with help from the specialist iron experts Kirkcaldy & Co. They found no obvious defect until they used a microscope, which showed that flaws in the iron had developed due to wear – not due to poor manufacture. Mr. Kirkcaldy told the inquest that "it appeared to have changed in character in parts through wear".[16] A 26ft length of rail had fractured into nineteen pieces – further undermining Oakley's statement. Marindin was scathing – the GNR's 84lb per yard rails were not strong enough for its new engines and he noted that some lengths of even 80lb still existed. He recommended replacing the whole with 90lb rail – although ¡careless work in doing this then caused the derailment at Little Bytham in March 1896.

In fact the rails that broke reflected even worse on the GNR than this. The line had been relaid in 1886 and the old rails from 1873 stacked in the goods yard for possible secondary use in sidings. At some stage before the derailment, two of the newer rails on the main line had been replaced by old rails, which it was found had been worn down to 70lb per yard and suffered microscopic cracking.

The derailment between Welham Green and Hatfield on 17th October 2000 is one of the best-known railway accidents of modern times, although not one of the most destructive. It demonstrated the resilience of modern coaching stock in that only four people died in a derailment at 115mph and they were all in one carriage which hit an overhead line equipment mast. However, the accident generated a panic about the fracturing of rails beneath high speed trains and ensured that newspaper journalists wrote 'learned' articles on 'gauge corner cracking'. It had a huge impact on rail travel for months: in terms of 'damage', this accident therefore probably had wider impact than any other East Coast line disaster, whilst it also demonstrated the problems in charging companies or individuals with manslaughter after such accidents.

Prior to the Hatfield disaster, in late 1999, a problem with a rail at Aycliffe in Co. Durham had given rise to widespread concern amongst Railtrack's London & North Eastern Zone engineers about 'gauge corner cracking', a technical phrase which was to gather great significance in the coming months. A review of the whole route identified a number of priority sites where similar problems were a significant risk and these sites were each accorded a priority level. Some of the highest priorities were identified on the high speed curves through the Hatfield area at Hatfield itself and at Welham Green just to the south. Priorities were decided in February 2000 and work at Welham Green scheduled for May 2000, to be done after the work at Hatfield. However, a decision was made that Welham Green was an urgent matter and so it was rescheduled for the third week of April. Rail was not successfully delivered to the site until 28th April and then the over-running work at Hatfield caused further delays for rerailing at Welham Green with dates being suggested into the start of the next year.[17] Problems at the site were well known. Rails laid in 1982 had been replaced in 1995.

The constant delays were motivated in part by worries over delays to trains. As the final report stated, Railtrack was "biased towards performance-driven decision"[18] and "train delays" was the most significant target. There was a marked reluctance to impose speed limits. At the same time the condition of the track was inspected weekly by staff from Balfour Beatty Rail Maintenance but they, together with engineers from Railtrack, had a difficult job making visual inspections of rails on a high speed main line with curves because of the staff 'protection' arrangements. At Welham Green, staff on the track would only have a four-second sighting of an approaching express and so inspection was often conducted from the cess rather than on the track.

On 17th October 2000 the 12.10 King's Cross to Leeds set out with a trainee driver at the controls and an experienced colleague alongside her to supervise. They were carrying 170 passengers and twelve staff. Half a mile south of Hatfield, just north of Oxlease Avenue bridge on the Welham Green curves, the train derailed as the left-hand rail – the outside of the curve and canted at 130mm – fragmented beneath the train in two sections. Marks on the locomotive wheels suggested it had possibly passed over the fracture and then the rail fragmented beneath the first two carriages. The lower part of the rail remained intact though damaged.

The locomotive, No.91023, and the first two carriages stayed on the track but the next eight all derailed at high speed which increased the rail fragmentation. Carriage 'C' hit signal mast K563. The buffet car bogies were ripped off and it tipped on its side, separating it from coach 'H'; it then struck two of the overhead line equipment masts and the second of these penetrated through the roof to the floor of the carriage. All those killed were in this carriage and two buffet staff were seriously injured. This was the first serious accident with Mark IV coaches and they proved the strength of a modern train.

Four people were killed and over 70 reported injuries. A further risk from the live overhead wires, which had been pulled down, was well managed by railway staff and they were soon switched off completely although current breakers would probably have operated anyway.

Pieces of the rail were taken away for analysis at Sheffield. As the final report commented, "the rail fracture was due to the

The high speed derailment at Hatfield might not have resulted in any fatalities, except a carriage struck an overhead line post as it turned on its side.

(image provided by the Health and Safety Laboratory)

presence of multiple pre-existing failure cracks". In fact there were two sections that disintegrated. The first section of 35m length broke into over 300 pieces and there was then a 44m section that remained intact, followed by a further 54m which also fragmented. The rails on the curve had been subjected to fatigue caused by trains with 'out of round' wheels with flat sections, also by poor jointing and poor packing under the rail. In these conditions stresses might develop into fractures or cracks and at Welham Green there was found to have been extensive cracking which became known as 'rolling contact fatigue'. However, the press picked up on the idea of 'gauge corner cracking' and subsequent official reports indicated some routine confusion in the use of the two terms even by rail engineers.[19]. The first report on the accident identified 'gauge corner cracking' as a form of rolling contact fatigue. What actually happened is explained by "surface-initiated fatigue cracks developed into deep transverse (downwards) cracks that

severely weakened the rail" and were inadequately identified by inspection practices – mainly because this feature had not previously been understood. It was also found that existing ultrasound testing methods were not always effective, especially when there was 'spalling' on the surface or cracks were at an angle.

But this was not just a technical matter, it was also a political one. The Chairman of Railtrack criticised the structure in place for investigating accidents[20] but the privatisation of the railways had always had its opponents and the causes of the accident showed up evident weaknesses in how the permanent way was being managed by Railtrack and its contractors. "The poor condition of the rail in the derailment zone indicated serious failures in the maintenance regime" the final report commented.[21] Authors Barry and Slater concluded baldly, "the Hatfield crash was not an accident".[22] The rails should have been visually checked every week and, although this was generally done, there were variations in how effectively it was done which were closely related to the inherent risks in examining the rails of a high speed line whilst trains were running and often with only one look-out. However, Barry and Slater blamed "…systematic underinvestment of Railtrack in track repair, the lack of engineering expertise in the Railtrack board, and the failure to maintain an adequate programme of monitoring of the state of the railway infrastructure. The company did not have a detailed register of its assets and their condition. Assessments of the condition of the track that had been made were not systematic, co-ordinated or acted upon".

It is a criticism that echoes the attacks on the management of the Great Northern more than a century earlier.

In the aftermath of the tragedy, Railtrack imposed emergency speed restrictions throughout the country at any site which had been identified for rail replacement because of gauge corner cracking. Speeds were to be reduced by one third, but to 20mph where fragments were breaking off the rail surface – a process termed 'spalling'. The resultant impact on the rail system was chaotic for months and criticism of the systems for regulating the railways and ensuring safety were widespread. The imposition of temporary timetables forced Railtrack into disputes about compensation with the train operating companies and, ultimately, caused such damage to the organisation that its replacement became inevitable. A nationwide search for more 'broken rails' was still discovering 'five a day' in mid-December 2000[23] and costs were being put at £150million.

The inquiries and legal proceedings were protracted. Interim reports were produced on 20th October and in January 2001 but the final report was not published until July 2006. Balfour Beatty[24] "failed to manage effectively… the inspection and maintenance of the rail"[25] and, in turn, Railtrack had failed to manage Balfour Beatty.

In February 2002 the Health & Safety Executive submitted proposals to prosecute under the 1974 Health & Safety at Work Act. Cases were brought against six individuals, Balfour Beatty and Railtrack for manslaughter and gross negligence. On 1st September 2004 the manslaughter charges against Railtrack and its junior staff were dismissed and in July 2005 a Judge dismissed these charges against Railtrack and Balfour Beatty executives. Charges of corporate manslaughter against Balfour Beatty were also dismissed. In July 2005 Balfour Beatty pleaded guilty on Health & Safety charges and two months later Railtrack was found also guilty, but individuals were acquitted. The result was that Balfour Beatty was fined £10million and Railtrack £3.5million though the former appealed against this and succeeded in reducing its fine to £7.5million in July 2006.

Points and crossings

In December 1877 a Grantham to Boston local train approached the junction points at Barkston[26] South Junction but derailed on a check rail. A disaster could have resulted since engine and tender blocked the up line, but the only fatal victim was guard John Russell whose van to the front of the train was smashed, "its unfortunate occupant being killed on the spot and his body horribly mangled".

The later destructive derailment of a Hull/York to King's Cross express at Doncaster Balby Road bridge on 16th March 1951 attracted particular attention because it occurred only a few yards from a similarly terrible disaster in August 1947. A2/2 Class No.60501 *Cock o' the North* left Doncaster on the up slow line, which had been laid on the formation of an old siding in 1910. This joined the up main at Balby Road bridge– where the up fast was canted four inches on a curve. Due to this configuration, which was enforced by shortage of space, the up slow had a speed limit of 10mph; in the days before speedometers were standard this was regularly exceeded – by double the speed or more. Controlling the speed anyway would have been more difficult as the train was assisted in the rear by a tank engine.

Cock o' the North joined the up main with no problem, but the rear bogie of the third carriage or the leading one of the fourth derailed and the others followed. A signalman described seeing sparks coming from beneath the third carriage: "I saw the coach sway off the rail. I shouted to my mate and the next thing I knew all the coaches were coming for us. I jumped into an alcove as the coach smashed into the stonework of the bridge pier. The train seemed to be gathering speed and was pumping hard."[27]

Two survivors from the worst affected carriage, the third, described their experiences: "We knew there was going to be an accident when the train started to vibrate and sway. Another passenger told us to pull our legs up, and we all hung on the sides. Then there was a long rending crash, a tumult of noise, and to our horror we saw the carriage behind coming past us by the side of our window.

"The whole of the corridor caved in on us. The carriage seemed to rise in the air and come apart, and the next minute it was all a mass of wreckage. There was a woman standing in the midst of the debris with timber all around her."[28]

One of the carriages was caught against the brick pier of the bridge and under pressure from those following it; in the words of a policeman, it was "twisted like chewing gum". The accident report referred to it as having been "virtually wrapped around the pier' and almost all of the fourteen deaths were in this carriage, including three from one family. Two people were recovered from beneath the carriage bogie. The train was derailed back to its tenth vehicle. The scene was close to houses and railway facilities, so rescuers were soon on the scene including a "frail-looking, grey haired woman who recklessly ignored dangers" in order to help[29] – and who was one of the last to stop working.

Initial attention focussed on whether Driver Wadsworth had been exceeding the speed limit – he probably had been but not, apparently, more than seems to have become normal. So attention shifted to the track and the trailing 'V' crossing. In order to even out the cant, oak packing had been put underneath the left-hand rail but some of this had decayed and inspectors also found one missing bolt and another loose. "The strength of a crossing depends largely on the integrity of the transverse bolts" the accident report commented, but as well as one bolt missing the inspectors found two others with fatigue cracks "which probably led to their failure". Unsurprisingly then, the inspection concluded that "the disaster was initiated by the bursting of the crossing" though it was also recommended that passenger locomotives be fitted with speedometers.

FOOTNOTES

1. *Daily Telegraph*, 11 October 2003
2. *The Observer*, 11 March 1849
3. As noted previously, this term was more commonly used at this time than the later and more correct 'Flying Scotsman.'
4. *The Times*, 26 March 1877
5. *The Times*, 11 August 1880
6. *Newcastle Courant*, 13 August 1880.
7. *The Times*, 14 September 1880
8. Name sometimes spelt as 'Teesdale'.
9. *The Times*, 14 August 1880
10. Rails were classified in weight per yard.
11. *The Times*, 11 March 1896.
12. Wilson made allowances for inaccurate recording of times at signal boxes and so concluded 70mph was about correct, but the career of this illustrious driver clearly hung in the balance. His train was a third quicker from Potters Bar than the average for 20 similar expresses.
13. Some locomotives had still not had them fitted.
14. *The Times*, 4 May 1860.
15. *The Times*, 24 April 1860
16. *The Times*, 30 November 1895
17. *Train Derailment at Hatfield: A Final Report by the Independent Investigation Board*, London, 2006, pps 100-123.
18. *Final Report*, p. 123
19. *Final report*, p.16
20. *Financial Times*, 6 December 2000
21. *Final report*, p.79
22. A Barry and D Slater, *The Technological Economy*, London, 2004, p.93
23. *Evening Standard*, 11 December 2000.
24. As indicated earlier, this was a separate section of Balfour Beatty operations (Balfour Beatty Rail Maintenance Ltd.) and the name changed during the aftermath of the accident; for reasons of simplicity, it is referred to as Balfour Beatty from this point.
25. *Final Report*, p.3
26. Commonly spelt 'Barkstone' at that time.
27. *Doncaster Evening Post*, 22 March 1951
28. *The Times*, 17 March 1951
29. *Manchester Guardian*, 22 March 1951.

Fourteen people died in the derailment at Doncaster in 1951, caused by the excessive speed and derailment of a departing express.

(Peter Tuffrey)

5

CARELESS SHUNTING

Many accidents which might be classified as due to 'careless shunting' could perhaps be equally readily categorised under errors by drivers or signalmen. However, in this section we can look at some accidents that owe their origins to issues concerning how shunting was carried out. There were hundreds of these, but often the results were relatively minor – as on the occasion when the Scottish express travelling at 50mph hit a brake van that had been carelessly left on the main line at Essendine; the heavy locomotive knocked the van out of the way into the six foot, from where it caused considerable damage to the passing carriages – yet crucially there was no derailment. There was not always such a lucky escape.

At Raskelf, between York and Thirsk, on the foggy night of 24th April 1868, a mixed goods train slowed to prepare to shunt and detach some cattle vans at about 5.30am. It was a lengthy train of 55 wagons and a guard's van, in which the guard had several companions. They included Mr. Scott, steward to Major Stapylton of Myton Hall, and his labourer Auld, another labourer, and three railway labourers on their way to York.

The goods guard knew that a coal train was running behind theirs, so he jumped from his van and began walking back down the line with his red flag towards Raskelf distant signal – which was 315 yards from where he got out. It was his duty to put 'on' the distant signal to warn the following train.[1] Before he had got even 100 yards the coal train appeared out of the fog, travelling at about 25mph, and whistling frantically. One of the labourers in the van heard the noise and shouted "She is coming into us." The three railway labourers and one of the Myton Hall party were able to leap to safety, but Scott and Auld were less lucky. The coal train ploughed into the guard's van, smashing it to pieces and killing the two men who were "pitched a considerable distance".[2] Two valuable racehorses, Chelsea and Virtue, were on their way from Richmond to Newmarket by this train but were not injured.

This accident reveals much about operating practice in 1868, quite a lot of which seems to have positively invited disaster, leaving Colonel Hutchinson of the Board of Trade aghast at the practice displayed.

The first train was the goods from Newcastle to York, due to leave Darlington at 3.30am. Invariably it ran late and this morning was no different, a situation made worse when the night foreman at Darlington, Lowcock, directed its guard "quite unusually" to pick up four cattle wagons and to drop them off at the wayside station of Raskelf. The cattle were accompanied by Scott and his two labourers, who wanted to travel in the guard's van. In making this arrangement, the foreman was "creatively interpreting" rules about stopping at stations at night – he had refused to allow the cattle wagons to go forwards on the 11.30pm train as it would have been dark when they got to Raskelf, but he now expected it to be light on the train's arrival.

In fact the North Eastern Railway had issued an order in December 1862 restricting unloading at night with the intention of preventing goods trains detaching when station staff would not be on duty – the daylight factor was incidental to the main concern. However, the goods train was also not timetabled to stop at Raskelf at all and, given the primitive time interval system under which the goods trains were despatched, this was an obvious risk.

When the goods got to Thirsk it was shunted again so that the cattle wagons were at the front, rather than in the middle, and the three platelayers joined the train. The guard did not tell Thirsk staff that he would be stopping at Raskelf.

None of this might have mattered, except that a coal train was scheduled to run behind the goods from Darlington. Due to an apparent error in the timetable, this train was scheduled to leave Thirsk after the goods and to arrive in York before it – with no provision to overtake. At Darlington, no-one told the coal train's driver – Riddell – that the train in front of him would make an unscheduled stop at Raskelf and at Thirsk no-one told him because the goods guard had not told the staff there. In fact at Thirsk Riddell asked if he could go in front of the goods and was refused.

Riddell therefore determined to follow the goods train "as closely as possible" – which he did by observation. When the fog began to gather he worried about losing sight of the goods and increased his speed, until "the fog became so dense as to cause him to lose sight of the train in front". When he saw the goods in front emerging out of the fog, Riddell put his engine into reverse and leapt off the footplate – the rather pluckier fireman stayed at his position.

Hutchinson was unimpressed by almost everyone, but he stated that "the main cause of the collision is to be attributed to the neglect of the night foreman at Darlington" for "transgressing the spirit, if not the letter of an order" and for failing to warn the coal train driver. The coal train driver was also censured for driving recklessly, whilst the goods guard had failed to warn staff at Thirsk. However, the most obvious failings lay in the procedures of the NER, including its tolerance of trains following each other 'on sight' and a bizarre practice where a guard could jump off a train to run back and put the signal behind to danger – albeit only a distant signal in this case.

Particularly in the early days of the railways, careless shunting of goods wagons at wayside stations proved a frequent hazard for the express passenger trains that inevitably seemed to be due just after an error had been made.

The serious accident that occurred at Dunbar on 3rd January 1898 bore similarities to many other accidents where a goods train was shunted on a main line in front of an approaching express – the same pattern as at Arlesey in 1876 (see Chapter 2) and elsewhere. However, by this time much was understood

Two illustrations of the Dunbar collision, showing the wrecked engine and both passenger and goods stock, with significant damage to the passenger carriages.

about how to prevent a possible accident, including the need to provide a complete block section between any following train and the shunting movements ahead – rather than rely on a close-by home signal with insufficient protection against 'signal passed at danger'. None of this knowledge helped to prevent the Dunbar disaster.

The double-headed 11.30pm from King's Cross was heading north from Berwick with two North British Railway locomotives whilst staff at Dunbar station were attempting to shunt an up goods train out of its way from a position on the up line across the down line and into the South Sidings on that same side. At a critical moment, several wagons of the goods train derailed on the diamond crossing and so both lines were blocked – but this should only have been the cause of minor delays as signals were protecting the points. However, signalman McPherson at Dunbar East had already and irregularly 'accepted' the oncoming express from Cockburnspath[3] even though he knew he had the goods train shunting across its path only a few yards from the home signal and against the block regulations. He later tried to justify himself in that he had thought the goods would be out of the way, but he had done something that block regulations expressly forbade. A space of a quarter of a mile should have been left clear in advance of the down home signal before the

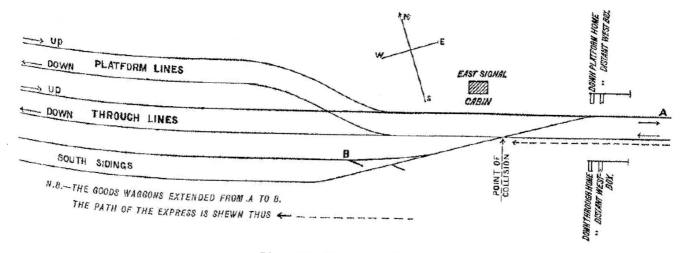

Plan of the Dunbar accident.

train was accepted. McPherson then offered the train to Dunbar West signal box, which cleared its signals for it.

The diamond crossing was protected by a home signal about 80 yards to the east and also a distant signal 681 yards further in the rear. Both signals were clearly visible for around 1,000 yards. The signals and points at Dunbar East were fully interlocked and so the signals were set at danger against the down express.

McPherson had told the goods train staff that the express 'was on' but none of them seem to have understood that he had accepted it. According to his own account, McPherson left his box to help with the re-railing, but the frantic efforts of the men were thwarted by the difficulty in getting the final wagon – with all four wheels off – back on the line.

A shout of warning from an onlooker that the express was coming gave the men just enough time to jump out of the way. Then the speeding express ploughed straight through the goods train, crashing right through the third wagon and causing "utmost consternation" as the leading locomotive derailed and carriages piled up. Driver Steedman had a "most marvellous escape" having jumped or been thrown from the footplate but a bogie carriage was crushed by the heavier Aberdeen carriage. The passenger train ran against the side of the goods train so that every window on one side of the train was broken. Passengers were thrown about and a Mrs. Ruddock was "pitched from her seat into the arms of a fellow passenger".

The goods train was scattered in all directions with some wagons ending in a heap 100 yards away, whilst Colonel Yorke made the rather odd observation that "three others seem to have disappeared". The first locomotive came to rest across the down platform line 160 yards along.

As rescuers struggled to get into the wreckage of the second and third carriages they could hear screams from within. When they eventually found their way into a ladies only compartment they found two sisters on their way to their father's funeral in Perth – one was dead. The members of a 'Cycling Trio', on their way from Brighton to perform at Kirkcaldy Fair, were brought out alive but injured. A baby was found under a seat still alive.

In the aftermath, the press noted that Steedman insisted the distant signal had been at 'clear' and his fireman initially refused to say anything at all. However, in evidence to Colonel Yorke, the driver said he had begun to brake from 60mph about 300 yards from the distant signal but the greasy rails prevented him from stopping the train – which he said was travelling at about 25mph when it hit the goods. Yorke thought this story "quite incredible" given that the train had Westinghouse brakes and a minimum of 981 yards in which to stop. It was unfortunate for Steedman that a senior officer from the Glasgow & South Western Railway[4] was awake at the time and felt the brakes go hard on just before the impact whilst Steedman's own guard thought the brakes went on very late and the speed at impact to be 55mph.

Yorke calculated that Steedman made several errors which in some respects were due to him assuming that McPherson had acted correctly in 'accepting' his own train since, although he knew Dunbar East's signals were at danger, he could see that Dunbar West's beyond were 'clear' for him and the rules said there could be nothing in between – but McPherson had broken the rules. By the time Steedman realised his assumption was mistaken, he was too late.

It took many hours to restore normal services; the passengers on the 'early train' from Berwick had to get out and walk around the scene of the disaster, which must have been somewhat sobering for them. The dead woman's body was later taken to Perth and buried at the same time as her father.

Colonel Yorke was forthright in his summary: "…it will be gathered that the collision was in no way due to accidental causes, but was the result of direct breaches of duty on the part of signalman McPherson and driver Steedman… the responsibility for this fatal disaster must undoubtedly rest upon these two men, who had both been on duty for less than an hour, and I have sought in vain for any justification of their action."

Yorke felt that McPherson's offence "seems to be the greater" as he had broken the regulations and so perhaps misled Steedman. However, the latter had "committed the most serious offence that a driver can be guilty of, viz., the failure to obey a danger signal".

Yorke also criticised some of the working practices of the NBR and referred to another accident at Falkirk, only five weeks earlier. This prompted the company's chairman, Lord Tweeddale, to robustly blame the railwaymen when speaking to his shareholders, saying that the report: "…confirmed all previous experience of the difficulty of entirely eliminating the element of human fallibility, however much they surrounded their servants with mechanical safeguards and framed regulations designed to be implicitly obeyed".[5]

On 6th September 1915 the 5.45pm down express from King's Cross hit a goods wagon in the dark at Newark Maltings, just north of Northgate station. The left-hand side of the engine was damaged and a guard heard "a loud report and the train was suddenly checked and violently shaken". The train split in two behind the second carriage. The locomotive, Atlantic No.1455, stayed on the rails as far as the crossing with the Midland Railway half a mile ahead, but the carriages derailed and the seventh fell over on its side, killing one and injuring fifteen. The fatality was a child, who fell through a window as the carriage turned on its side. Lt. Col. E. Druitt, a Board of Trade railway inspector, was on the train and then led the inquiry.

The chain of events had started when a horse shunter left two wagons in the No.1 siding outside Gilstrap's Malt Kilns, which was adjacent to the down main line, leaving enough space for three further wagons to be accommodated without fouling the connections to sidings 2 and 3. Later a steam locomotive was used by shunter Whittington to shunt four more wagons into the sidings; then he placed twelve or thirteen wagons in siding No.3 before putting another ten or eleven into siding No.1 from the north end. He then left, without taking care to check whether they had knocked into those already in the siding. The siding had capacity for twenty wagons between the 'fouling points' at either end, but in fact some wagons had been pushed too far at the south end. Although it was not dark, Whittington did not bother to look and just assumed that because the total was fewer than twenty the wagons would not have knocked into each other. He had just returned to shunt the wagons in siding No.3. At this point his shunting must have fouled a wagon from No.1 which was knocked over and in turn fouled the down main line. Shunter James Whittington accepted that the provisions of Rule 184 (c) had been infringed, as he had not checked the number or position of wagons in the siding by actual observation.

FOOTNOTES

[1] Press reports make several references to the signals being handled by the train crew. *The Times* said "the fireman of the goods train had put on the signals on account of the coal train that was following". This appears to have been because the station staff, who would normally do the signalling, did not work at Raskelf at night.

[2] *The Times*, 27 April 1868

[3] Cockburnspath was over seven miles away – the long gap explained by two intervening boxes being switched out at the time. This may have influenced McPherson's judgement that he had time to shunt the goods without delaying the express, even though the goods was early.

[4] This was Charles Cockburn, Superintendent of the Line from 1895 to 1921.

[5] *The Times*, 25 March 1898

6

TECHNICAL FAILURE

Infrastructure Failure – Broken Engines and Boilers – Broken Wheels – Goods Wagons

Failure of the equipment has been a regular theme in railway accident history. There are many instances of rail accidents caused in the early days by failure of brittle iron components such as wheels and axles, even occasionally by exploding locomotives, but there is only one occasion on the East Coast line when fatalities were caused by a failure of the infrastructure.

This was the collapse of Penmanshiel Tunnel, seventeen miles north of Berwick, on 17th March 1979. The tunnel had been opened by the North British Railway in 1846 and had given many years of sterling service despite its relatively unknown internal features. The arch of the brickwork, which was mainly four or five rows of bricks thick, was not in direct contact with the rock above. One result was that there was a 'large void' above the brickwork near the northern end of the tunnel to which apertures gave access for inspection purposes. This was one of the reasons why British Railways objected to the re-routing of the A1 over the tunnel in 1971.

In 1979 British Rail was engaged in a series of works to improve the tunnels of the East Coast line to make them suitable for trains carrying the higher 8ft 6in containers. At Stoke and Peascliffe it had successfully lowered the track in the tunnels and by March 1979 there had already been considerable progress at Penmanshiel. Work on lowering the up line had been completed and work on the down line was well advanced – the trackbed had been lowered and only some tidying-up remained to be done before the replacement concrete slab track could be laid.

Early on the morning of 17th March some JCB machines were at work when the Railway Works Inspector saw small pieces of rock "apparently bursting off the vertical face". He decided to get some shoring put up and began to walk out of the tunnel. He had only gone a few yards when there was a loud noise and much of the tunnel collapsed over a distance of about 30 metres. The fall engulfed one of the JCBs and also a dumper truck with their respective drivers, though other men in the tunnel were able to escape. The rock filled the tunnel from floor to roof.

The cause of the accident was not apparent. The tunnel had no history of problems and the work ongoing at the time of the collapse was not producing any undue vibrations. However, nothing other than speculation was really possible as the collapsed material was never removed, although examination of the brickwork did reveal some inconsistencies in construction.

Rather than try to rebuild the tunnel, it was decided to by-pass the site and construct a new open line about 40 metres away from the old tunnel. This work exposed a geological anticline intersecting the line of the tunnel which indicated an unstable wedge of broken rock above the tunnel. However, the use of gelignite in constructing the new alignment produced no evident damage at all.

The British Railways Board and the tunnel works contractor were prosecuted for health and safety offences and tried in Edinburgh in May 1980. The Board pleaded guilty and was fined £10,000 whilst the contractor pleaded not guilty and this was accepted. The BRB was criticised for not having done a thorough geological survey but the Accident Report concluded that a survey would have been unlikely to identify the problems. The renewed route was opened on 20th August 1979 and a memorial to the two dead men erected on the hillside above.

An infrastructure failure that could have been a lot worse than it actually was occurred at Hatfield on 20th February 1966. Although it resulted in no deaths or injuries, and was not even a 'railway accident' as such, it had far-reaching consequences in terms of the 'lessons learned'.[1]

On that Sunday the line was closed for work to improve the track bed of the up fast line just north of Hatfield station. This involved deep excavation of the subsoil and refilling the resulting trench with fresh sand and ballast. This included work under the centre arch of the three-arch brick-built bridge No.62, known as 'Wrestler's Bridge', which carried the old Great North Road across the line. By 1966 it had been reclassified as the A1000 but still carried a substantial amount of local traffic.

At about 10.50 that morning, as excavation work was under way, part of the eastern arch over the up slow line collapsed, rendering the whole structure unstable, and the rest of it was demolished as a matter of urgency later that day.

Despite the fact that there were neither trains involved nor any casualties on either the railway or the road above, a full Ministry of Transport inquiry was called. Colonel D. McMullen conducted it and in his report published on 29th July 1966 he concluded that the primary responsibility rested with Mr. A. B. Henwood, the Divisional Civil Engineer. Henwood had been aware of the poor condition of bridge 62, the eastern pier of which had subsided by a few inches over several years and there were some cracks visible. He had written to the Eastern Region Chief Civil Engineer expressing his concern and recommending its demolition, yet he had not considered that deep excavation close to the pier's foundations would be a potential hazard and had not told anyone in charge of the permanent way gang.

Col. McMullen's final paragraph is interesting. It reads: "I think this [regular inspection] is especially important for highway bridges over the railway because many are carrying loads greatly in excess of those which it was necessary for them to carry when they were designed. The design methods then used were, however, in many cases conservative in the light of present day knowledge and provided considerable reserves of strength. The British Railways Board is now undertaking a comprehensive review of the strength of all highway bridges for which they are responsible. I hope that where a realistic assessment shows a bridge to be of sub-standard carrying capacity, appropriate measures will be taken to restrict its use accordingly."

Broken Engines and Boilers

On 12th November 1847 a fast first class mail train of the York, Newcastle & Berwick Railway derailed at speed – 40mph – whilst crossing Newham Bog, near Lucker in Northumberland. The bolt on one of the engine's springs broke, derailing it, the tender and the luggage van immediately behind it – though miraculously the guard sitting on top held on to the rail and survived unscathed. As the *Newcastle Courant* reported, "One of the spring pins of the engine gave way, which caused the ploughs[2] in front of the engine to tear up the sleepers."[3]

The engine and luggage van plunged into the bog. "The engine was completely buried in the bog, only a portion of the funnel remaining visible."[4] All accounts agree that the passengers then got out and, with the guard, went to find the driver and his fireman – both of whom were discovered buried "nearly overhead" in the bog and underneath the luggage van. According to the account in *The Times,* the rescuers cleared the bog away from their faces but were unable to dig them out for half an hour until a gang of platelayers arrived with spades.

At this point the accounts of *The Times* and *The Observer* diverge – the former says that the injured driver was taken to Berwick but his partner was totally unharmed and "walked about afterwards as if nothing particular had happened to him".*The Observer,* though, reported that the fireman was so "shockingly scalded and bruised" that "it is reported he has since died". Newham Bog may not have contributed to the accident, but the instability of the track formation in this location has continued to be a problem into the 21st century. The *Courant* took the view that "no blame attaches to anyone" although as technical knowledge progressed such events would no longer be seen as 'accidents' but would reveal clear trails of responsibility.

This type of accident did not usually end so seriously. More common was the sequence at Werrington Junction on 26th June 1882. The iron connecting rod of the locomotive, which linked the driving wheels together, snapped at speed causing heavy damage to the locomotive and two carriages. Six were derailed and two turned over but fortunately there was only a handful of minor injuries[5] as the train was lightly loaded.

Boiler explosions were regular events in the early days of the railways when the technical ability to prevent disaster had not yet overtaken the ability of enginemen to abuse their machines through neglect or the ability of the boilermakers to ensure security. Gradually improved methods of construction, testing and inspection together with better safety equipment such as safety valves which could not be tampered with led to increased reliability.

On 2nd February 1850 George Barker of Hurworth was tending his land about two miles south of Darlington alongside the tracks of the former Great North of England Railway[6] when he was "alarmed by a loud explosion". He saw a southbound goods train and "perceiving a great body of fire and steam proceed from the train, he ran to render assistance". The explosion was so loud that it was heard in Darlington by Mr. Bell, the company's locomotive superintendent, who also set off to help. Barker was easily first on the scene and found what he took to be a dead body between the lines and the train's tender thrown across the down (northbound) line. The "dead body" proved to be James Wilson, the locomotive's driver, who later died.[7] Barker searched for any other bodies and found the stoker, John Tinkler, in a ditch and the guard, Frances Howe, 25 yards away in a nearby field. Tinkler was dead and Wilson died a few days later. Barker reported that the engine gave the appearance of having "burst".

An inquest on Tinkler opened at Darlington on 4th February, but was adjourned awaiting evidence from Driver Wilson – who then died, so the inquest reopened except for being on two bodies rather than one. At the first session it was confidently reported that "it appeared the accident had been caused by the explosion of the boiler, owing to there having been too little water in it and the cold water having been let in when it was in a heated state".

The train had set off from Darlington heading for Richmond behind locomotive No.35, an "old" locomotive[8] that had previously been in an accident, but whose boiler was reported to have been in excellent condition. The train had five timber wagons and 21 of coal. Although Bell and everyone else agreed the accident had been caused by the lack of water and a burst boiler, no-one was sure why this had happened. There had been plenty of water in the tender, so either the enginemen had been negligent "or pipes might have got stuffed up". Captain Wynne investigated in great detail, starting with the movements of No.35 that day; he found that it had made a return journey to York with Driver Davidson, who then handed it over to Wilson full of water. The engine had then spent an hour and a half doing nothing, followed by two hours of shunting. Wynne theorised that Wilson let it get low on water during this time and he was seen at the water column before heading off for Richmond – after which the farmer had noted it as moving very slowly prior to the explosion.

Wynne concluded that Wilson had let the water get too low so that the engine had become too hot – and he had then suddenly let in too much cold water onto the hot surfaces. However, Wynne added a comment that the boiler did not have "a plug of easily fusible metal…which is meant to act as a guard against the danger arising from suffering the water to become too low in the boiler". So this was a case of technical failure, but one exacerbated by careless handling of a pressurised boiler.

The boiler explosion at Peterborough on 14th January 1865 did not even involve a train out on the line – it occurred during testing of repairs and took away three lives with it. As a case it attracted considerable press coverage, the nature of which is a salutary reminder as to how reporting has changed – in an age of explicit horror films, it is now inconceivable a newspaper would report a story in the way that the Peterborough boiler explosion was reported.

Boiler repairs were not conducted in New England Works but in a large running shed much closer to Peterborough station, but on that Saturday afternoon most of the men who worked there had already gone and just a dozen or so were left, some of whom were working on No.98; this was a Grantham-based engine which worked from there to London or York with Driver Edwin Brown. Brown had noticed problems with the boiler leaking "in the barrel" and thought "the smoke box was very thin", so had driven the locomotive to Peterborough for repair on 16th December 1864.[9]

At Peterborough on the fateful afternoon George Kightley was supervising the final work and the steam testing of the boiler which had been repaired with two patches. They lit the fire at about 2.00pm but it took until 4.00pm to get a sufficient amount of steam up. Once they got to 20lb pressure a series of leaks became evident, most of which were dealt with by caulking, and then they took the pressure back up. Hanging around being something of a nuisance was seventeen-year-old Frank Hoyle, an articled pupil to Archibald Sturrock, the locomotive engineer. Hoyle boarded the footplate and thrice set off the whistle, but he was blown off the footplate by an escape of steam and injured his foot. Hoyle, who had to fight off later accusations that he tied down the safety valve, later recalled seeing steam escaping from a new rivet head in the firebox but said he did not worry as no-one else seemed concerned.

Steam testing was still continuing at 125lb when the locomotive "exploded with a report which shook all the buildings in the neighbourhood and put out most of the gaslights."[10] The running shed, 160 yards long, was almost totally wrecked. When rescuers arrived they were able to pull out six men from the wreckage and these were able to return home, some injured. However, under the boiler was found "the trunk of a man, stripped of clothing, and the head and legs reduced to a pulp." This was Charles Chamberlin. Kightley was recovered, badly injured but expected to live. Charles Mackness was found dead. At the time of the explosion fifteen-year-old William Corby had been sitting on top of the boiler and he was blown into the air. His body "appears to have been struck against an iron girder twenty yards off the scene and literally to have been smashed to pieces". His feet and legs were picked up eight yards away from the rest of his remains. "His head was completely shattered, and half his head was found in his cap whilst on the girder upon which he struck one of his braces and part of his stockings yet remain, and his blood has bespattered the skylights." *The Leeds Mercury* also told its readers that "pieces of flesh and intestines, and stray particles of clothing continue to be picked up and are reverentially laid by". Another newspaper added the detail that Corby had been blown through a brick wall into the adjoining shed.[11]

The idea that there had been interference with the safety valves was put about by the Works Manager, who told the coroner: "It is supposed the safety valve was closed and thus the steam, not having the usual means of escape, burst the boiler." However, Captain Tyler from the Board of Trade doubted that Hoyle was at fault; in his evidence to the Coroner, he said that "it would have required the boy should have held both the valves down for some time to have produced danger". However, Tyler criticised the practice of steam testing – he pointed out that the South Eastern and Great Eastern Railways tested using water pressure, which was much safer. Archibald Sturrock agreed, but this is a case where the verdict of 'Accidental Death' seems especially weak – it was plainly not

an accident, but poor work, that cost three lives.

The incident provoked fury amongst engineering experts because all the rules and laws by then in place regarding boilers were flouted. An article in *The Engineer*[12] fulminated: "Now we should like to know of what earthly use is all the talking or writing in the world against such recklessness as this – a recklessness equal to carrying out an operation which consists in exploding a boiler in the repairing shed, to see whether it will not burst when put on the line. Of what use are all the newspaper writing, all the juries, all the Government inspectors, in the world, if these things can be carried on in broad light of day?...In fact, this case, however flagrant in reality, will be forgotten much sooner than any other incidence of railway slaughter, as the people maimed are not travellers but servants of the Company. The Compensation Act does not apply here...as to the relatives of those killed outright, the company is probably quite safe against action for damages against them."[13]

There was also a fatal boiler explosion a quarter of a mile east of Dunbar station on 1st September 1882. This killed the locomotive's driver, his fireman and a publican. The explosion was so violent that windows were broken in nearby cottages and the body of the driver was torn in two. According to press reports, the firebox of the locomotive was found thirty yards from the tracks in a cornfield and its dome "even further" away. Part of the front of the boiler was found in a potato field 400 yards from the scene of the explosion. The fireman was killed even though he was not on the footplate at the time. The explosion also threw a number of goods wagons off the line and these were hit by another goods train.

Broken wheels and associated parts

In the early days of the railways iron proved susceptible to failure, often with tragic consequences. There were also some remarkable escapes, such as when a carriage axle fractured on the 'Flying Scotchman' whilst crossing the viaduct at Bawtry on 14th February 1874. It was thought that, had the braking characteristics of the stock been different, then the following carriages might have careered off the viaduct with serious loss of life.[14] In fact, no-one died. On another occasion, the disaster was exaggerated in initial reports: after the derailment at Carlton on Trent on 29th June 1858, the first reports spoke of "an accident of very alarming character".[15] After the tyre on a tender wheel broke, it was said to have been "instantly shaken off the line, plunged down an embankment ten to twelve feet high, carrying with it the whole of the train and heeling over into a field by the side of the line". It was reported that all the carriages turned over and that some passengers had been thrown through the windows, though no-one had been killed. Reports the following day corrected much of this, pointing out that there was no embankment and only the first two carriages had been slightly damaged although the driver had been "pitched over the chimney of the engine" but had not been injured! Nonetheless, it was a warning as to the risks when equipment made of iron failed to stand up to the rigours of express travel.

As will be seen with the Marshmoor accident, described below, the effects of extreme cold on iron were understood in the mid-Victorian period but without any certain remedy. Cold, and the parsimonious attitude of the North British Railway, were blamed for the failure of an axle on one of its carriages on 18th January 1855. This happened to one of its third class carriages, marshalled into a train from King's Cross which had just entered the first tunnel when its driver realised something was wrong – had this happened a few minutes later, death and disaster might have been the result. As it was, Colonel Yolland's investigation blamed the carriage axle and he arranged for it to be analysed by the Great Northern workshops in Doncaster since the NBR was unable to tell him anything about its provenance. Writing from the Board of Trade, Captain Galton had a stiff message for the North British directors: "[Col Yolland] states that the iron of which the fractured axle was composed would appear to have been of a very inferior description throughout, and to point out the responsibility which the Directors will incur if any consideration of economy should induce them to allow of the use of inferior materials in cases where the safety of the public is involved."[16]

Another, more remarkable, tunnel escape occurred on 27th August 1860, when the leading axle of a locomotive built by Hawthorn & Co. in 1852 fractured inside Wood Green Tunnel whilst working an up express from Edinburgh. The locomotive lurched wildly off the up track and apparently 'onto' the down track and then back again. Remarkably no-one was killed or injured, though many were very frightened by fear of sudden death in a dark tunnel. Reports commented on how normal schedules meant that up and down expresses often passed in the tunnel, but fortunately not on this occasion.

Another miraculous escape was at Little Bytham on 4th April 1863, when the leading tyre on an engine wheel split whilst it was running at 40mph with a lightly loaded Manchester to London express. The whole cavalcade veered off the tracks, but was prevented from running down the embankment by wagons in the adjacent siding. One passenger carriage ended up miraculously suspended, with one end skewed across the track and the other suspended in mid-air above the embankment by telegraph wires which had been knocked out of line but not broken. A man and his wife were injured, but escapes were termed 'miraculous': "One young lady was found with her head under one of the seats amongst some carpet bags and hampers, and her feet in the air. It was feared that she was dead, but upon being extricated, and recovered from the fright, she was found to have escaped without a single bruise."[17]

On 1st November 1906 the fragmentation of an axlebox of a van in the Glasgow Sighthill to London express goods derailed it near East Fortune, east of Edinburgh. This could have led to serious disaster as wagons had fouled the down line and the 2.20pm down express from King's Cross was expected imminently, but fortunately Driver Hopkin of the goods was alert to the danger. He ordered his fireman to reverse the engine sufficiently that he could uncouple it from its train, then leapt onto the footplate to move it forwards whilst sending the fireman to the front to change its lamp indications to red for danger. Hopkin managed to get a few hundred yards up the line, so that the driver of the express had about 800 yards warning – managing to sharply reduce its speed so only a minor collision was the result.

A minor derailment at Gateshead led to the death of a panicking passenger in August 1869. A local train from Sunderland to Newcastle was leaving Gateshead station and approaching the south end of the High Level Bridge when the rear two carriages derailed. One carriage jolted along on the sleepers for 30 yards and then one of the passengers, Robert Head, manager of a steamship company, jumped out in terror and was crushed as the carriages fell on him. The signalman in the cabin on top of the High Level Bridge saw the derailment and shouted to the driver to stop. It was too late for Head – "On the mangled remains of Mr. Head being removed from beneath the prostrate carriage, life was found to be quite extinct."[18] The accident was thought to have been caused by a faulty wheel flange on one of the carriages, which had become caught in the check rails on the High Level Bridge.

However, turning to the more serious accidents caused by axles or wheels, the accident at Marshmoor, between Potters Bar and Hatfield, on 26th December 1870 was one of the worst of the era with eight killed, but unusual in that two of the dead were passers-by hit by derailed passenger carriages.

The accident happened on a freezing evening with temperatures at 20°F and press reports commented that the frozen ground made "the road like iron". The 4.25pm semi-fast train to Peterborough was well-prepared at King's Cross – its wheels were tapped twice, although not intentionally. Nonetheless, as it started to slow to 30mph beyond Bell Bar signal box and approached Marshmoor crossing for its first stop at Hatfield, the tyre of a brake van disintegrated. Gatekeeper Harry Town, who was standing in his cottage doorway on the up side, noticed a momentary "jumping" of the brake van and after the crossing it broke away from the engine. The driver, John Fuller, felt a "little jerk" and assumed his engine was slipping, so let out some sand. His fireman heard a "cracking of timber". Then his train split, but Fuller continued on to Redhall signal box, one mile further north of Marshmoor, for fear that the carriages would run into him if he slowed. Then he slowly returned.

Whilst the engine carried on, the carriages derailed in all directions, first hitting a stack of sleepers and then colliding with the crossing keeper's house of a Mr. Hawkins so that Town saw "fragments flying and some carriages leap towards the east of the line". Van No.387 was dismembered and its roof landed on the other side of Marshmoor Road; one carriage leapfrogged over another and the roof of a third class carriage (the second carriage) hit the wall of the level crossing gatehouse at a height of 15ft. Another pitched across the up line and smashed the crossing gates. Two carriages killed the wife and sister of a signalman whilst they were at the lineside near the level crossing and injured others waiting at the gates. The carriages that hit the gatehouse bounced back towards the line. "The mangled bodies of the killed… were laid out on a bank by the passengers" on a night with snow all around. One of them, a cattle dealer from Stilton, had £100 in his pocket. An unusual feature of the accident was that eight were killed but only one left injured and alive, whilst all the passenger deaths were from the third carriage.

The guard ran out to put fog signals on the up line. An up

coal train was brought to an emergency halt just in time, just touching one of the derailed carriages. Town watched with astonishment as a gentleman named McFarlane crawled out of a ditch, then assisted in removing four bodies from the wreckage as well as the severed head and arm of a man.

The coroner held his inquest in the schoolrooms at Welham and it was a matter of comment that no Board of Trade representative attended at the start. Poor Town was cross-examined on his rescue work and was asked whether the severed head was of an old or young man; Town had to explain that it was crushed beyond recognition.

One piece of broken tyre was found 130 yards before the level crossing and two others near to it. They were labelled 'Cammell, Sheffield, cast steel, 2, 1870'.[19] The iron tyre had been fitted to the iron wheel of the van. Questions were then also asked about Beattie's patent fastening, which involved hammering clips into grooves after the tyre was fitted and which was meant to ensure that when a tyre shattered the wheel stayed intact; this had also failed at Little Bytham in April 1863 and many companies had gone over to Mansell's alternative. The GNR explained that it did not use Beattie clips on anything except brake vans but later correspondents on the subject returned to the issue of axles – a three-axle van would not have been so debilitated by one broken tyre. Evidence was produced to show that the South Eastern and London & North Western Railways disagreed with the GNR over the reasons for not fitting Mansell's patent to brake vans.

After all the debate, the Coroner returned to the subject of the cold saying that "it was a danger against which it was impossible to guard".

The technology at the time could not really furnish an explanation of the splitting of the tyre, Lt. Col. Hutchinson suggesting a combination of the very "rigid" track on such a cold night, an over-tight fit of the tyre to the wheel and a possibility that the metal was "too hard". He did not mention that the open spoke wheel had not been able to handle the impact, nor that the axle had snapped under the additional pressure, nor side with the view of newspaper correspondents that vans and carriages with three axles rather than two would be proof against such disasters as they were more stable and would not "drop". The Great Northern twice refused Hutchinson permission to test the pieces of broken tyre at Doncaster, even though he visited the works there. The jury at the inquest agreed the tyre caused the accident, but refused to apportion blame.

Broken wheels and other technical failures were not entirely a problem of the nineteenth century. For example, on 1st September 1955 the unique W1 Class 4-6-4 No.60700 derailed at Peterborough due to a fracture in the leading bogie frame.

A High Speed Train derailed on 16th June 1998 at Sandy in an accident that showed the safety of high speed rail travel as the accident was probably at a higher speed than any up to that time. A wheel on the last passenger vehicle (there was a power car behind that) disintegrated and all the wheels of the carriage derailed. Crucially the carriages stayed together and in line as the train took a mile to stop, during which it avoided any lineside obstacles, with only the derailed carriage ending slightly out of line. Although injuries were minimal the incident

had huge impact on East Coast Main Line services as all similar units – the bedrock of the line – were taken out of service for checks. For several days sundry suburban electric multiple units were pressed into 'front line' inter-city service.

Goods wagons

Passenger traffic in the mid-nineteenth century included some ambitious overnight excursions, such as the train in June 1870 which – by doing both journeys overnight – allowed the citizens of West Yorkshire a day in London. The return trip left King's Cross at about 9.20pm with over 350 people in 23 carriages. Less than a mile south of Newark, near Clay Lane Bridge, one of the guards felt "a succession of jolts" and then the engine derailed "and turned end for end". The momentum of the train behind it forced it up the bank and then it fell down again.

At first it was a complete mystery as to what had happened. Almost every carriage had damaged sides and some had broken axleboxes. On the up line, though, were a few wrecked goods wagons, one of which had fouled the down line in advance of the excursion and derailed its engine. The pier of the bridge was marked by a deep indentation where the chimney of the locomotive had hit it as it derailed, destroying some of the carriages that followed as they were forced between the engine and the goods wagons. Sixteen passengers died and both men on the engine, the driver of head injuries and the fireman after losing both legs. The scene was made worse by being in the middle of the night and dawn was breaking before much could be done – "the groans of the wounded and dying rang through the air, and in the dim light of morning many passengers ran to and fro, some bleeding and bruised…"[20]

The goods wagons had come from the 12 midnight Doncaster to London. At Clay Lane Bridge the driver had felt a sudden jerk, then his tender had split from the 29 wagons behind. He continued on for a little, expecting the wagons to coast up behind, but they did not, so he set back to find them. Seven of the wagons had derailed and a truck of potatoes had fallen into the six foot space between the two tracks, fouling the down line. Captain Tyler concluded the accident was caused by an undetected flaw in an axle of the potato wagon, built in 1852.

In an unfortunate postscript, the police of Newark were heavily criticised by the *Leeds Mercury* for apparently looting the dead passengers. The Mayor of Newark said they were removing rings from the fingers of the dead so they could be catalogued and returned to family members, but it was felt necessary to hold a 'protest meeting' to defend the town's good name. Five of those killed had taken out rail insurance for the journey at 2d each – their families received £100 in compensation.

On 5th January 1946 Driver Slinger was in charge of the 3.40am up goods from Low Fell to Doncaster – a regular run for him and no great problem for his B16 4-6-0 No.842 with 44 four-wheel wagons and a brake van attached as they set out through County Durham. The train was brought to a halt at Ouston by signals, but had no difficulty restarting despite the rising gradient there. Slinger saw more signals against him as he approached Bridge House; as on previous occasions, he

A night scene after the crash south of Newark, with carriages piled up and spectators gesticulating wildly.

(Author's Collection)

slowed down to pick up the relief signalman for Ferryhill, Gavin, and then the signals were cleared so he could move forwards to the box.

Slinger slowed his train to walking pace as the signalman held out his hand lamp for Gavin to climb on to the footplate and then gently opened out again, satisfied that there was no 'pluck' of the train which might indicate that it had split. However, later Gavin was to claim that he had noticed just such a movement and had said something to Slinger, but probably too quietly for the driver to have heard. Giving evidence later, he thought he had spoken on the lines of "he hoped he had not pulled the train in two".

The signalman at Bridge House noticed a gap in the train of four yards behind about the seventh wagon as the train passed his box and sent a message to the signalman at Browney – 'Train Divided.' However, he was unable to warn Guard Wear who remained blissfully ignorant of the fact that he was separated from the locomotive and the front part of the train.

Slinger continued onwards down the gradient, also unaware that the rest of his train was following him at a gathering pace. The goods had got up to about 30mph when it was checked again, this time by the signals at Browney having been set against it in order to advise of the splitting of the train. However, with the descending gradient, this added the risk that the runaway wagons might collide with the back of the front portion – but Browney's signalman had thought this a better

risk than a collision on Croxdale Viaduct. Slinger's fireman left the footplate to speak to the signalman and then they both saw the sidelights of the runaway portion's brake van approaching. There was no time to do anything before the runaway collided with the stationary front portion, Slinger having had no chance to restart it.

The impact derailed the B16 locomotive and its tender so that they partly fouled the down line, whilst seventeen wagons piled up on top of each other to create a greater obstacle behind. Two of the wagons went down the bank and disturbed the signal wires for the down home and down distant signals, so that they changed to 'Off.' The impact also knocked the down distant block instrument off its shelf in the signal box.

The Browney signalman, Johnson, might have averted further disaster if he had anticipated the collision and immediately sent an 'Obstruction Danger' warning south to Hett Mill box to hold any northbound trains. However, he was too slow and this left the 11.15pm down King's Cross to Newcastle unprotected behind V2 No.4895 – Johnson was unaware the signals were showing clear. The overnight express struck a minor blow against the derailed goods engine and then derailed as it hit the wreckage of the wagons. Driver George Furlanger could do nothing, having seen no warning until his engine started to 'screech' – his first thought was that "it was falling apart". The locomotive and its tender derailed on their sides and the second, third and fourth carriages were wrecked

After the collision between a diesel-hauled express and cement wagons near Thirsk in 1967. The locomotive, No.DP2, was scrapped but lived on in the Class 50s which were based upon it. (Ken Hoole Collection)

with the fifth landing on top of them although there were many comments made that its electric lights continued to shine throughout. Most of the ten fatalities were in an articulated twin carriage, which was fortunately lightly loaded. Furlanger's clothes caught fire but he was saved by his fireman.

A passenger in a sleeping car to the rear of the express was the Home Secretary, James Chuter Ede. He was unhurt and was taken by police car to his South Shields constituency. However, there was an additional casualty when one of the soldiers drafted in to help collapsed and died in hospital later in the day.

The cause of this disaster could be easily traced to the division of the goods train, though human decisions had exacerbated rather than prevented disaster. The cause was traced to the drawbar of an old ex-Lancashire & Yorkshire Railway wagon, built in 1914. It was found that a slot in the shank was not central and that the thickness of the metal either side was less than regulations required; this had caused the failure but it was not known why imperfections that were visible to the eye had not been attended to.

The collision at Thirsk on 31st July 1967 is famous because it caused the demise of well-known prototype diesel locomotive, DP2, which had the misfortune to arrive on the scene of a cement train derailment. The high-speed collision that resulted killed seven and injured 45 and raised even more

doubts about 'Cemflo' cement wagons.

'Cemflo' wagons were specially designed for cement trains, mainly between Cliffe in Kent and Uddingston in Scotland run on behalf of Associated Portland Cement Manufacturers. The train involved in the collision was the 02.40 from Cliffe, which at the time of the disaster had 26 four-wheel wagons although two had earlier been detached at Peterborough. Whilst travelling at its prescribed speed limit of 45mph on the slow line near Thirsk, the twelfth wagon became derailed and the train split; wagons 13 to 20 went down the adjacent embankment but the 23rd slewed across to the down fast line. Approaching at speed on this line was the 12.00 King's Cross to Edinburgh, hauled by English Electric's prototype DP2; the driver saw dust ahead and braked 'as a reflex action', but was unable to reduce the speed by much and at about 15.17 the locomotive hit the cement wagon, derailing it and seven of the express train carriages. The first carriage suffered serious damage to its left-hand side.

Despite the fairly remote location, the accident was witnessed by a farm worker and the first ambulance arrived by 15.40. The accident caused chaos on the main line, but this was alleviated by hastily reopening the closed Harrogate to Northallerton line for down train diversions.[21]

Although the accident report later referred to there being "no apparent cause for the derailment", most of the evidence pointed towards problems with the 'Cemflo' wagons. These had been built in two batches in 1961 and 1963-5, but had been bedevilled by incidents with broken springs and underframe cracks so that their permitted speed had been reduced from 60 to 45mph when loaded. Two derailments had already been caused by broken springs but other reports commented on the known "violent oscillation" of the wagons. The guard on the cement train said this was "often severe" and a trainspotter had seen one of the wagons "oscillating from side to side" on the day of the disaster. Another witness saw one of the axles apparently "drop heavily" on the crossover at Pilmoor.

Tests on the wagons showed that 'hunting' developed at about 24-27mph and was made worse if couplings were slack – which had been the case between wagons 12 and 13. Safe speed was estimated to be only 38mph for a wagon designed for 60mph and they were limited to 35mph almost immediately. The UIC link-type suspension was widely criticised, having an average life of only 5,000 miles. The conclusion was that wagon LA233 had derailed "as a result of excessive lateral oscillation". A major express brought to grief by poor goods wagon design seemed a very Victorian-style disaster for 1967.

FOOTNOTES

1 With thanks to Allan Sibley for this contribution.
2 British trains did not normally operate with 'ploughs' or even 'cowcatchers', so we assume this to mean guard irons.
3 *Newcastle Courant*, 19 November 1847
4 *The Observer*, 14 November 1849
5 *The Times*, 28 June 1882
6 Several references identify the GNoER as the company concerned although it had been the York, Newcastle & Berwick since 1847.
7 *Parliamentary Papers*, Vol.51, p89, record Howe as injured not killed. At the inquest, it was reported that Howe was between the tracks, Tinkler in the ditch and Wilson in the field. Thus Howe and Wilson appeared to have swapped places during the retelling.
8 So the press referred to it, though it was built by Hawthorn in 1845; perhaps this is a comment on the pace of change at the time.
9 *The Standard*, 25 January 1865
10 *Leeds Mercury*, 16 January 1865
11 *Birmingham Daily Post*, 17 January 1865
12 *The Engineer*, 20 January 1865
13 A Parliamentary Bill to provide compensation for relatives of those killed in boiler explosions had failed in the previous session.
14 *The Times*, 3 April 1874
15 *The Times*, 1 July 1858
16 Captain Galton to NBR Board, 15 March 1855.
17 *Penny Illustrated Paper*, 11 April 1863
18 *Newcastle Courant*, 6 August 1869.
19 Johnson, Cammell& Co. were well-known Sheffield ironfounders who specialised in wheels and rails. The firm later merged into Cammell, Laird.
20 *The Times*, 22 June 1870
21 Michael Back notes that the regular signalmen on this line had been made redundant, so BR had to find enough qualified men to re-open it in haste having checked that all the equipment was operative.

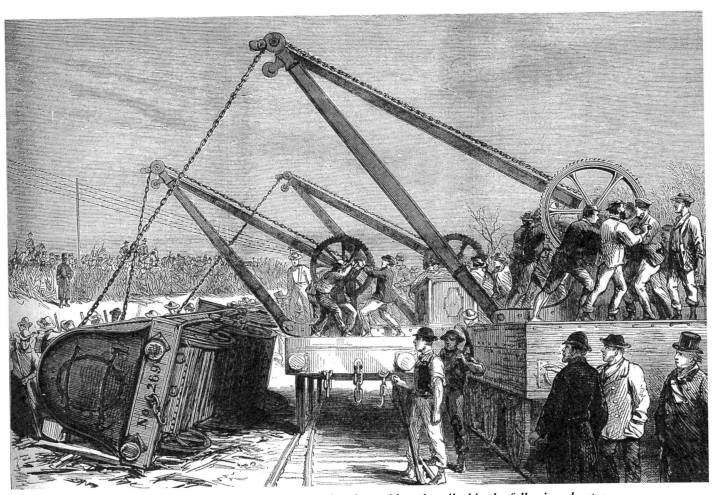

Recovering the overturned locomotive at Abbotts Ripton after the accident described in the following chapter.

(Author's Collection)

7

WEATHER AND DISASTER
Fog – Snow, Cold and Heat – Water

Fog

For all of the nineteenth century and the first half of the twentieth the single greatest hindrance to the safe and efficient working of Britain's railways was fog. Its most significant effect was that drivers could not see the semaphore signal arms and oil lamps. The British engineer Edward Alfred Cowper invented the explosive detonator or 'fog signal' in 1841. It became widely used quite quickly but 'fog working' – the use of detonators to give audible indications of signals to drivers – was a very labour intensive, expensive and inherently dangerous operation at first until mechanical detonator placers came into use. The situation was improved when the Clean Air Acts of the 1960s led to a decrease in the massive consumption of coal for domestic and industrial purposes and the dense and long-lasting 'smogs' in urban areas were gradually eliminated. Weather-related dense fog still afflicts some areas such as the Vale of York but the development of the electrically powered colour-light signal with its focussed beam and various forms of in-cab signalling have also reduced the impact of this type of fog on railway operation.

There were scores of fog-related accidents. When there was no fatality, some accidents attained almost comic proportions as a chain of events unfolded. One example of this occurred during dense fog in January 1871 north of Peterborough; in the first incident, the driver of a goods train failed to spot signals or coal trucks left on the line at Little Bytham and ploughed into them. This closed the line for hours, with a 'Scotch Express' delayed for four hours at least. A further train delayed was a northbound goods at Tallington, but the driver of another northbound goods also failed to spot any signals in the fog and ploughed into the back of it, his locomotive mounting up on the rearmost wagons. Fortunately the guard on the waiting goods had tired of waiting on his own and had gone into the station. This accident resulted in a large amount of destruction and four breakdown gangs were summoned, it still taking more than 24 hours to clear the mess, during which a few trains were diverted via "a siding at the back of the station"[1].

The signalling at Barkston[2] Junction, north of Grantham, in 1874 suffered not so much from technical inadequacy as poor design. On 10th January John Whittle was driving the 'market train' from Boston to Grantham and approached the signals protecting the junction at Barkston in heavy fog. For some disputed reason he missed the distant signal and then spotted the white 'all clear' of the home signal – or he thought he did, but it is probable that he had become disorientated in the fog.

In fact Whittle had spotted the signal on the up main line which the Barkston signalman had cleared for the up Scottish express, the 10.45am from Edinburgh with Driver Cobb. Both signals were set very close to the points, so that in the swirling fog it might have been possible to mistake one for the other and Whittle put on steam to move forward to the points at walking

pace. The signalman soon realised what had happened and held out a red lamp – Whittle reacted quickly by putting his engine into reverse, but he was too late. His train was hit by the express travelling at about 30-40mph. The express "crushed the back carriage immediately in front of the brake van and made sad havoc amongst the leading carriages"[3]. The rear carriages of the local train were thrown over the embankment "and crushed into an indeterminate mass".[4] Whittle's engine was knocked forwards 100yds up the line.

The express engine bore much of the damage to its boiler, which caused steam to blow back back through the firebox, scalding to death its fireman[5] and badly injuring the driver. A down luggage goods, passing at the same time, was hit by wreckage and several wagons derailed. However, others attributed its presence with being a saving grace – "the luggage train adjacent kept the Scotch express on the line and saved the lives of many of its passengers".[6]

Fortunately the local train was lightly loaded, but a "powerful man in sea faring dress and wearing sailors' high boots" was found dead at the back. No-one knew who he was and he did not have a ticket to show where he had come from.

Colonel Yolland investigated for the Board of Trade, finding concerns in the conduct of Whittle but also in the fact that no-one at Barkston had thought to send out the platelayers with fog signals until after the accident. However, the signalling attracted his ire – although main and branch signals were interlocked, this only prevented them from both showing red, whereas they could still both show the white 'all clear'! Their position too close to the points was also a problem and the Great Northern re-installed them 60 yards from the junction on 19th March. He also recommended changing to the absolute block system.

Whittle was charged with manslaughter of the fireman and hauled up before the Assize Court at Lincoln in March 1874. The defence argued the signals were poorly sited and had been too close together and Whittle was acquitted. It was very rare for a railway worker to be convicted by a jury on such a charge.

Flagrant disregard of rules and common sense caused the serious accident in fog at Hornsey on 28th January 1882 in which two passengers died, with a third dying later. During the evening rush hour at about 5.10pm, a blanket of fog descended on north London with great speed so that within a few minutes visibility was reduced to barely four feet. One man later complained that it was so dense he had been unable to find his way home on foot from Hornsey station, but several minutes elapsed before the station master sent a lad to find some men to do fog duty. The fog caused delays along the Great Northern line at Wood Green and the 5.20pm Moorgate[7] to Enfield was held in Hornsey station. Six minutes later there was then an enormous bang and the train shunted forwards along the platform, to the astonishment of the guard who was standing

THE LAST (WE TRUST) OF A RIGOROUS WINTER: SNOWED UP ON THE RAILWAY.

The recent snowstorms: a block on the railway. An illustration from 1886 demonstrates the impact that snow could have on railways, with the train guard forcing his way through drifts to speak to concerned passengers.

(Author's Collection)

beside it, but it was so foggy that none of the station staff initially realised what had happened.

In fact the stationary train had suffered a rear end collision from another train, running from Victoria to Barnet. The impact destroyed the rear carriage, with the guard being fortunate to be outside it, and its roof was torn off and landed on the up platform. The body of the rear carriage was crushed beneath the wheels of the following train's locomotive, killing a girl of sixteen and one other passenger. A passing up mail train from Scotland was stopped and took the injured to King's Cross.

Major Marindin had no problems in identifying the immediate cause of the accident – a train had passed Hornsey down distant and home signals at danger in dense fog. Drivers on both trains agreed about the problem of the fog; George Johnson, the driver of the train to Barnet and thus under suspicion, said that after Finsbury Park the fog had been "like running into a wall". William Daniels, driving the Enfield train, said he had been unable to see any signals or lights until a faint glimmer from the station gas lamps at Hornsey. However, Johnson claimed to have driven at about 8mph to Hornsey whereas the jury at the inquest concluded his speed had been nearer to 18mph – in conditions of four feet visibility.[8]

Johnson's train had stopped at Finsbury Park when the fog descended; it was allowed forwards past the cleared down starter signals to the advance starter, which was at danger, but the signalman at No.5 box was rather surprised to discover his train had gone completely. In fact Johnson simply missed the signal in the fog and assumed it was 'off' like the previous signals. After some delay in getting access to the telegraph despite using the 'VU' (Very Urgent) code, the signalman sent a message forwards to John Rowsell[9] at Hornsey box to say "I think train has run past my starting signal slow." Rowsell was working in difficult conditions and had not received any 'be ready' message (giving notification that a train was being 'offered') from Finsbury Park, whilst the fog had descended so quickly that he did not have a fogman available who could place detonators and give hand signals. Just at that moment another signalman arrived to act as fogman, quickly followed by the sound of a collision. Shortly after the Enfield guard came to the signal box to report the accident, but it was so foggy the signalman could not see him at first.

At the inquest, the jury ruled neglect against George Johnson who had driven much too fast in impossible conditions. However, it also criticised the station staff at Hornsey, whom they thought had been too slow sending for fog signallers. The third victim died several days later at the Royal Free Hospital, necessitating a separate inquest. Major Marindin blamed Johnson, but also criticised the Hornsey signalman for being slow to send for a fogman from the list that he kept in his box.

Fog accidents were generally the result of both the weather and incautious behaviour by railway staff – normally drivers. This was the case in the accident at Peterborough North on 7th December 1927, when Driver George Franklin took his Gainsborough to King's Cross excursion into Peterborough North at approaching 30mph although the permanent speed restriction even for non-stop trains was 10mph. To make matters worse, Franklin was driving in extremely foggy conditions so that his fireman admitted it was difficult seeing even to the smokebox of the locomotive. The fireman, Whillock, did not know the road so could only have been of limited help with looking out for signals. Having restarted from a signal check at Walton up main home signal, Franklin ran past Spital Junction and Peterborough North up home signals at danger and the frantic efforts of the Spital Junction signalman, who despairingly put out the red flag.

Franklin's engine, 4-6-0 No.5034, hit the rear of the departing LMS Leicester to Peterborough East train, telescoping the two rear carriages and badly injuring one man who died later. Franklin was reported in the press as saying that "the fog was extremely dense, and he never saw Peterborough North until he entered the station at barely 10 miles an hour"[10]. The inquiry could only blame Franklin, who had driven excessively fast and passed two signals at danger, covering the distance from Westwood signal box to the station at an average of 21mph despite the fog and speed restriction. Franklin was considered to have placed too much trust on Whillock to assist him. After the enquiry, Whillock admitted he did not know the line and was "absolutely lost" in the fog.

Accidents in fog continued to be a feature of railway operation even after the Second World War, though more rarely resulting in loss of life. At Hitchin on 19th November 1958 there was a spectacular multiple collision involving three goods trains and a light engine that had no fatal consequences but caused the complete closure of the East Coast line and huge disruption. Although this is perhaps not a 'disaster', therefore, the involvement of four separate trains is almost unique. Driver Howlett, on the footplate of a 9F 2-10-0 and hauling the 3.25am down goods to Peterborough, made a series of errors as his train approached Hitchin. Dense fog developed at about 4.00am and Howlett misread signals, passing the Wymondley auto-stop signal at danger and failing to reduce his speed, with the result that his train ran into the back of a preceding freight which was just restarting after a three-minute signal stop. Although the only damage to Howlett's train was the derailment of the 9F, the wagons of the other train were scattered across the up main line. Although the Hitchin South signalman was able to place detonators, the driver of the approaching Leeds to London express freight was unable to stop and hit the wreckage at about 35mph. The engine of this, a V2, was derailed along with seventeen wagons which in turn struck a Class L1 2-6-4T standing on the up slow line, which was overturned.

Howlett's thoughts as he watched this amazing scene of chaos unfold from the relatively unscathed perspective of his own train can only be wondered at. It would have been worse except for the quick thinking of the Stevenage North signalman who managed to avert further mayhem by placing emergency detonators. The inquiry had no difficulty identifying the cause of this, especially as Howlett had passed signals at danger in fog only three weeks earlier.

Snow, Cold and Heat

The early railways were poorly equipped to cope with snow nor the way it gathered in cuttings or restricted the view at even a low speed. The GNR was badly affected by the open countryside between Peterborough and Grantham, the line typically being shut for several days in January 1854. When the snow stopped, two goods trains had to be dug out and rerailed at Corby and Little Bytham and at least one passenger train dug out. Passenger trains were embedded for three days; although the passengers were taken away by other means, the railwaymen had to stay with the train through the worst of the weather. Certainly in the early days, this was the area that seemed to suffer most from snow and the line was closed regularly. Sometimes even attempts to keep it open contributed to the problems – in January 1881 the 'Scotch Express' collided with a snowplough which had got stuck at Essendine, injuring the driver of the latter and the line was completely closed for a while.

The next accident to be described, that at Abbotts Ripton,[11] was one of the most serious in the history of the Great Northern Railway and had far-reaching consequences in terms of 'lessons learned'.

On 21st January 1876 Joseph Bray was assigned to drive a Great Northern Railway coal train south from New England Yard at Peterborough. Due out at 5.35pm with 33 wagons, Bray did not leave until nearly 6.00pm and headed out into the dark, snowy night across the Fens to Holme. It had been snowing since 4.00pm and, as his guard later reported, "the flakes grew bigger, as big as a two-shilling piece, and they seemed to stick to everything they touched". Another driver, Edis, later said "I never had seen snow in such large pieces in my life." In the words of another driver, "I was never out on a worse night…it was freezing, blowing and snowing." A routine run on an unpleasant night turned out to be a momentous one that Bray would never forget.

Running late, Bray expected to be shunted at Holme to allow a following southbound 'Scotch Express' to pass but all the signals showed a clear white light. He concluded that the 'Scotch express', due out of Peterborough at 6.18pm, must be running very late, perhaps because of the weather. It was also late because it had made a special stop at Doncaster to pick up Lord Colville, Deputy Chairman of the Great Northern Company. The signals at Connington[12] and Wood Walton also showed white. Then he saw the Abbotts Ripton distant signal also showing a clear light. However, Bray was now certain that he would be shunted into a siding and, not trusting visibility in the swirling snow, slowed enough to call out to the Abbotts Ripton signalman at about 6.40pm. The signalman called out "Come on back; look sharp, you are stopping the express", never fearing anything else since the signals were interlocked with the points which would protect the express from the goods in its way. Bray started setting back, but as he did so there was a tremendous crash as the express ploughed into his shunting goods about four wagons back from the engine. The goods guard, already shunted well back into the siding, saw his train split into two.

The express locomotive and its stock splayed across the tracks, straddling the northbound down line. Passengers were thrown about – a surgeon from Spalding found himself in the arms of a valet to the Russian ambassador, Count Shouvaloff, who was also travelling on the train.

Bray was dazed for five minutes or so, his engine knocked forwards, and then was woken from his confusion by a relief clerk, alert to the dangers. The clerk, Usher, had been travelling on the 'Scotch Express', but now placed fog detonator signals on the down line and sent a man back along the up. With his own guard on the footplate and a red lamp to warn approaching down trains, they set off up the line towards Huntingdon but had gone little more than 500 yards when they saw a down express approaching. The guard, William Hunt, cried out "For God's sake, Joe, blow up, for here's a train coming up." Bray 'opened the whistle' and the guard waved the red lamp, then they carried on to Huntingdon without knowing what had happened behind them though the fireman, Faulkner, saw that the other train was slowing. On the way they passed a red signal – the only one Bray saw between Peterborough and Huntingdon, though his guard reported seeing a "little speck of red light when we got up to the starting signal at Abbotts Ripton". At Huntingdon they stopped another northbound train, the Manchester goods.

Meanwhile the Abbotts Ripton signalman, Johnson, was badly shaken and his signal box had been invaded by passengers from the wrecked train, "all bothering me …to telegraph to their friends". The Spalding surgeon rushed in and berated him for not blocking the line, but he could only point at his instruments. In the confusion, he temporarily forgot about a down Leeds express approaching from the south.

The train Bray had passed was the 5.30pm down express to Leeds, driven by William Wilson. Wilson had passed nothing but white signals for miles, with the Abbotts Ripton distant showing a "beautiful white light" in the words of his fireman, but was suddenly alarmed by the explosion of fog signals followed by the sight of a red lamp. He shut off steam and cut the speed to about 15-30mph, but then knew little "until I found myself among the ruins of the break".

Wilson's fireman had a similar experience. James Falkinder found himself "crawling up the bank on the west side and behind the engine… I found the hedge, and caught hold of a woman who was sitting there, who I thought was my mate". Their guard also had a lucky escape: "My van was smashed to atoms. I found myself in the ditch at the bottom of the cutting after the collision."

The down Leeds express had ploughed straight into the wreck of the 'Scotch Express': "The engine of the Leeds express literally cut its way through the tender of the Scotch train." Its engine glanced off the upturned 'Scotch' one and eventually off to the side of the line. The following carriages broke free and swept over the wrecked 'Scotch' carriages, "utterly crushing and destroying those beneath". This was the cause of the death and destruction, and most of the thirteen killed were at this point. Ben Jolliffe, a farmer trying to help ladies out of the carriages, was "crushed beneath the ponderous weight" of the Leeds engine. Elizabeth Sanderson and her sister, who were struggling to get out, were killed. Two ladies in another compartment were also crushed, yet a bottle of champagne in the luggage net of their compartment survived intact. Lord Colville survived, but two youths in the same compartment were killed. Also killed was Dion Boucicault, son of a famous actor and dramatist, and grandson of Dionysius Lardner.[13]

Among the many injured was the driver of the 'Scotch' express, Catley, whose hand had been crushed and a finger had been severed. Nonetheless, he acted to put out the fire of his stricken engine before it could spread to the wooden carriages.

Meanwhile a guard of the Scotch express, Day, had been thrown to the floor of his van but gradually recovered his senses. He placed fog signals behind his train to protect the wreck from the north, but had time to check that the Abbotts Ripton distant signal was still showing a fateful white. His fog signals stopped the up Manchester and Leeds express from adding to the already fearful wreckage. This was driven by William Edis, forming the 6.28pm from Peterborough, and had left that city eleven minutes late, running into blinding snow but clear signals. There was confusion at Wood Walton, where the signals showed white but the signalman waved a red lamp, and Edis brought his train to a halt. He could see a white distant

Carriages piled on top of each other and rescuers working in a blizzard - a famous image of the Abbotts Ripton disaster.
(The Graphic)

for Abbotts Ripton ahead, so had restarted – only to meet Day along the way. Noticing all the signals still at white, he told a porter to cut the wires so that the arm would move to the danger position.

Many of the railway staff seemed to have shown great reluctance to speak to the signalman at Abbotts Ripton, Charles Johnson. Typical was guard Day who said, "I did not tell the signalman that his signals were showing white lights." Many seem to have assumed it was the signalman's fault. However, Wilson recalled his days as a lad porter at Claypole and that "I have frequently known signals to stick on such a night." As a driver, "I have observed the signals not working properly from frost or snow, but I have never had occasion to report them." To cover himself, Wilson wrote a statement that all the signals had been 'white' on the night.

However, Simpson, a guard on the down Leeds express ran across to the signal box to check that the lines were now 'blocked', which they were, and also went down the line to meet the next train from the north, the up Leeds express. He joined Edis on the footplate and as they advanced cautiously to Abbotts Ripton they saw the problem with the up distant signal: "The spectacle glass of the lamp was covered with snow.

Abbotts Ripton – 'The Scene on Saturday Night' - blazing wreckage, an overturned locomotive and the signal box - with one 't'.
(Author's Collection)

The red glass was before the light, but the snow which covered the spectacle made it show a white light. The arm I noticed was up at 'danger'."

The fireman on the up Manchester express, Reuben Murfitt,[14] also noticed something wrong with the Abbotts Ripton down home signal: "I noticed that the arm… was loaded with snow, and it appeared to be half down and half up. I could see the arm distinctly. I could not see the lamp glass or spectacle. It showed a perfect white light, not as if the snow were in the way to prevent its shining properly… I do not think I have ever seen a lamp glass covered with snow. I never saw anything like that snow before… I have never known the signals stick through the snow."

Simpson then went back to the signal box to confirm that the lever was set to 'danger', before lighting a fire to warm the distressed survivors. Another guard on the down express noticed the white light of the down distant, but not the position of its arm. He then walked to the intermediate Stukeley signal box, noting that its signals showed more white than red, and remonstrated with the signalman there – who confirmed all his signals were set to danger. Usher also noticed the strange mix of red and white near Stukeley.

Meanwhile, the station master at Holme had failed to respond when his signalman told him that the coal train had run past the signals and had done nothing as the 'Scotch' express followed as Holme had received 'line clear' from Connington and his men had wiped snow away from the signal spectacles. It was one of the platelayers, who had been at work since 6.00am, who noticed that signal arms failed to return to danger as the snow had weighted they down. The station master watched platelayers rather tardily "working the balance weights at the foot of the signal posts" so as to knock the snow off the arms. However, as soon as the second southbound express passed, the signal arm refused to return up to danger due to the snow and so the red spectacle would not cover the lamp.

The down home and up starting signals at Abbotts Ripton showed a white light long after the crash because some of the train vehicles were on the wires. It took a 36lb iron chair tied to the balance weight to shift one signal arm to danger, because the engine was on one of the wires. Signal fitter Joshua Pallinder also found that snow on the signal cables kept the signals down at 'all right' as well as snow on the arms. But this problem was well known – Pallinder told how he had been out to clear snow from the signals repeatedly the previous winter, but this night was worse and he had to go up a ladder to clear it from the arms. However, the GNR's Chief Signal Inspector, based in Retford, claimed that in 30 years he had never known "a single instance" of snow stopping a signal from showing the proper indication. Henry Oakley, the GNR general manager, told the Board of Trade inspector "I never heard from anyone in our service that a signal had given a wrong indication." Both men were subtly ridiculed by Captain Tyler in his Accident Report, who listed six of the junior employees who mentioned signals sticking in snow. Ice also formed on telegraph wires between Great Ponton and Peterborough, bringing them down. This brought an end to a problem for the Holme signalman, who found that "fighting" for space on the wires prevented him getting messages through; in fact the Huntingdon South signalman prevented his Abbotts Ripton colleague from sending a message for help for twenty minutes. "Fighting" was a bizarre practice where stations would struggle to control the wire by moving the telegraph handles "rapidly and irregularly from side to side".

In the aftermath, the GNR was heavily criticised by relatives who received false reports or were prevented from going to Huntingdon. Nothing was reported about Boucicault's death for two days, despite his inscribed watch having been found. He was buried at Huntingdon and his father offered to pay for a drinking fountain in that town as a memorial. A coroner's jury found a verdict of accidental death due to the 'inefficient' block system, but criticised the GNR directors for running heavy mineral traffic without an extra line of rails.

Captain Tyler investigated the accident for the Board of Trade. He thought errors were made at Holme, where the station master was slack in not realising the reason why the coal train had run past the signals and where the lack of a speaking telegraph to the intermediate boxes between there and Abbotts Ripton had been a handicap. If he had "displayed greater activity and a moderate amount of forethought and caution" the first accident might have been avoided. However, it was finally the failure of the signals to act as designed at several places which caused the first accident and also the second. The signalman at Huntingdon South was also censured.

Although the coroner's jury had blamed a failure in the block system for the accident, Tyler disagreed. He thought the block system could not fail – it was signals and telegraphs which failed. Very simply, the weight of snow on wires and arms prevented the arms returning to a 'danger' position. In the 'clear' position, a signal arm fell into a slotted post and the red glass spectacle was withdrawn from in front of the lamp; for 'danger', the balance weight worked to pull the arm up to the horizontal and move the red glass over the lamp. Tyler thought the weight of snow on the wires was a problem and he debated the relative advantages of a signal sticking in the 'danger' position. He criticised the running at speed in poor weather, implying that men feared the GNR's iron discipline if they were late, and he blamed the Leeds train's lack of continuous brakes for its failure to stop in time. The lack of 'speaking instruments' at Connington and Wood Walton had been a factor, also the failure of Wood Walton's signalman to place fog signals and excessive speed in poor weather.

His recommendations included suggesting two improvements for signals to make them less liable to stick in the 'all right' position and an extra slow line up Connington Bank. Yet the final words of the report were a stinging rebuke for the GNR, as he opined that "punctuality may be purchased at too dear a price". Yet that December there was another fatal collision on the same line just twenty miles away at Arlesey (see Chapter 2) when a goods train being shunted into a siding was derailed and then hit by an express.

According to some sources, the driver of one of the trains was depressed by his role in the affair and, several years later, committed suicide.[15]

The Abbotts Ripton disaster did not result in any dramatic changes to the GNR's preparedness for snow and only a few months later another serious disaster was only narrowly averted. At 4.45am on 14th April 1876 an overnight Scottish express to King's Cross was brought to a standstill in blizzard conditions near Corby Glen; the snow was so heavy that it had brought down the telegraph poles, reportedly over a distance of fifteen miles to Peterborough.[16] According to the eye witness account of a passenger, the guard then struggled back through waist-deep snow to protect the rear of the train as best as he could given that the luggage train would be following.[17] The guard got far enough back to give some warning to the luggage train, although it was claimed its brakes then "broke", but the rear-end collision that occurred was only minor and resulted in one or two slight injuries. "No-one could fail to see how marvellous had been our escape" wrote G. Martin Tait. The stuck train was hit at low speed by an up express goods from Manchester.[18] However, a second disaster in the snow had been successfully avoided, although passengers did not get to London until 4.00pm – over nine hours late.

However, three significant changes were implemented following the Abbotts Ripton disaster. Firstly, the Great Northern and other railways changed the practice whereby signals normally indicated 'clear' or 'all right' to one where 'caution' or 'stop' became the 'normal' position. Secondly, the Great Northern and most others with the notable exception of the North Eastern Railway abolished the use of 'slotted post' signals. Both these measures were successful in helping to ensure that signal arms could not be frozen in the 'clear' position. Thirdly and uniquely among the principal British main railway companies, the Great Northern adopted Edward French's design of what became the familiar centre-balance 'tumbler' or 'somersault' arm signals.[19]

With improved technology, the railways became better able to cope with snow and – though services still tend to get stopped – generally free from disaster. However, in January 1939 heavy snow caused the railway system to revert to a method of working more typical of the 1830s than the 1930s and the result was another disaster at Hatfield. Before he published his report, Lt. Col. Woodhouse made a perhaps unguarded comment about the main cause of the accident being the "extraordinary climatic conditions" but in fact there would not have been an accident if other factors – including incautious driving – had not intervened.[20]

Days of heavy snow had had a serious effect on the main line in all areas south of Newark in January 1939, mainly because it had built up on the telegraph wires and brought them down in many places. As a result, the block telegraph between Welwyn Garden City and Hatfield failed at 6.30pm on 25th January and the main line had to switch to the 'time interval' system of working as laid down by the Block Regulations. This was, of course, the same system as had been abandoned many decades earlier as not giving sufficient security against a tail-end collision.

Problems continued into the next morning. The signalman at Welwyn Garden City, Jakes, therefore had no means of communication with Hatfield and followed the Regulations which applied when the block system failed. This meant that every train was to be stopped at Welwyn so its driver and guard could be warned of the time interval arrangements; Jakes was convinced that he spoke to every driver, but did not think he had been able to speak to every guard and one of the exceptions was Driver, the guard on train 250 from Cambridge. He then let the trains depart at ten-minute intervals.

By this time the LNER was struggling to maintain a service through Hatfield where several lines joined and delays had built up north of the station in both directions. By the time of the disaster, four trains were standing on the up main line and two goods trains on the adjacent up goods line. The rules stated that trains required to stand outside home signals during the use of time interval working required hand signalmen to protect their rear, but none was on duty at Hatfield.[21] In this situation, the guard had to go back to place detonators and to give hand signals whilst the fireman should also go back to meet the guard. By the time of the accident, the first of the four passenger trains had only been standing for 24 minutes, but the first of the goods trains had been waiting for over four hours.

Driver Fiske on train 250 stopped twenty yards behind another Cambridge train just outside Hatfield station. Following the regulations for trains 'standing outside a Home Signal', he sent his fireman, Barham, back to see the guard. The latter, Harry Driver, was perhaps a little slow to get out of his compartment – although, of course, no-one had told him the block system had broken down – and the two men had only just started to walk back to protect the rear of their train when they heard another train approaching round the curve.

This was train No.269, the 7.15am from Peterborough, with Driver W. Merchant who had also received a warning from Jakes. Drifting smoke from the stationary trains, and the position of the goods trains standing on the adjacent track, meant that there was a limited view ahead for any train approaching from the north on the main line. However, the report of *The Times* that drifting smoke and falling snow "formed an almost opaque screen" was not widely supported by other witnesses, most of whom thought the snow had stopped and a thaw had started. Whilst Barham waved to attract attention, Driver placed a detonator on the line when the approaching locomotive was barely an arm's length away and clearly risked his life in doing so. The explosion of the detonator actually dazed the guard. The result was that Merchant was alerted by the explosion of the detonator and the sight of Barham and first saw the standing train ahead when he was only 125 yards from it, having gained a clearer view past the goods train.

In this situation of general breakdown, the 7.15am Peterborough to King's Cross (train No.269) collided at 10.09am with the rear of the 8.25am from Cambridge (No.250) which was standing on the up main line near Mount Pleasant bridge about ¾ of a mile north of the station. According to

Barham, "the engine seemed to disappear right inside the guard's brake, and the coach just went up in a mass of splinters".

The force of the impact drove the Cambridge train, which was reported as standing without its brakes on, forwards by twenty yards or so. This train was made up of articulated carriage sets which, though they had steel frames, had wooden bodies which were little protection against impact. The two rearmost sets were "demolished" by the impact and the underframe of the rear carriage was "crumpled and distorted in a remarkable fashion", according to Lt. Col. Woodhouse's report. The carriages rose up, coming into contact with the bridge arch and certainly above the level of the Peterborough locomotive's chimney; the body of the rear carriage was torn off its frame and thrown across the two down lines.

Train No.250 was pushed forwards and in turn collided with the train in front of it, No.238. This was also from Cambridge and standing with its brakes off, which then was propelled forwards another fifteen feet.

One passenger in the 8.25am Cambridge train, a woman, was killed and there were numerous injuries. The wooden coach bodies crumpled like paper; two people sitting opposite each other in a compartment found "their seats were so closely jammed together that they could not extricate themselves without help". One woman thought the train had been destroyed by a bomb.

Two men were on their way to their weddings, with mixed fortunes. One was standing up looking out of the window, anxious about the time, when the impact knocked him to the floor; he crawled out of a small opening in the dismembered carriage, clambered up the side of the cutting on to Mount Pleasant bridge and hailed a passing road coach on its way to London – saying that he might still be on time. However, the Rev. Stratton, on his way to get married in Eastbourne, had to be detained in hospital.

How did this happen? One theory was that train 269 was headed by V2 2-6-2 No.4813, which was barely two months old and of a new and powerful type. Sir Nigel Gresley, the Chief Mechanical Engineer, and others suggested that the driver might not have been familiar with the power of this new engine and its ability to accelerate; if this were so, it was hardly praise for the LNER's driver training programmes. This contributed to an argument about the speed at which Merchant was driving – though he said he never exceeded 25mph, Gresley thought "nearer 40 than 20" was likely from the impact damage. Merchant's claim was that he was only travelling at 5-10mph when collision occurred was believed by almost no-one. However, all agreed that the standing goods trains on the down goods line restricted the view, but the simple fact was that Merchant was driving too fast given he had only a limited view ahead. Woodhouse concluded that the speed must have been more than 20mph or Merchant would have been able to stop within 200 yards; he thought it probable that speed was over 40mph until Merchant saw Barham. The inspecting officer, Woodhouse, also conjectured that Merchant might have been expecting one train to be standing ahead but had not allowed for the possibility that there might be several. Although the weather had started the chain of events which led to disaster, it was the failure of railway staff to adjust that caused this accident.

Class V2 No.60885 was derailed in the multiple collision at Hitchin on 19th November 1958; underneath the pile of wagons on the left was L1 2-6-4T No.67785, which was knocked over. (David Percival)

There was also comment about the LNER's failure to deploy hand signalmen. It was noted that Hatfield box had had trains standing for more than four hours, but no flagmen were on duty although they were required to protect trains held outside the home signals.

Accidents that were due to solely to the cold do not feature, but cold could have some impact on the humanity who operated the railway and it is likely that the effects of the cold led to the driver error which caused the very serious fatal accident at Barkston on 19th January 1936. The direct cause of this disaster was undoubtedly a driver passing signals at danger but, when he was prosecuted for manslaughter, the fact of the freezing conditions played heavily on the minds of the jury when acquitting him.

The early hours of a Sunday morning in January should have been a relatively quiet time on the line north of Grantham, but on this occasion there had been a build-up of traffic and additional freight trains were being run.

As a result the intermediate signal box at Peascliffe was unusually manned on a Sunday morning and, indeed, at 6.00am saw a change in shift from signalman Ward to his colleague Hebblethwaite. It was a fine but very cold morning, with some patchy fog. The change occurred at a busy time, with three down workings in quick succession being forwarded from Barrowby Road box, past Peascliffe and onwards north through the tunnel to Barkston South box.

Hebblethwaite had a busy start to his shift. A train of mineral empties steamed north and then, within five minutes, a ballast train followed. This train was going to track relaying work at Barnby near Newark and was also going to pick up extra railway workers at Barkston. Some men were already on the train, crowded into the guard's van at the rear. The ballast train was checked by Peascliffe's down home signal and Hebblethwaite had time to tell its driver that a headlamp was out and needed relighting. Then it steamed off, labouring through Peascliffe Tunnel towards Barkston.

As the ballast was slowly approaching Barkston, where it was due to pick up the other men, the Barkston South signalman received a frantic bell signal from Peascliffe – 'train running away'. Then Hebblethwaite rang his colleague to say that two light engines had passed his signal box, running through signals at danger and travelling "at speed". The Barkston signalman acted quickly – sending a man out to tell the ballast train driver to accelerate rather than slowing down, but he was too late. The driver and fireman of the ballast train felt an impact from the rear, which was also heard by the signalman at Peascliffe. As the ballast train passed the signal box at Barkston South, the signalman could see that the brake van was missing from the back and the rear wagon was damaged. As the train passed by he sent the emergency bell signal ahead to Hougham box – 'Stop and Examine.'

Two light engines coupled together had left New England Yard early that morning at 5.35am to return to York; they were 4-4-2s Nos.2199 and 2198. Travelling at about 45mph, they passed all of three Peascliffe's signals[22] which, according to Hebblethwaite, were certainly at danger or caution, and Barkston's down outer home– which may have been as the ballast train was only just passing. The driver on the leading engine, Ward, said that he saw no tail lamps on the ballast train and so ploughed into it without slackening his pace. The brake van was "demolished" and the rear five ballast wagons also destroyed. The engines carried on for 300 yards without stopping, sustaining minor damage and derailing the front axle of one of them. The sixth wagon from the rear of the ballast train derailed as it was hauled through Barkston station, fouling the up line, and the seventh later derailed at Hougham.

This might have been only a minor accident except the brake van was carrying a dozen men on their way to the relaying works. Parts of the brake van were thrown backwards over the engines into a ditch. Five men were killed instantly, three died later and four were seriously injured.

The injured, and later the dead, were pushed silently by hand on a railway trolley to Barkston station where Dr.Jausch arrived to tend the dying. There ambulances gathered to take them to Grantham hospital whilst the dead were laid out in the waiting room of one of the line's quietest stations. One of the ambulance men told a reporter, "When we got there we could see that things were bad. We took six or seven doctors and another ambulance came from Sleaford. It was very cold and conditions for the doctors were difficult."[23] A railway worker also described the scene: "Along the banks of the cutting in which the collision occurred were bits of the van in which the dead and injured men had been travelling. A little farther on I saw the bodies of two of the platelayers lying in the four foot way on the up line. In the six foot way between the two tracks I came upon a headless body of a man, and on the outside of the down line there were two."

Suspicion initially centred on Hebblethwaite who controlled a distant, outer home and inner home or 'starting' signal, with track circuits between the home signal and starting. It was obviously considered possible that he had forgotten to return the distant signal to caution after the ballast train, but he insisted that it had remained at caution behind the mineral and not been cleared. There was also doubt about the Barkston South distant, which was the last signal passed by the light engines before the collision.

The driver of the leading engine was David Ward, who had worked south earlier that night on a fish train. Ward stated that it had been so cold that the glasses on the locomotive cab had become covered with ice and, in order to see, he had had to lean out; this had caused his eyes to water, but he was still certain that all the Peascliffe signals had been clear. He denied confusing Barrowby's down starter signal with Peascliffe's distant – losing track of exactly where you were was always a worry. He stated categorically that Barkston South's distant was 'off' or clear and that he would have seen any tail lights on the ballast train if they had been operating.

Ward's fireman, Harold Calvert, contrived to give evidence that exactly equated to 'I saw nothing'. He said that he "was not well acquainted with the road" and denied seeing any signals at all – but if the driver was struggling with the cold, Calvert should have been providing some support. The driver of the second engine, Smith, followed the same line – he said that smoke prevented him seeing any signals except for Barkston South's down distant which he said was 'off.' He saw no tail lamps, of course, and his fireman Robson saw nothing at all.

A crucial additional witness was the signalman that Hebblethwaite had taken over from – also called Ward, in this case G. C. Ward. The signalman had left Peascliffe box to walk home and had seen the light engines approaching rather fast so soon after the ballast; this had caused him to look back and he was certain that Peascliffe's distant signal had been showing a yellow caution light.

Lt. Col. Woodhouse led the inquiry and was therefore forced to consider Driver Ward's word against that of Signalman Hebblethwaite. The testimony of G. Ward the signalman weighed heavily, though, and Woodhouse decided that in all probability the distant signal had been at caution. He thought it possible, if "extremely unlikely", that Hebblethwaite had forgotten to return his home and starter signals to danger. He was less sure about the Barkston South distant signal, which

may have been slow to be returned to caution, but the position of this had little to do with the cause of the disaster.

Woodhouse clearly took the view that David Ward was lying to cover his responsibility. He noted that Calvert had appeared to disagree with his driver as to where he was standing on the footplate at a given moment. Whilst laying the blame largely with Ward, Woodhouse did note that Ward 'might have been slightly dazed by the cold and by the strain of looking out for signals.' In these conditions, Ward might easily have mistaken the green Barrowby starter as being the Peascliffe distant and, assuming the box to be unmanned as usual, had not then looked for its other signals.

Ward later added an additional line of defence, that smoke from the ballast train had further obscured his view, although, of course, if he was unable to see the signals he should have assumed them to be at danger. However, the cold is worth bearing in mind – to be face first into a freezing wind at 45mph for mile after mile would indeed have been a challenge for any man.

Ward, Smith and Calvert were all charged with manslaughter. In an initial hearing at Grantham Police Court, their counsel argued there was "not a shred of evidence". They were tried at Lincoln on 15th and 16th June 1936. A model of the railway and the signals was shown in court and the severity of passing four signals at caution or danger explained by the prosecution. Mortimer Creasy, the LNER's Signalling Inspector, said that the block signalling system was "as perfect as human ingenuity could make it". Hebblethwaite came under a bit of pressure as he had not sent for a fogman despite visibility dropping below 250 yards – he rather lamely said he did not like to call a man out on a Sunday morning. Nor did he use the alternative precaution, double block working. Spencer, driver of the ballast train, said that there had been patchy fog and that the Peascliffe home signal was the hardest to see; he added that his train would have left plenty of smoke to make visibility worse. No evidence was presented against Calvert and the judge ordered the jury to find no case against Smith. Ward was then acquitted, the evidence about the frosted glass seemingly crucial. Justice Hawke then made an odd little speech: "This case has been conducted by men who are too wise to introduce side issues, and if I might imagine myself as a referee at some match I might say that it has not been necessary for me to blow my whistle."

The case illustrates a theme of these accidents – the extreme rarity of a railwayman being convicted of an offence following a fatal incident. In this case the fact remains that Ward had not exercised proper caution and had indeed passed four signals. If he had had difficulty seeing, the proper action would have been to slow to a more suitable pace.

The LNER invested heavily in the aftermath of this accident and on 17th October 1937 provided continuous track circuiting between Grantham and Barkston South with colour light signals.[24]

From the 1950s British Railways launched an energetic programme of replacing old jointed track with continuous welded rail but in the hot summer of 1969 this led to a minor national panic after a series of four accidents in a few weeks including one at Sandy.[25] Though this accident was not fatal, it is historically significant in being probably the accident with

The rear section of the derailed 'Tees-Tyne Pullman' at Sandy, July 1969. Note the dislodged rails from the down slow line.
(David Percival)

the highest train speed that had occurred up to that time and the lack of fatalities was due very considerably to the improvements in railway coaching stock. Given its occurrence at a time of some public tension and the similarities in significance to Hatfield a few decades later, it was therefore a noteworthy accident.

On the day of the accident temperatures had been very high and railway staff had been patrolling the line in case the track buckled. At a point very close to the actual scene of the disaster, rail temperature had been recorded at 119°F shortly before the 17.00 King's Cross to Newcastle 'Tees-Tyne Pullman' approached Sandy at around 92-94mph behind 'Deltic' diesel locomotive No.D9015 *Tulyar*. Rounding a curve, the driver clearly saw that the track ahead of him had buckled and was 18in out of line. The locomotive and first carriage rode through but the second and third carriages became derailed. The train became divided, the 6th and 11th carriages turning on their sides. Remarkably, there were only eleven injuries requiring hospital treatment from a total of 400 passengers.

The Ministry of Transport rushed out a report on this accident and also several other similar ones involving continuous welded rail. The rails here had been laid in 1959 but since 1966 repairs had been made by welding several short lengths into both rails, which involved de-stressing the track. The Permanent Way Inspector also noticed unusual sidecutting on the higher of the two rails, but the rushed report was curiously inconclusive about the causes of the buckling at Sandy. After further rumination, a Government spokesman in the House of Lords clarified technical changes: "The special measures the [British Railways] Board have now put in hand to increase the margins of resistance to heat distortion in continuous welded track take the form of increased ballast provision and of the re-adjustment of the continuous rails themselves to a higher stress-free temperature condition than has hitherto been deemed necessary. This work should be completed before the onset of the hot weather of 1970.[26]

Major Rose began a lengthy and detailed inquiry which did not report until 1974.

Water

Water was a serious risk if a line was poorly engineered, since rushing waters could then take away the trackbed and cause sudden derailment. This happened in the double accident at Carlton on Trent on 14th August 1857 in the middle of a most appalling night; although this was not a disaster in that no-one died, it claimed two trains and was therefore very serious. Exceptionally heavy rain had already swept away a large part of the nearby Midland Railway line at Fiskerton, closed the Manchester, Sheffield & Lincolnshire Railway between Clarborough and Gainsborough, and affected the GNR's loop line near Saxilby. At just after midnight a GNR up fish train passed through Carlton on Trent station, a few miles north of Newark, but went only one mile further before suddenly disappearing into a void. "The driver suddenly found his engine sinking under him and diverging from the rails", plunging into rushing water. A few moments later a down overnight express approached from the south and "dashed into the flood, the rails rose and fell once or twice, and then the engine capsized, taking several of the passenger carriages with it and plunging them into the water."[27]

Although first reports suggested the disaster was caused by water from the flooding River Trent washing away the tracks, it was actually caused by insufficient drainage through culverts provided beneath the line to enable water to escape from the surrounding fields, so that it rose over the line with a scouring effect. To make matters worse, a deep ditch ran beside the line and this proved a dangerous trap for many struggling to escape. Passengers trapped in the carriages, which were filling with water, could only be rescued by ripping the roofs off. James Withers described how carriages were "literally smashed to pieces" and he only escaped through a hole that had been made in the roof. One widow narrowly held on to her small child, who was in danger of being washed away. Several passengers felt that they had escaped cold and watery deaths although only two were injured badly enough to require extensive attention.

In order to escape, parts of carriage roof were laid across the water to form a causeway to Carlton village. The passengers struggled to Carlton on Trent station, where another up train was being held. What happened there was a subject of some debate – Withers thought that the station master only allowed this train to go forward to collect more survivors "after a very protracted debate" whereas the surgeon from Sutton on Trent said that "Mr.Grylls the station master also acted not only with prudence but much promptness in the affair."[28] Temporary repairs were quickly made although it took rather longer to remove the two trains which partly blocked the formation, so "a tramway of sinuous form" was constructed "to afford a passage for the regular trains through the wreck".

FOOTNOTES

1. *The Times*, 21 January 1871. The 'siding' was actually the up goods line but there was no down equivalent.
2. The name was commonly referred to as 'Barkstone' at this period although also known as Jericho Junction after a local farm.
3. *Huddersfield Chronicle*, 17 January 1874
4. *The Times*, 12 January 1874
5. Initial reports named him as Arthur Clayburn, later ones as Arthur Casburn.
6. *Nottinghamshire Guardian*, 16 January 1874.
7. One of the curiosities of this accident is the variation in press and official sources as to where the trains started; this one was described as starting from Aldersgate Street and the Victoria one also described as starting from King's Cross at 5.07pm – possibly because drivers were changed there; it left Victoria as the 4.23pm. Given the accident occurred at 5.30pm, the departure time for the Moorgate train also would appear confused.
8. Trains did not have speedometers so speed was usually an estimate though after accidents speeds were calculated roughly from passing times recorded at signal boxes.
9. Also reported as 'Razzell.'
10. *The Times*, 13 December 1927
11. Abbotts Ripton – or Abbot's Ripton? As Captain Tyler used the former spelling in his official report, that is used here, but *The Times* used the latter. The name has also been spelt with or without apostrophe and without or without two 't's, making a choice from four.
12. Spelt here in the railway version, but more correctly spelt 'Conington'.
13. Lardner was a 'popular scientist' who was initially sceptical of railways but later made a fortune from writing and speaking about them. He was equally enthusiastic about women, fathering the first Dion Boucicault and eloping to Paris with the wife of a railway director. The director followed him to an hotel there and beat him, and then beat him again in the courts. See the present author's article in *Backtrack*, May 2010,

pps.316-7.
14. The accident report confuses who was on which train. In its index Murfitt is listed as fireman of the up Manchester and gives evidence in the text about his journey from Peterborough with Edis, yet in the introduction is referred to as Wilson's fireman – Wilson was driving the down train. There was also a Faulkner as fireman on the coal train and Falkinder on the down Leeds!
15. Over a century later, well-known railway historian and itinerant lay-preacher Prof. H. P. White was asked to preach to a Sunday evening congregation at Abbotts Ripton. As he told it himself, his opening remarks that he had always wanted to preach there due to the railway accident were not received with any great enthusiasm.
16. *The Times*, 17 April 1876. This was a letter from a passenger, glad to still be alive.
17. This was a special working carrying luggage of the passengers on the preceding express.
18. S. Hall, *The Railway Detectives*, Shepperton, 1990, p.47
19. The design was also used in South Wales and Ireland.
20. *The Times*, 1 February 1939
21. Block Telegraph Regulation 25g stated that no train should be held outside the home signal until hand signallers were available.
22. A down distant, home and starter.
23. *Manchester Guardian*, 20 January 1936
24. Information courtesy of Michael Back.Mr. Back has also seen signalling plans at the National Archives showing only two Down signals for Peascliffe box, yet the Accident Report is unequivocal in showing three.
25. S Hall, p.131
26. *Hansard*, 5 November 1969
27. *The Times*, 16 August 1857
28. *The Times*, 17 August 1857

This 'sketch by a passenger' contains a fair amount of artistic licence, including the locomotive perched precariously in mid-air after the Arlesey collision on 23rd December 1876, as described in Chapter 2. (Author)

8

DERELICTION OF DUTY

Few accidents were caused by dereliction of duty alone, but there have been a number of accidents which could have been prevented if individuals had done what was expected of them.

There were many hundreds of minor incidents caused by individuals neglecting to carry out their duties properly, but only a small proportion led to major disaster. One which very nearly did, but in the end cost no lives, resulted from the carelessness of an engine cleaner at New England shed, Peterborough, on 15th July 1865. The firelighter came to engine No.352 to start his work but failed to check – as was his duty – that the brakes were firmly on and also left the engine in forward gear. The 'washer out' and the engine cleaner also worked on No.352 and also failed to check that it was left safely braked.

At about 2.30pm that afternoon the relief signalman at New England cabin was surprised to see an engine heading out from the sheds at about 20mph. The Inspector who was with the signalman saw that something was wrong, but assumed that a cleaner had tried to move the engine and lost control. A hedge restricted the view of the two men who, in a panic, set the points for the main line whereas a runaway engine should have been sent into a siding. It passed through Peterborough station at about 25mph, gaining ground on a mixed goods and passenger train which had left a few minutes before. The Inspector telegraphed the station and an engine was sent out in pursuit of the runaway. Reports in one newspaper that a 'telegram' was sent to warn the crew of the goods train to speed up seems rather unlikely as there was no means of delivering it![1]

This train was normally a goods, but on market days had carriages attached at the rear for passengers for Yaxley, Holme and Ramsey; these were fairly full. About 1¾ miles along the line, the light engine caught up with the train and smashed into the carriage at the rear. Up to 40 passengers suffered various injuries, with the seven most serious being taken back by the 'chasing' engine to Peterborough. The three New England men lost their jobs.

Some of the early cases highlighted public debate over who was to blame if an accident occurred due to the bad management of the line. Such was the debate when there was an accident at Stamford Cutting, two miles south of Christon Bank station in Northumberland, on 22nd December 1851. Patrick Morton, a clerk with the Electric Telegraph Company, was killed and three drovers injured[2] – all had been travelling in the guard's van of a goods train that was hit from behind on a moderately foggy night. A Tweedmouth to Newcastle cattle train had left Tweedmouth with two locomotives heading a train of 42 wagons and a second class carriage that was, according to reports, about 250 yards long. The guard seems to have been inexperienced and lacked proper equipment, such as fog signals, but there was an inspector of some description also travelling. Whether the presence of the drovers, presumably to look after the animals, was a distraction is perhaps also possible.

At Chathill the train was running late and already at a time when it was bound to conflict with the next southbound passenger train. The station master should have given orders for the train to be shunted, as the rules said this should always be done if a passenger train was due to follow within fifteen minutes. The station master later blamed the travelling inspector, who seems to have been on one of the engines, although that man did not interfere in any way. Nonetheless, the train was allowed to proceed southwards which it did – very slowly. There was another neglected opportunity to shunt it at Christon Bank. By the time it had struggled onward to Stamford Cutting, between one and two miles south of Christon Bank, it had slowed to a crawl on a rising grade of 1 in 150 and was losing traction on the icy and slippery rails. The inspecting officer's report said that speed slowed to only three quarters of a mile in twenty minutes.

At this point one of the drivers became concerned about the following train and sent his fireman back down the train to tell the guard to warn the following passenger train. In fact the speed was so slow that, knowing an express would be following, the guard had already got out of his van to walk back and warn the following train – the line relying on a time interval system of signalling. He took his lamp with him and planned to listen for its approach – the fog having got worse. He had gone barely twenty yards when he saw the express approaching and so disaster was inevitable.

On the footplate of the passenger train they spotted a red light at the rear of the cattle train about 60 yards in advance, but it was too little warning. The passenger train ploughed into the van at the rear and it "shivered to pieces"[3] with the death of Moreton and injury to his fellow travellers. Several passengers on the express were reported to have been severely injured.

The coroner held an inquest in a nearby road side inn. The jury saw this as a classic case of bad railway management and blamed almost everyone they could. They found the main cause of the accident to be 'death by neglect', blaming the goods train guard for not placing fog signals and the directors of the York, Newcastle & Berwick Railway for not issuing him with any; it seems therefore a bit harsh to blame the guard for not placing them! They thought the directors "guilty of great blame and culpable neglect" in allowing the lengthy goods train to set out when the following passenger was due, for having a 'double train' with only one guard – and an unqualified one at that.

They also took exception to the Superintendent of the YN&B, who had attended the inquest and produced a printed set of instructions which they considered "an attempt to throw the blame on an unfortunate guard".

The investigating officer identified four railway staff as having contributed to the disaster – the guard, the Chathill station master, the driver of the second engine and the travelling inspector. Regulations required the guard to have a "constant supply" of fog signals, but he had none. The driver was blamed for being too slow to send warning to the guard. The inspector's presence should have led all to be more alert to the rules, but instead had "a contrary effect".

The guard attracted great interest. His normal job was as a porter at the goods warehouse, but about every fortnight he went out as guard on this train – as he had been doing this for three years, Captain Wynne thought he should have known his duties rather better. The Captain added a footnote, that such occasional work for porters was known on other railways. Wynne was concerned about "so many individuals concurring in disobedience of orders" and that "regulations are not enforced with that strictness which is so essential to safety". He also thought the load of the train was excessive given the locomotives and weather conditions. All this pointed to lax management by the railway company but, unlike the coroner's jury, Wynne did not point the finger at the directors quite so obviously.

The directors responded in their own way – by dismissing the driver, guard and inspector, but they excused the stationmaster at Chathill on the grounds that the "train was under the special charge of the inspector".[4]

It was noted in Chapter One that on the North British Railway there was almost a licensed disregard of danger signals in the early 1850s. This culminated in the fatal accident at Calton Tunnel on 7th December 1854, although on this occasion the dereliction of duty was by the signalman not the driver. Due to the intensity of the traffic, telegraphic control was in operation from a central office at St. Margaret's. However, Captain Galton, reporting to the Board of Trade, noted that the electric telegraph regulations were "habitually neglected…and it is stated that this neglect has occurred with the knowledge of one of the principal officers of the Company".[5] The 11.45am goods from Duns arrived at Leigh Junction and there took on a banking engine for the climb through the tunnel. It made very slow progress and was just emerging from the other end at about 7mph when the 2.00pm Berwick to Edinburgh via Kelso train hit it in the rear. The driver of this train said that there had been a danger signal at St. Margaret's but the telegraph officer signalled him to come forwards with a green light, though warning him there was a goods train ahead of him. He increased his speed after he saw an 'all right' signal at the tunnel entrance. The collision caused the passenger train to split and, because it was unbraked, some of the carriages began to run backwards. The guard in this section found his brake to be damaged and unworkable, so he began to crawl along the carriage roofs to get to the brake van at the other end – there being no corridor, of course. However, he had not got very far before the descending carriages collided with a light engine that had also been permitted to proceed towards the tunnel. A passenger died as a result of this second collision.

The directors had insisted that the regulations be complied with but the telegraphic staff and train drivers were led by William Smith – the same man who, in Chapter One, was referred to as having a rather flexible attitude to danger signals. Smith resigned two days before the accident but his foreman confirmed that the disregard of regulations was well known to Smith. This, together with an accident near Tranent on 25th November, led Captain Galton to conclude that "there is a general want of system in the manner in which the North British Railway is worked". Galton also found that NBR drivers worked on average more than twelve hours a day; in the week ending 25th November 1854 four of them worked for an average of sixteen hours per day!

One of the most spectacular examples of failure to meet duties was the double collision – and subsequent conflagration – in the northern of the two Welwyn tunnels in 1866. This attracted a lot of attention because it was so unusual – *The Times* introduced its first report by saying the line had been "blocked by a disaster the magnitude as well as the character of which is entirely without precedent". Three goods trains collided in the tunnel, with the result that the tunnel itself was converted into "one huge furnace and its air shafts into a species of burning crater".[6]

On the night of 9th June 1866, an empty goods train left King's Cross Goods and headed down the line for Peterborough. In the northern Welwyn tunnel, a boiler tube burst and dampened down the locomotive's fire so that it could not proceed with the whole train. The driver sent his fireman back to speak to the guard, who was illicitly sharing his brake van with a former GNR friend who now worked for the Metropolitan Railway. The driver wanted the guard to walk back to Welwyn station but the guard, Joseph Wray, suggested they set back down the gentle gradient to Welwyn instead. He conveyed this brusque message by leaning out of the window of his van. The train driver, Liser, quite properly refused to do this and decided instead to uncouple his engine and work it forwards light to Stevenage. Wray should have left his van to run back and warn following trains, but presumably was having a good time with his companion – John Rawlins – and did not bother.

The train should also have been protected by the signalling system; the cabins at Welwyn and Knebworth[7] were connected by telegraph and Welwyn was not supposed to let a train into the tunnels unless Knebworth had telegraphed to say the previous one had come out. After the event, the two signalmen disagreed about the telegraph messages, but the upshot was that a following Midland Railway goods steamed into the tunnels after the Welwyn signals cleared to let it pass. The Midland goods hit the back of the stationary GNR train since the tunnel was full of smoke and no lamps could be seen; the Midland engine derailed. Wray was killed and Rawlings died a couple of days later. Driver Liser on the footplate of the first engine, which had uncoupled ready to move forwards, received "a bit of a bump" from his trucks but then an up 'Scotch' meat train passed him as well – heading into the wreckage.

The train, loaded with fresh meat for Smithfield, collided with the wreckage and also derailed. The two collisions were about three minutes apart. Amazingly, the enginemen from all three trains survived without serious injury, although the driver of one had to dig himself out of the coal which had piled forwards over the footplate. The guard of the up meat train was found injured on the track. About four hours later the wreckage caught fire, probably after naptha from men's lamps ignited wood shavings used to pack furniture in the Midland's load although another account assumed reasonably enough it was coals from the locomotives.[8] This then ignited casks of oil and about 30 trucks were engulfed.

The footplatemen survived unscathed and went looking for their guard colleagues. Wray was found "in the midst of the ruins of his brake, frightfully crushed and quite dead, and with him another man, a fireman in the employ of the Metropolitan Railway, whom it appears he was conveying surreptitiously down the line…"

A large number of men gathered at Knebworth to help retrieve the trains but conditions became so bad they could only haul out part of the meat train. By the time another 200 men arrived from the London end, 36 wagons[9] were on fire; heat, smoke and repeated explosions made entering the tunnel impossible. From the ventilating shaft some 60ft above the railway, smoke and flames billowed forth "with sounds resembling a mighty cataract or river, [which indicated] the character of the conflagration that was raging underneath".[10] With no access to water, the railway authorities could do little except allow the fire to burn itself out although this must have put the structure of the tunnel at considerable risk. Access was possible by about 6.00pm, some help having been received when the Marquis of Salisbury lent his fire engine from Hatfield House.

As hundreds of navvies worked through the night to clear the wreckage, trains were diverted via the Hertford branch from Welwyn Junction and from there by Eastern Counties to Cambridge and back to Royston.[11] The inquest on Wray and Rawlings was held at the Cowper Arms, adjacent to Welwyn station.

Wray had clearly neglected to do his duty and paid for this with his life. For the Board of Trade, Captain Rich clearly identified Wray's neglect of his duty as the primary cause of the disaster but was unable to sort which of the two signalmen was in error. Radford, at Welwyn, insisted that he had received a telegraph message saying the 'empties' were clear of the tunnel. At Knebworth, John Harding insisted that he had improperly been sent two trains without sending a 'train out' message back. As the telegraph messages for 'Out' and 'No' were similar, Rich thought an error by the Welwyn signalman most likely. The coroner's jury agreed on 'accidental death' but "declined to express an opinion as to the signalmen".[12] In some ways this disaster was very similar to the one in Clayton Tunnel on the Brighton line, which involved passenger trains with consequent heavier loss of life. It also achieved a small mark of recognition in classic literature when, in *Howard's End*, E. M. Forster had a character pass through "the North Welwyn Tunnel, of tragic fame".[13] There was another accident in the tunnel on 6th February 1920, when a goods train became divided and was run into by a fish train, with one guard slightly injured.

The collision at Manors in 1926 had several unusual features. At about 10.50pm on 7th August, the 9.47pm Newcastle–Monkseaton–Newcastle electric train collided at about 35mph with a goods train which was crossing over in front of it just west of Manors station which is on the northern edge of Newcastle. The train was one of the intensive third-rail electrics serving the city's suburbs at that time and had run fast to Monkseaton and then was supposed to call at all stations back to Newcastle. It managed to stop at all stations as far as Heaton, then rushed through Manors station where it should have stopped before hitting the goods which had been cleared to cross in front of it.

There were about 150 passengers on the train when it ran straight into a loaded grain wagon, with the front motor carriage jamming up against the wall under Manors Junction signal box. The steps of the signal box were torn away and some of the debris fell 60ft into the street below. Fortunately there were only three passengers in the front carriage and only sixteen in total were injured, the frames of the stock standing up well to the violent collision.

As rescuers arrived on the scene, their first concern was for the driver or 'motorman', whose chances of survival appeared slim. However, railway staff led by Inspector Gill could find no sign of a body. In the darkness they searched for a considerable time before concluding that he was not there. The guard recalled seeing the motorman, William Skinner, standing beside the train at Heaton station – but where had he gone and how had a train continued without him? A clue was found by Inspector Murray as he searched the cab – the deadman's handle was tied down by two handkerchiefs triple-knotted together; Murray removed them as evidence, one red and one white.

A search back up the line eventually revealed Skinner's body under Heaton Park Road bridge, which was supported by iron columns with only inches clearance from the trains; this was at 3.00am, more than four hours after the accident. The body was on its back with one arm extended across the live rail. Skinner had clearly been killed at this point by his head hitting the bridge columns and he must have been leaning out of the van door a considerable way to have fallen out altogether. The train continued without him – despite being fitted with a deadman's handle which should have put on the brakes if there was no pressure on it. But it did not because, as Major Hall reported, "this control had been deliberately rendered inoperative". Although no-one could explain why, Skinner must have left his position, gone into the guard's compartment, opened the door and leant out; in order to do this, he had had to fix the controls so that the train continued running without his presence.

The dead man's handle required relatively light pressure of 1lb 12oz to hold it in a position short of the 'tripping point'. Fixed in this manner, the train had been able to accelerate down the 1 in 200 gradient from Heaton to Manors, rushed through a station at which it was meant to stop and only then started to slow as the gradient rose – a distance of more than a mile without a driver. It had passed the Tynemouth line home signal (there were four tracks at this point) which had been set to protect the goods. The guard reported that he had then tried to put on the brake, but had been thrown to the floor in the collision before he could do this.

Was William Skinner a bad driver? He had been trained for the electric trains in 1922 but drove them only rarely. The guard

An artist's view of the scene in Welwyn Tunnel after the multiple collision and fire. Although it ably conveys the chaos and destruction, the artist's grasp on scale is somewhat wayward – the men appear to be midgets in comparison with the width of the track and the bore of the tunnel. (Author)

thought he had a tendency to "run very fast into the stations". Nonetheless, Major Hall concluded that Skinner had been guilty of "a most serious offence" which might have led to many deaths had the train been busier. Whether this should be classified as a fatal collision is another matter, of course, because the only death was the driver and he was not with the train at the time of its disaster.

A whole succession of mistakes contributed to an accident at Darlington on 11th December 1968 which could easily have been very serious. Air-braked MkIIa coaching stock had been introduced in September that year, depending on the connection of a two-pipe system throughout the train. This was poorly designed, so that it was necessary to cross the two pipes over in connecting the locomotive to the first carriage whereas on Freightliner trains the two pipes were connected in parallel. One pipe was the brake pipe and the other the main reservoir pipe; to avoid getting them wrong, the 'heads' were slightly different in design (though not different enough) and painted red and yellow.

The coaching stock for the 11.00am Newcastle to King's Cross only arrived in the station at 10.47am and this led to some shoddy practice in the haste to change the locomotive and put 'Deltic' No.D9017 on the front. Inspector Gordon was busy on another platform and did not check that a brake test had been carried out; carriage and wagon examiner Scott insisted that he supervised the coupling-up but no-one else saw him, Driver Crow failed to carry out a brake test – and Guard Thorn did not even realise one was necessary as he did not know the locomotive had been changed!

The man who coupled up was the secondman, E. Gray, who was more familiar with Freightliner working than air-braked modern coaching stock. He undoubtedly coupled up in the way he was used to, with the two pipes in parallel. His mistake was made easier because the locomotive did not have red and yellow heads, but two painted white – very poorly.

Driver Crow then allowed Gray to drive the 'Deltic' even though he was not passed to do so. Although they managed to stop safely at Durham, the problems told against them as they approached the signals into the No.1 platform at Darlington. The locomotive's brakes – and the guard's efforts with his hand brake – were too little and they ran straight through the platform before derailing at about 20mph on the catch points beyond. The inquiry identified a whole series of errors which contributed to this, but Crow took the brunt of the blame. However, the pipes were poorly designed – at the inquiry it was demonstrated that "it was easier to couple up the hosepipes incorrectly than correctly, despite the intention that it would not

77

"squeezed into derailment". Travelling at near 100mph, the rear bogie of the third carriage and the first bogie of the fourth came off the rails to the left-hand side. The effect was that the rear bogie of the fourth carriage then took the fork at the points towards the down slow line while the front of the train continued on the fast line.

The rear carriage struck parts of the eastern end of the overbridge across Darke's Lane at the south end of the station and became detached from the rest of the train. Travelling almost sideways, it seems to have become airborne as it passed over the bridge and it went up the ramps at the end of the island platforms and jammed under both canopies blocking the two fast

be possible to do so". After the accident, the Chief Engineer agreed to change the heads so that they were "completely incompatible"; fortunately it had not needed someone to die to achieve this safety improvement, but the risk should have been obvious.

Potters Bar

On 10th May 2002 the four-car 12.45 King's Cross to King's Lynn, electric multiple unit No.365 526, was approaching Potter's Bar station when it derailed on facing points.[14] This was one of three serious disasters in succession that created the impression of the East Coast as Britain's most afflicted railway. Getting unusual insight was the line's Chief Signalling Inspector, Roger Badger, who was travelling in the cab as part of a familiarisation exercise and felt a series of sharp jolts as the train approached Potters Bar at near its maximum speed.

Both driver and inspector first thought the jolts were a mechanical problem but then all the lights went out, quickly followed by a full automatic brake application. The signalling inspector, with his eyes focussed on the signals, also noticed that signal K539 ahead of them flickered from green to red and then back to green. "I have lost everything… we are off the rails" Driver Gordon Gibson shouted to his senior colleague.

In fact as the third and fourth carriage had passed over the crossover at the south end of the station, the right-hand switch rail had begun to close so that a bogie on each carriage was

lines. For passenger Wing Commander Rose, it was "like being in a tumble drier". Rose reported that "I floated up out of my seat. I blindly reached out and managed to get hold of the luggage rack." The front three coaches continued until they stopped north of the station.

Six passengers on the train were killed and a woman pedestrian, walking along the road beneath, died after being struck by debris. Acting correctly, the Chief Signalling Inspector got out of the train and placed detonators on the up lines. Indeed there was a considerable risk to up trains and a driver approaching on the up slow line saw "the rear carriage tumbling towards me across the island platforms. It was coming at me very fast. My immediate thought was that it was going to hit me. I did the emergency brake stop."

An interim report was produced within days of the accident which noted that nuts on the points were out of place; witnesses from the works contractor Jarvis gave evidence that two detached nuts at the crossover had been replaced nine days before the crash. On 20th May they produced photographs to argue that the points had been damaged deliberately and a few weeks later blamed Railtrack for sending Jarvis's staff to inspect the wrong points after complaints of rough riding.

The technical investigation concluded that parts of the points moved as the train passed over, causing the derailment. The right-hand switch rail closed against its stock rail as the third carriage passed over. The previous train, one for Peterborough, had used this crossover, No.2182, to cross from down fast to down slow without a problem.

So the immediate cause was quite simple, but why had the rail moved at all? This was a tale of three stretcher bars which together held the individual rails of the set of points rigid and exactly apart – they were the mechanisms which moved the points and took the pressures to hold the switches in place with the correct gaps. The lock stretcher bar was the initial cause of this because it had fractured at its right-hand end when not properly restrained by the front and rear adjustable stretcher bars. Excess stress fatigue built up, causing the bar to crack, because it was not designed to take the stress without support from the front and rear bars. These were both lacking some of the nuts that held them properly in place and there were probably also problems with the point machine.

So what had happened to the nuts? Here the final report noted that the points design had been in use since the 1980s but that the mechanics of the system used to secure the nuts was not properly understood; a story was unearthed of nuts being secured in place at Wood Green by taking a chisel to the threads. The contractor's track gangs had not been trained in the process of installing stretcher bar assemblies. Staff did not know about locking and positioning stretcher bar nuts.

To add to the reports of incompetence, it was revealed that several complaints had been made about the rough ride across the points. A check had been arranged – but the wrong track had been looked at.

The men on the track worked for Jarvis Facilities Ltd. but standards and supervision were the responsibility of Railtrack as the infrastructure controller and the latter was recommended to devise and introduce a specification.

The inquiry was not able to report with certainty how the nuts came to be missing. They thought that the nuts on the front bar of the points came loose so that it could no longer resist the tendency for the switch rails to move apart and this put pressure on the lock stretcher bar which was worsened by a similar sequence at the back. Jarvis very quickly floated the possibility of malicious action in removing the nuts and this attracted much press comment. The report, though, concluded that "the possibility of a malicious act cannot be ruled out, although the panel considers this to be highly unlikely". In an exposed position close to station platforms, only a railwayman might have been able to remove the nuts without attracting suspicion.

The rear stretcher bar had received some attention on 1st May 2002 and it was still possible that there had been interference with the threads and nuts – but "extremely unlikely". In March 2004 Jarvis and Railtrack accepted liability in advance of the final report in February 2005.

In the media fallout that followed, there were demands that the track contractor, Jarvis Rail Ltd., and Railtrack PLC should be prosecuted for gross negligence amounting to manslaughter. However, in October 2005 the Crown Prosecution Service (CPS) announced that there was no realistic prospect of a conviction on this charge and that it would not be bringing a case. In March 2010 Jarvis Rail went into administration. The following July, the inquest jury returned a verdict of accidental death on each of the cases – over eight years after the deaths. In October 2010 the CPS reiterated that it had no intention of bringing a prosecution.

The coroner's inquest did not take place until summer 2010, when it lasted seven weeks. The jury concluded the points had been unsafe and had not been maintained properly. The Coroner wanted an apology for it taking eight years to get the inquest finished. Stories about malicious damage were discounted and a trade union official said that Jarvis executives should "hang their heads in shame" for claiming it.

The conclusion of the inquest cleared the way for the Office of the Rail Regulator to start proceedings under the Health & Safety at Work Act of 1974. These proceedings can result in a fine of up to £20,000 or can be referred to a higher court for a heavier fine and the case was sent to St. Albans Crown Court. In November 2010 Louise Christian, a solicitor representing some of the families, commented that "the prosecution is being taken against a company which is in administration and another not-for-profit company which is owned by the Government. It can only result in a fine, so the extent to which it can produce accountability may be limited".[15]

When the case started it was effectively a trial of two dead companies and "the Judge and spectators all recognised the strangeness of the proceeding".[16] On 13th May 2011 Network Rail, the successor to Railtrack, was fined £3 million with £150,000 costs for failings with regard to the shallow-depth adjustable stretcher bars on the Potters Bar points. With Jarvis in administration, charges against them had been dropped. One newspaper commented that "Railtrack was misconceived in structure and badly run in practice... was managed by people whose egos exceeded their talents".[17] There were many criticisms of the post-crash process, from the three years taken to publish a final report to the nine years spent deciding on legal issues – by which time both the two main organisations involved had ceased to exist.

Crossings

Train passengers put their safety in the hands of drivers, signalmen and track workers, but road users trusted to the crossing keepers who were once such a common feature of the railway scene. For most of the time, the crossing keepers did their jobs well but the sheer frequency with which road and rail crossed each other made disaster perhaps inevitable.

The crossings at Riccall, on the A19 road between Selby and York, became a famous cause of complaint as the busy road was often blocked by the demands of a main line railway. The northern crossing, Riccall Gates, was half a mile north of Riccall station and by 1952 had become one of the most demanding crossing posts in the North Eastern Region of British Railways. The road crossed the railway at an angle of about 60 degrees but railway visibility was generally good – a down train could be seen 800 yards away but this was reduced to 250 yards if a train was on the up line.

Gatekeeper George Ogley had a demanding job, requiring constant communication with Riccall North and South signal boxes; he had to the clear his own signals and attend to the opening and shutting of the gates – often against a backdrop of impatient motorists. At 7.53pm on 16th July 1952 Ogley closed the gates for an up goods train having been advised by Riccall North box and at the same time South box offered a down express to the North which was accepted. Ogley cleared all his signals – up and down – and the goods passed at 7.58pm. He paused in his discussion of cricket scores with a friend and was distracted by a waiting car that started hooting as soon as the goods had passed and whilst he was restoring the up signals to danger. Ogley then made a series of errors – firstly putting his down signals back as well and then opening the gates for the car – the approaching express being hidden by the diminishing bulk of the goods.

John Newby's car, an Austin A70, started out over the crossing, at which point Ogley realised his error as the 'Tees-Tyne Pullman', hauled by an A4 Pacific, swept into view at 60mph or more. By frantic gestures, Ogley tried to encourage Newby to cross faster but he seems to have become confused and, instead, stopped. Four seconds later the car was hit by the express and carried half a mile along the line. Both people in the car – Newby (61) and Doris Newby (36) his wife – were killed.

Ogley had worked at the crossing for sixteen years and made a momentary error, which he tried to rectify. He possibly had 'family worries' to distract him, but had also been talking to a friend. Colonel Walker concluded that the accident was caused by "simple human error" but the car's progress was never fully explained. One witness said that "it moved steadily on to the line and seemed to stop there". Ogley was convicted of manslaughter at York Assizes and sentenced to nine months in prison.

FOOTNOTES

1   *Northampton Mercury*, 22 July 1865, accessed by Ray Townsin
2   *Railway Accidents*, return to the House of Commons,
3   *The Times*, 3 January 1852
4   Letter from YNB to BoT, 5 March 1852.
5   Letter from Galton to Board of Trade, 15 January 1855.
6   *The Times*, 11 June 1866
7   There was no Woolmer Green box at this time.
8   *Annual Register*, Vol.108, p.66
9   Rich reported 30 were damaged by fire, and also a GNR engine.
10   *Annual Register*, p.67
11   There was no loop via Hertford at this date.
12   *Annual Register*, p.68
13   *Howard's End* was published in 1910, so the fame of the tunnel crash must have been quite enduring.
14   As with Hatfield in 2000, a succession of reports was issued. This account is largely based on the final report of the Rail Safety and Standards Board of 12 February 2005.
15   *Daily Telegraph*, 11 November 2010
16   *Financial Times*, 18 May 2011
17   *Ibid.*

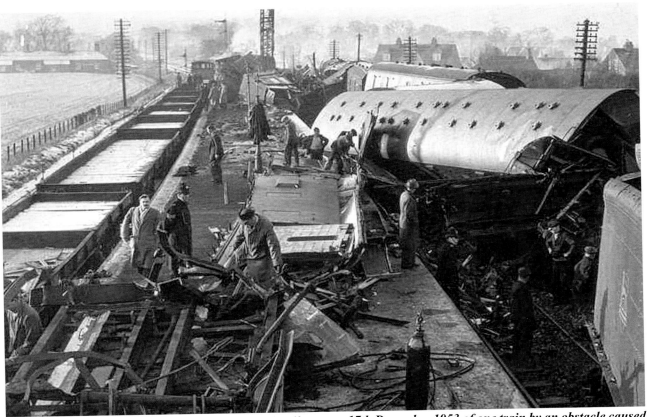

The recovery operation at Longniddry, after the derailment on 17th December 1953 of one train by an obstacle caused by another – see next chapter.

(Midlothian Museum)

9

EXTERNAL CAUSES

Terrorism – Loose objects – Fire – Vehicles on the line

On rare occasions, railway accidents are caused by factors which are completely external to the railway itself. Such disasters can include deliberate acts of vandalism by the public, including terrorism, and also disasters caused by careless use of level crossings. In recent years the most famous example has been the disaster at Great Heck, caused by a motorist and reputed to have resulted in one of the largest car insurance claims of all time. However, there can have been few incidents as curious as the injuries to a fireman on an express train near Cramlington in 1848 who, in the night, was suddenly attacked by a group of owls who pecked his face and knocked a tooth out.[1]

Terrorism and other malicious acts

The East Coast Main Line escaped any involvement in the sporadic Irish-American terrorist plots of the Victorian era, which most affected the underground lines in London and the termini of the southern companies. That worse was to come in the twentieth century was presaged in the use of two bombs against the unlikely target of the coal bays at King's Cross goods depot in early 1939. These caused little damage, but the police then picked up brown paper parcels containing hot water bottles and rubber pipes which they put in their cars – to rather more damaging effect.

However, on 26th July 1939 a sulphuric acid bomb exploded in the Left Luggage office at King's Cross, killing Dr. Donald Campbell, from Edinburgh, and injuring fifteen people. Campbell was a lecturer in Latin from Edinburgh University. There was a similar explosion at Victoria soon afterwards. The explosion took place under the 'receiving counter,' where smoke had been seen escaping from a suitcase just before the blast, but detection work was hampered by the apparent loss of the record books. These were two amongst a series of explosions and in the next few days there was a number of arrests in Brunswick Square and chaotic scenes at Euston as Irish people tried to get home. IRA agents in New York told the press there that their policy was to avoid deaths and that Campbell's had been a 'regrettable' accident.

Hoaxes became a more serious problem as well in later years. When a ganger found a large tin with protruding wires buried in the ballast at Tempsford in August 1957 he thought he had averted one of the worst possible disasters for the railway. He flagged down an approaching engine, the police were called and all trains diverted. But the 'bomb' contained only a clock mechanism.

Railways were also subject to attack in both the First and Second World Wars. On 21st November 1941 Goswick station was bombed and machine-gunned as a local passenger train was standing there; six people were slightly injured and the station was kept closed until 1946. There was also a famous attack on York.

One of the most famous 'political' incidents, which narrowly avoided being a disaster, was the derailment of the 'Flying Scotsman' during the 1926 General Strike. In Northumberland the main line ran through an area steeped in mining history where feelings were running very high and there was some annoyance around the running of trains with volunteer crews. On 10th May an attempt was made to stop trains by removing a rail and the victim was the 'Flying Scotsman' (although it was doing little 'flying') – the fireman on the day was a student volunteer from Edinburgh University. However, some sources claim that the main intention was to disrupt 'blackleg'

The wrecked cloakroom at King's Cross after the bomb explosion.

The wrecked carriages of the 'Flying Scotsman' near Cramlington in 1926. In the famous incident during the General Strike, Merry Hampton *turned on its side following a relatively slow speed derailment.*

(National Railway Museum)

coal traffic.[2] A group of miners had taken a rail out of the down track and had started to work on the other rail when the train appeared. Engine No.2565 *Merry Hampton* and four carriages were derailed close to milepost 9. However, injuries among the 270 passengers were almost non-existent as trouble had been expected and the speed was very low, though the engine turned on its side. The fireman had a burn to his leg and one passenger had a leg trapped by wreckage.[3]

Historians have given symbolic significance to the incident, calling it "a symbol of the dangerous passions the strike had aroused".[4] The incident caused some consternation and led to Parliamentary questions. Details were scant as the press was disrupted by the strike and the Home Secretary was asked if he thought there had been 'foul play'. William Joynson-Hicks replied rather obscurely "I am like a parrot. I may think a good deal and not say much." Colonel Pringle conducted a standard accident investigation and a key witness was Mr. Robert Martin, a civil engineer who had been patrolling the line in advance of the train between Benton Quarry and Plessey. Martin had six other volunteers helping protect the track. He reported that people from "Dudley Council Houses" had attacked him near Annitsford station with stones and clods. When he reached an old signal box between Dam Dykes Crossing and Cramlington, which was in use as a PW store, he was attacked again. He also noted attempts had been made to steal equipment.

Fearing an attempt to attack the train, Martin had flagged it down from 40mph at Cramlington station and warned the driver before getting into a carriage. They then crept forward at 20mph. After the derailment, some of the passengers and staff chased men across the fields but caught no-one. There have been allegations of bad feeling between the middle class volunteer staff and passengers, and the mining families; in one version, miners' wives who rushed to help any injured passengers were told instead to "wash their dirty selves and their dirty homes".

Pringle had little trouble concluding that derailment was caused by the removal of fishplates and the toppling of a rail out of its chairs. It became a criminal case; ten men were rounded

up in midnight raids on 5th June but two were soon discharged, with eight men found guilty and sentenced to between four and eight years in prison. The eight – seven miners and one labourer, all in their twenties – were charged with having "maliciously displaced a rail with intent to overthrow the train and endanger the safety of persons travelling on the railway". Much was made of the fact that, had one person died, they would have been tried for murder. One of the main witnesses was a miner, Lyle Waugh, who was related to a policeman, although the defence alleged he had been a ringleader of the group. The harshest sentences went to Arthur Wilson who was found to have led the act of removal of the rail, Robert Harbottle who entered the signal box and Thomas Roberts who damaged the track. "The accused received the sentences apparently unmoved, but some of their relatives cried out in court and afterwards gathered in a weeping group outside." Although this was a minor disaster in the annals of the East Coast Main Line, it continues to be seen as having enduring and symbolic fame.

During the General Strike there was also a serious fatal accident on 10th May 1926 at St. Margaret's, just outside Edinburgh, when a Berwick to Edinburgh passenger train ran into the rear of a goods train. It could be argued that this accident was the result of malicious action albeit indirectly, but equally arguably it could be seen as the result of amateurish operation of trains by non-professionals. During the Strike there had been considerable difficulty in operating trains from Edinburgh to Berwick; Stemp, the LNER's Area Superintendent, complained that anyone who tried to operate a signal box had been subject to intimidation. This meant that drivers never knew which boxes were open or closed. The signal box at St. Margaret's suffered badly as it was overlooked from the main road nearby and the signalman there had to take shelter in the nearby Railway Works between trains, creeping out to alter the points and then scuttling back again whilst standard regulation signalling had to be abandoned. Only after police and then soldiers were stationed at the Works did things improve.

The collision took place between a passenger train and some trucks in a short tunnel. There was no suggestion that this was caused directly by malevolent action, but there was criticism in Parliament of railway workers who refused to help in the rescue by manning the breakdown crane. As it was, some of the wreckage was in the tunnel and a few of the rescue workers were overcome by fumes. Three people died. Colonel Pringle investigated and found errors by the volunteer signalman and also that the driver exceeded safe speeds when hand signals were being used.[5]

Very few accidents on the East Coast Main Line have been caused by purposeless human action deliberately intended to cause destruction although all railways suffer from occasional acts of vandalism. In the case of the fatal derailment of an overnight express at Connington[6] South on 5th March 1967, much consideration was given at the time as to whether harm had been caused deliberately and there was also speculation as to the mental state of the perpetrator. All the more shocking was the fact that this key individual was the signalman at Connington and the accusation was that he had deliberately moved the points as the train was passing.

That March night the 22.30 King's Cross to Edinburgh was hauled by 'Deltic' locomotive No.D9004 and included three Post Office vehicles and a sleeping car. The rear portion of the train derailed on a facing connection to the down goods line at Connington; the rear carriages derailed at 75mph, the train split and the last four carriages ended up on their sides. Five passengers were killed.

The Connington South signalman was Alan Frost, 20, who was officially believed at the time to be of good character although locally some considered him eccentric in some ways. However, he gave some confused evidence to the investigating officers and his actions had been puzzling; he had sent a 'train out of section' bell signal back to Abbots Ripton before the train had reached the correct point and also a message to Connington North to say the 22.30 was "coming to a stop" when he already knew it was derailed.

Frost denied having put his down home signal back to danger too soon but the damage to the interlocked points suggested that this must have been the case. The facing points were found locked and bolted after the accident but much later, after rumours began circulating about Frost's behaviour, the investigation came round to the possibility that the facing points had been unlocked and reversed as the train passed over them. To do this, lever 27 would have had to be unlocked. The mechanical interlocking system meant that the crucial lever 14 could only have been moved if three other levers operating points ahead of it were also moved; as a result, there was much studying of the speed with which various movements could have been accomplished. The whole interlocking system was designed to make accidents impossible and tests showed that for it to happen by mistake the sequence of moves would have had to be done in about two seconds – so it was not likely to have been an error. This could only be "the result of a premeditated series of actions which involved tampering with the electric lock on the facing point lever".

What was being suggested could only have been done deliberately by a determined individual with split-second timing. Frost would have had to stand with the home signal lever catch disengaged – using one hand – and his other holding the catch on another lever to instantly unlock it and then pull the points. He would have had to time the move to perfection before the front wheels of the locomotive triggered the down main track circuit, which would have locked lever 19.

The accident report concluded that "the derailment was directly caused by the actions of the signalman on duty in Connington South signal box… who unlocked and opened the facing points whilst the train was passing over them". Facing a possible manslaughter trial, Frost told a policeman that he had unlocked the points accidentally while swinging on the levers and had then panicked and grabbed the points lever by mistake. Frost had by this time left railway employment and a warrant for his arrest was issued at Norman Cross, a roadside hamlet south of Peterborough, in August 1967.

Although Frost had a sound official reputation in his short railway career, according to press reports of it at least, after the investigation it emerged that he had been discharged from the Royal Marines for "hysteria and immature personality" – which was not known when he was taken on as a signalman. Nonetheless, he managed to get another post as a military bandsman after the accident. He was charged with manslaughter as well as unlawfully operating signals so as to endanger passengers and went through an eleven-day trial at Nottingham in November 1967. The judge instructed the jury to acquit him on the manslaughter charge and Frost pleaded guilty on the other, for which he was given two years.

Was the Connington South accident a deliberate act or the result of foolishness? It has been much debated, but the inquiry pointed distinctly to the unlikeliness of the necessary sequence of events having been completed with no deliberate intent.

Loose Objects

Very early in the morning of 30th September 1862 a coal train of 30 wagons from Peterborough was steadily wending its way towards London when the engine struck an object on the line as it approached Offord station. The locomotive derailed, running up against – and demolishing – some 20 yards of the station's wooden platform, before turning over as it ran off the side of the line.

The guard, who had been shaking his greatcoat dry now that the rain had stopped, ran out to put out the detonators and then, with the station's night porter, chased along the lines looking for the driver and fireman. They found them, some fifteen yards from the engine, buried under trucks with terrible crush injuries. The driver, John Johnson, was quite dead, but they heard the cries of the fireman, Henry Lee, who was wailing and moaning. Although Lee said he did not wish to be moved, they took him to the station porters' room where he died within an hour. The guard was immediately able to locate three pieces of broken metal as the cause of the derailment and recalled having passed a northbound goods train which was carrying several wagons of machinery.

The safe loading of goods wagons was vital to keeping the railway free from accidents so even the humble goods loader at a wayside station had a serious responsibility. Some small stations had sizeable goods traffic, the significant example here being St. Neots where George Bower ran a foundry manufacturing equipment for gas works and agricultural machinery.[7] During 29th September 1862 Bower's firm had loaded four threshing engines for export to Russia via Hull and they had been picked up by the local goods to Peterborough.

The iron pieces found at Offord were from a large iron flywheel and this was traced to one of Bower's threshing machines. Bower quickly accepted at least some of the responsibility, though he was mystified as to the cause of the wheel coming loose – given that another of his engines lost its flywheel near Corby Glen, he could hardly have been otherwise. Of the four engines loaded, the largest (No.1) had had its flywheel and chimney loaded separately; of the three others, one had reached Hull with its flywheel in place (No.4), one had lost its flywheel at Corby (No.3) and the other (No.2) had caused the Offord accident.

The inquest paid great attention to Bower's employees who had assembled the engines and loaded them, noting that the flywheel of each was keyed to its shaft by a single key. One of them, John Bennett, assured the inquest that "Every nut and everything that could get loose I tried and found all secure." Other evidence showed that the engines were all 'dropped' two or three inches onto their trucks – James Ayres, who worked at the foundry, commented that "I heard they dropped them down in the truck." Bower assured the inquest that "I do not wish to implicate the Great Northern in this matter" but then went on to comment on the poor loading facilities at St. Neots.[8] He told the coroner's jury that he would be giving £10 to the relief fund – both dead men had been married, one with two children. The efforts of the vicar of Buckden resulted in another £8 15s being collected.

Given the prevalence of open goods wagons, it is surprising that accidents of this type occurred so rarely and this was a testament to the skills and care of the men who loaded wagons in the many hundreds of sidings across the country. However, the spectacular derailment at Longniddry Junction near Edinburgh on 17th December 1953 was caused by a series of errors in a goods siding over a hundred miles from the scene of the eventual disaster.

An up extra parcels train, the 00.41 Edinburgh to King's Cross, was approaching Longniddry Junction and its station at about 60mph on a dark winter night hauled by A2 Pacific No.60530 *Sayajirao*. Its driver and fireman had no warning as it was suddenly derailed, with the engine being thrown clear across the station's 15ft-wide up platform and down an embankment. The engine rotated through 110° before coming to rest and its fireman, R. Mackenzie, was killed. The tender was left 40 yards away and most of the 28 parcels vans were wrecked. The derailed vehicles largely destroyed 123 yards of the up platform and 23 yards of the down one. The cause of this was a set of narrow gauge railway points which had fallen from a down goods train.

The set of points came from the 9.45pm goods from Heaton. This train had initially been in the care of Guard Brownlee who had checked his train before leaving; he had noted the truck that contained several sets of the points and that the load overhung the rear of the wagon by about a foot. The points were roped down but did not fit conveniently within the shape of a rectangular wagon and were "somewhat to one side".

At Tweedmouth Guard Hartley took charge of the train and he tested the rope. Passing Aberlady Junction, three miles after Drem, Hartley looked forward from his van and saw sparks flying. The points were in the truck nearest to his van and he could see that the load had shifted so that at least one set of points was hanging over the 'near side' of the wagon by about one and a half feet. Hartley tried to attract the attention of his driver by putting on his van brake and releasing it repeatedly, but this had no effect. Approaching Longniddry signal box, he got hold of his red tail lamp and waved it to attract the signalman's attention. This plan actually worked in that the Longniddry signalman sent the 'stop and examine' bell signal in advance which did indeed happen – but too late.

The overhanging set of points struck a water column on the down platform of the station and bounced off, the points landing foul of the up line. Within seconds they were hit by the speeding parcels train, with fatal results. Only afterwards did the goods train stop.

The inquiry focussed on the wagon load and how it had been secured. It had originated from Robert Hudson Ltd. at Gildersome West on 14th December, where eight sets of prefabricated 2ft gauge points were loaded with the 'double' end in the well of the wagon and the single end resting on its end. The securing of the load was done by Porter Kellett, who had only been with the railway a few months, and supervised by Foreman Wood. One of the key questions in this story was about railway staff failing to get up onto the load to check the ropes properly; in this case Wood said Kellett got onto the wagon, but Kellett denied this.

Kellett only used one rope to secure the load and this rope was actually an old rope and a new one joined together. Some experts thought an additional centre rope should have been used, but the District Inspector's opinion was that this was not necessary. The wagon was checked once more at Heaton, but again no-one climbed up to check the rope. However, the opinion of the Loads Inspector from Glasgow was that the pieces of track should have been tied together first and then to the wagon – which would have prevented one from falling off.

Pieces of the set of points were found amidst the parcels train wreckage and the rope which had supposedly secured the load was picked up in five pieces – three pieces of new rope and two of old. The old rope was "dry, limp, weathered and abraded" so it was simple to conclude that it had broken through chafing. The Loading Manual rules for using two ropes had been disobeyed though Colonel McMullen noted "I do not blame Porter Kellett for this." Putting packing round the points would also have prevented the chafing.

Fire

Throughout the Victorian and Edwardian eras, until electric lighting began to replace gas, the fear of fire in the aftermath of an accident was considerable – and added to the terror of incidents such as Grantham in 1906. Fire did break out and add to the destruction in goods train accidents, such as at Welwyn in 1866, often involving fires started from the locomotive coals. However, accidents in which fire was the cause were very rare and in most cases the fire was put out before any lives were lost.

In the earliest days of the Great Northern, the then practice of stowing luggage on the roof of a passenger carriage was a clear fire risk since sparks and hot ash could land there. Captain Tyler was twice forced to condemn this practice, once after a fire on a train near Newark on 27th February 1867.[9]

The fire was burning so fiercely that platelayers could see it as the train approached them and so they were able to signal to the driver to stop. However, none of the guards, footplate crew or passengers was at all aware that the luggage and the roof of one of the carriages was ablaze.

Tyler made the connection between this incident and another on the GNR on 2nd September 1868.[10] On this occasion the driver of the down 'Scotch Express' happened to look back as his train passed through the cutting north of Huntingdon and "he then observed that the cutting appeared to be illuminated". He realised that there was a fire on the roof of the fourth or fifth carriage, so brought the train to a stop and ran back. With help arriving, he pulled off the sheet which covered the luggage to find that the fire had burnt through it and taken hold of a hamper of stuffed animals. Meanwhile, the passengers in the carriage had got into a panic, with "screaming and crying", some climbing out of the windows or using their own keys to open the doors – which were still routinely locked. The guards arrived, shouting at passengers who had got down to the up line.

Tyler noted that twelve passengers had been in the burning carriage and that none of the guards had noticed the fire. He advised the stowing of luggage on roofs should cease.

A shocking fire incident caused the deaths of six boys of Ampleforth College on 26th June 1941. A large group of boys was travelling with one of their masters, the Reverend D. Pozzi, in a separate portion of three carriages attached to the rear of the 12.45pm King's Cross to Newcastle – itself running in two portions. The Ampleforth carriages were to be detached at York for the onward trip to Gilling station and the corridor connection between its front coach and the rest of the train was locked as regulations were said to have required at the time.[11]

The boys were aged 14 to 18 and those in the second carriage (the third was a brake) had no direct adult supervision. By the time the train was north of Grantham, they were fairly bored. Colonel Trench's report commented that "there is no evidence of any unduly rowdy behaviour" but immediately continued to say "some of them were, however, flicking matches at one another". One match went down the side of the upholstery and the cushion caught fire. With some of the windows open and setting up a strong draught, the fire soon took hold and spread along the backs of the seats. Attempts by the boys to put the fire out by carrying water from the lavatory in mugs and hats were hopeless and eventually one of them went to get the master.

Pozzi found the fire well established and told someone to pull the communication cord. The cord acted on each coach separately, so the driver noticed a small drop in the vacuum pressure. He and the fireman looked out, but could see nothing. Pozzi went forwards to the front coach of their section and pulled the cord there; this produced another drop in vacuum pressure and the driver did an emergency stop near to Westborough signal box.

This in turn alerted the guard, who looked out to see bags being thrown out – and indeed boys jumping out – before the train had even stopped. By this stage flames were already appearing above the carriage roof, so he rushed back to help the boys escape from the choking smoke. The guard, Dear, climbed into the carriage and shouted to see if anyone was in there, then tried to uncouple it from the one in front. This

became too dangerous, so instead he uncoupled beyond the first Ampleforth coach. All three carriages were destroyed.

An inquest was opened in the waiting room at Hougham station but then transferred to Grantham, reaching a verdict of 'accidental death by burning'. Jerry Stewart, age 14, admitted to having flicked lighted matches. The Coroner concluded that there had been "a good many" of the boys smoking and using matches, but there was no suggestion that fire had been started deliberately. He also thought that cigarette ends had been left lying about and had possibly been thrown about.

Following this accident, instructions were given that corridor doors should no longer be locked but several later incidents showed this was slow to be applied.[12]

Two further incidents in the next few years could both have resulted in similar loss of life, but fortunately did not. In the first, a carriage of a southbound express caught fire on 23rd June 1949 near Penmanshiel and the train was actually brought to a stop partly in the tunnel. A cigarette end or lighted rubbish started a fire which spread with astonishing speed due to the panelled walls having been sprayed with a cellulose lacquer. A couple was trapped in their compartment, 15ft from the scene of the fire, within fifteen seconds of it having started. Although one woman was badly injured, there were no deaths as the corridors were open and the train stopped within 75 seconds.

Penmanshiel occurred in a period when fires were causing significant concern, centred around the use of cellulose lacquers which were inflammable. An internal Ministry of Transport memo concluded that "the present situation has more than ordinary and acceptable risks".[13] On 8th June 1950 five people died in a similar fire at Beattock on the West Coast Main Line.

Then on 14th July 1951 railway staff and watching cricket players at Huntingdon were astonished to see flames and smoke pouring from the 3.45pm King's Cross to Leeds express. This was the 'West Riding', normally formed of articulated twin carriages from the pre-war streamlined 'West Riding Limited' but on this occasion partly formed of other spare but similar stock. In fact smoke had already been noticed by passengers some time before; they told the pantry boy, who told the guard: "The guard then went forward and, lifting the seat, saw that the smoke was coming from the corner of the floor, between the edge of the carpet and the side of the coach. He assumed at once that it was due to a hot axle box underneath, and decided to write a note, which he could throw out of the window as the train passed through Huntingdon in about another 10 minutes, asking for the train to be stopped for examination at Peterborough, half-an-hour further on. He told the passengers what he proposed to do, and then returned through the train to his compartment in the ninth coach to write the note."[14]

However, the problem got worse and passengers decided to pull the communication cord, but it took them precious time to find one: "There were only two at each end of the twin set, the one over an external door in the vestibule, and the other in the toilet compartment. Throughout the entire length of the main body of the two coaches, where the passengers were seated, there was none; neither was there any notice to inform passengers where it was to be found. In these circumstances, it is not surprising that they were unable to find the chain quickly when the need arose. Mr. Boardman eventually found it, but

Following the fire at Huntingdon, additional doors were cut into the inner ends of the pairs of first open carriages which were then used for the 'Talisman' until 1963. (David Percival)

not until he had first searched the rear end of the coach; other passengers were also looking for some time, but failed to discover it."

Fortunately the communication cord was eventually pulled and the train brought to a halt. A fire had started under a seat in the second carriage, quickly spreading to three others as they were open carriages with little by way of a physical barrier. As the train stopped, evacuation was difficult because the streamlined stock only had external doors at the outer ends of each twin set.

One woman had to rush back from the restaurant car to rescue her baby, which had been left in a forward carriage in a travel cot which had caught fire. Others, stuck one and a half coach lengths from a usable exit, broke windows and jumped out – in several instances, windows could not be opened. Twenty passengers were injured, nine requiring a stay in hospital.

The A3 Pacific hauling the train was later found to have a firebar missing and it was determined that the fire was caused by a lump of burning coal bouncing beneath the train and lodging in a hole in the floor beneath the bogie at the rear of the second coach. A contributory factor was the use of nitrocellulose lacquers on the interior trim, also a factor at Penmanshiel. After these problems, some of the combustible materials – including foam carpet underlay – were removed and additional doors cut in some of the articulated twin carriages. Wood, hair, leather cloth covering the sides of the coaches, and sponge rubber floor covering, all contributed to the fire hazard.

This series of fires resulted in several angry exchanges in Parliament and the checking of 23,800 passenger carriages – of which 8,000 were found to have inflammable surfaces. The problems with the communication cord were also raised in the same debate.[15] Speaking in the Lords in a debate after the publication of the accident report, Lord Lucas ridiculed the training of railway staff in handling fire: "This [passenger] noticed a wisp of smoke coming between the seat and the side of the coach. She called the attention of a passing pantry-boy who was going down the centre corridor of the coach, and he, in turn, informed the restaurant car conductor. The conductor informed the guard. The guard made an examination and came to the conclusion that the smoke was caused by a hot axle-box. He decided to throw a note out of a window as the train drew up at Huntingdon, about ten minutes travelling time away, asking for the train to be stopped at Peterborough, half-an-hour further on. He wrote the note in his compartment in the ninth coach, went to the restaurant car to search for a potato, to attach, I presume, as a weight so that he could throw the note out of the window; but he was unable to find a potato."[16]

Another result of this was a change in the rules to ensure that a train should be stopped immediately fire was detected.

Fires that started outside the railway boundaries were also a risk, but usually railway traffic could be halted. For example, on 24th June 1866 a flour mill which was partly underneath the High Level Bridge at Newcastle caught fire. The wooden roadway surface on the lower deck of the bridge soon also ignited and the railway traffic above had to be halted. Due to the frantic efforts of workmen, fire did not spread to damage the railway bridge. The North Eastern Railway's engineer was brought back from London at record speeds to check the bridge, travelling from King's Cross to York in only 3 hours 34 minutes – including an eight-minute stop at Newark.

Fire also killed two footplatemen at Holloway on 17th August 1889, in a unique example of an accident caused by the contents of a goods wagon. A truck of barrels of naptha destined for Hackney Wick was being shunted at Holloway sidings along the line to points from where it was routed into siding No.7. A locomotive on an empty coaching stock train had been standing on road No.6 and for a reason that was never understood chose this moment to move forwards without any signal and was hit at the points by the wagon. The collision must have ruptured the barrels, which exploded on contact with the steam locomotive, dousing it and the men on the footplate in flames. Although one of the shunters rushed up and threw his coat over the burning fireman, Henry Parker, both men died of burns.

Vehicles on the line

Misuse of level crossings was a common cause of accidents and there were several fatalities in the early days when pedestrians simply ignored the warnings of the crossing keepers. These were not really 'accidents', of course – they invariably were the result of incautious behaviour. Some were just too elderly or infirm to cross the line on the level, such as the 94-year-old William Ashton killed on an occupation crossing two miles north of St. Neots on 27th February 1856, his body cut completely in half with the upper part scattered down the track. Some we know little about, such as the fatality at Claypole level crossing on 14th June 1860. George Marrison of the Railway Inn at Tuxford had his pub on one side of the line and a new house being built on the other. At about 7.00am on 1st July 1880 he let himself through the wicket gate beside the level crossing and was run over by a goods train, severing one leg and severely injuring his head. He died from his injuries.

Level crossings were seen as a risk from very early days, but when the main road vehicles were lightly built out of wood the risk was invariably to the road user. As motor vehicles became commoner after 1918, and especially during the 1920s, level crossings became the cause of some national debate. It is a problem that persists today – in 2009 a taxi driver was sent to prison for six months after driving round the barriers at Helpston with five young children in his car.[17]

However, few motor cars were substantial enough to cause disaster for a train, though lorries and agricultural vehicles did cause fatalities on other lines. Road users might face either death or prosecution, such as in the case of Thomas Rowlett who crashed through the gates at Arlesey in 1928, narrowly escaping being killed by an express train. He was prosecuted for negligent driving but the defence argued that his brakes had failed and so he escaped conviction. William Stoneham was killed at Offord Crossing in February 1930 whilst driving his motorbike.

On 2nd January 1941 at Haywards Crossing near Askern an army lorry was hit by a troop train, killing two men.[18] On 13th August 1943 a lorry crashed through the gates at Lincoln Road signal box at East Markham; three people in it, including two Women's Land Army workers, were killed and four injured when it was hit by a down Hull express.

A very minor level crossing attained considerable notoriety in 1948 when it was the scene of two fatal accidents within seven months, causing four deaths. Unusually, reports on the two accidents were published together.

Occupation crossing No.85 was 68½ miles north of King's Cross where the line crosses the fens between Connington and Holme at a slightly raised elevation so that any road had to rise to meet it. The crossing had an unusual history which contributed to the accidents. As far as was known, there had been an occupation crossing on the site, leading only to some farmland to the east of the line which was bounded on the far side by woodland and the drain known as Monks Lode. The lane, on both sides of the railway, was 'unadopted' and the crossing was therefore only 'occupational'. At some point in the 1920s a bridge had been built over Monks Lode so that the lane became of greater use and it was adopted as a public highway by the County Council which became responsible for maintaining it.

However, the crossing itself remained an occupation crossing, with the gates normally closed against the road, and no railway staff on hand to control it. Indeed, there was no signal box in the vicinity. In 1928 the LNER wrote to owners of the land to the east, who were producing increased agricultural traffic, to remind them of its status following concerns that it was being used incorrectly but beyond that no further action was taken.

The self-closing gates, operated by road users, became increasingly unfit for purpose as both road and rail traffic increased, then during the war great changes were made just to the south at Connington. About 80 yards to the south of the crossing a new Connington North signal box was built with additional marshalling sidings provided. The sidings received rubble and waste from London as the damage of the Blitz was repaired. At its north end the goods loop continued as a long siding as far as Holme; this formed a third track across the level crossing but the idea of building the North box closer to the crossing so that it could control the gates had never been implemented – perhaps because the railway did not want this additional responsibility. However, a goods train standing on the down goods line might obscure a crossing user's view of an approaching train on the down main.

Also during the war, a prisoner camp was built at Sawtry and German prisoners from there were often taken across the railway to work on the fenland fields. In December 1947 there was a minor accident at the crossing but the Railway Inspectorate had already begun to take a gloomy view of such situations and after an accident at Wormley on the Great Eastern section it took the view that councils should not adopt roads leading to occupation crossings. Just before the war there had been a serious accident at a similar crossing at Hilgay, near Downham Market. None of this did any good in hastening improvements.

Just after 7.00am on 1st March 1948, with the sun starting to rise on a very foggy morning, a 2½-ton Fordson covered truck owned by Huntingdon War Agricultural Executive Committee approached the level crossing carrying German PoWs from Sawtry camp to the fields east of the line. Although no-one can be sure that the gates had been left open, the lorry seems to have driven onto the crossing without pausing to listen for trains – which would have been difficult to see in the fog anyway. As it crossed the line, the truck was struck by a light engine running tender first from Peterborough to Connington sidings, travelling at only about 20mph.

Three of the men were killed outright and a further three died later, including the driver Gustav Baehr and the passenger who was sitting alongside him; there were only two survivors. The engine driver saw nothing of the lorry, which the engine seems to have ploughed through, leaving one set of wheels one side of the tender and the others the other. All the Germans were due to be repatriated within a few days.[19]

When news of the accident reached the camp, the German medical officer, Dr. Kuhlo, was sent out by truck to help; he was also seriously injured when his truck collided with a bus only a few yards from the level crossing.

A few days later another driver, this time British, had a narrow escape in fog at the same crossing and accident investigators took a census of traffic. They found 150 motors, 172 cyclists and 34 pedestrians used the crossing in 48 hours –

mainly at the hours of peak rail traffic. A permanent way man thought that road users had stopped closing the gates ten years or so earlier, so it was likely the lorry had driven on with no checks, as if it were a signalled public crossing. A local farmer reported an accident had occurred in December 1947 and complained that the new sidings had dangerously blocked the view of the railway.

There was a debate about whether signaller-operated gates could be installed, but it was too far from the signal box for conventional gates. So almost nothing was done, except the closing of the gates was enforced, and then on 16th October 1948 there was another fatal accident. Colonel Mellows, a Peterborough solicitor, and his friend A. F. Percival – clerk to the magistrates – had been to their regular shooting spot east of the line and were returning in wet weather and fading light. It was foggy, with visibility down to about 20 yards. Percival got out of the car to open the gates just after a King's Cross to Leeds express had passed and Mellows probably had one eye on a goods train waiting to follow it out of the goods loop.

As Mellows drove forwards with his dog in the car, Percival saw an up train coming but was too late to stop his friend. Possibly the driver hesitated, but he was struck by a Pacific-hauled empty stock train at about 50mph – the locomotive catching the rear end of the car. Mellows and the dog were killed, with the latter being buried beside the railway. Mellows's executors sued the Railway Executive for negligence, arguing that the simple practice of requiring trains to whistle at this known hazard would have saved his life. In December 1951 the judge found against the Railway Executive which then appealed – which it also lost. Lord Denning took the view that the Railway Executive could not simply ignore the fact that road traffic – and therefore risk – had increased and had a duty of reasonable care in common law.

This accident led to further discussion about re-aligning the road, and Lt. Col. Woodhouse suggested making it a public crossing with a gatekeeper or to be controlled from Connington North. The problem of the crossing being too far from the box was solved by moving the whole box to the crossing on 13th August 1954.[20] The crossing is still there today, substantially better protected, but it is even lonelier now the Connington sidings have closed.[21]

In 1962 a car had a sidelong collision with a slow-moving diesel locomotive at Farrar's Boiler Works Crossing in Newark because a previous user had left the gate open and the next car's driver had gone onto the tracks in the dark before realising it. At these crossings, users were required by law to close the gates after themselves. On 7th December 1963 a man driving a van containing a dance band lost his way near Naburn and drove onto the main line at Vicarage Lane crossing, where previous user had failed to close the gate properly. The driver got into a panic and, in attempting to reverse off, managed to get the van wheels stuck between the sleepers. The band members got out and started to empty the van whilst some of them set off towards where they thought a signal box or signals might be – but they went the wrong way. The van was hit by a diesel-hauled sleeping car express, but there were no deaths.

By the twentieth century the problem of level crossings was well understood and some of the crossings mentioned in this book, such as that at Lincoln Road, Tuxford, have been replaced by bridges. However, the East Coast line north of Peterborough is unusual for a British main line in the number of crossings that still exist – and some being used by quite major roads. Bitterly ironic, therefore, that the worst road-related accident, at Heck, involved a vehicle at a bridged crossing point.

The crossings at Riccall, on the A19 between Selby and York, have been scene of several incidents – at least two fatal and several near misses. A fatal accident in 1952 is dealt with in Chapter 8 and in August 1962 there was near disaster when a lorry laden with 16 tons of fertiliser left the road, ploughed across a field and ended across the tracks with a train approaching in the distance. Its driver said "The train was in seeing distance when we came to rest on the metals and I told my pal to jump out and run." Luckily the signalman was able to stop the train. The accident was caused when the lorry braked to avoid the queue of traffic waiting at the crossing gates.

There was a more serious accident at 0.15 on the morning of 15th November 1980, at which time Riccall Turnhead crossing was protected by automatic half barriers. Diesel locomotive No.47 042 was approaching the crossing on an overnight Freightliner train from Edinburgh to Stretford[22] and its driver could see the red lights flashing ahead and that the barriers were down. Nonetheless, he saw the headlights of a car enter the crossing, turn towards him as it moved around the half barrier and then away again. There was little the train driver could do and he struck the car at about 70mph.

The occupants of the car, Dr. Sharid Kar and Mrs. Anne Marie Narayan, were killed. There was no explanation for their deaths other than that Dr. Kar had decided not to wait at the barrier and had driven his car around it rather than wait the maximum likely 53 seconds for the train to arrive.

An accident caused by a member of railway staff breaking the rules occurred at Stobswood Crossing near Widdrington on 15th September 1959. This was an occupation crossing, but fully staffed due to high levels of road traffic to the nearby colliery following two accidents in 1935. A down goods train had just passed and the crossing keeper held the gates open to allow a lorry to cross without permission from the signalman. However, an Alnwick to Newcastle diesel train was approaching under clear signals and hit the lorry, killing the train driver. Following the accident, it was considered whether diesel trains needed to be strengthened at the front. Porter H. Ferguson was held to be wholly responsible although working practices at the crossing were clearly slack whoever was on duty.

In the aftermath of serious accidents, it is common for the press to offer pensive analysis. After the terrible disaster at Great Heck on 28th February 2001, one journalist opined that "it was caused by a set of circumstances that could, in all probability, have been neither prevented nor foreseen";[23] however, this seems less certain in retrospect, especially with several subsequent disasters where road vehicles brought trains to grief. The initial cause of the accident – a road vehicle ending up on the railway – had occurred many times before, but the modern high-speed train might have escaped with less damage had its derailed wheels not been deflected by points into the

The use of a telephoto lens has graphically emphasised the jumbled and torn wrecks of passenger and coal vehicles after the Great Heck collision.
(The Press)

Following the collision at Great Heck, the Freightliner locomotive ended up very close to nearby housing.
(The Press)

path of an oncoming coal train on the opposite line. The accident has gone down in mythology as "likely to prompt the biggest motor insurance claim in insurance history"[24] and the five-year prison sentence given to its main cause is perhaps the longest handed out for an accident on the East Coast Main Line.

The origins of the disaster are well known. Gary Hart of Strubby, Lincolnshire, spent most of the night talking on the phone to a woman he had met on the internet and then set off for Manchester in his Land Rover – towing a Renault car on his trailer. It was an ambitious journey for a man who had had virtually no sleep and he was, in the words of Sergeant Peter McKay, "a mobile catastrophe waiting to happen".[25]

At about 06.10 Hart was travelling at speed on the M62 and approaching its bridge over the East Coast Main Line near Great Heck, north of Doncaster. Some initial reports suggested he suffered a 'blow out' but it was accepted that he had fallen asleep when his vehicle left the motorway and ran down the embankment and through the railway fencing – 115m distance in all. The M62 bridge over the railway was protected by safety barriers, but Hart's vehicle left the motorway before the barriers started – one of a number of slender possibilities that combined

to cause this tragic disaster. It came to rest with its left front wheel on the up line and one tyre flat; Hart, now wide awake, first tried to reverse off the track and then frantically rang for help. The jackknifed trailer became detached from the Land Rover and ended on the bank with the car clear of the track.

At 06.13 his Land Rover was hit by a Newcastle to King's Cross express travelling at or near full speed of 125mph and the front vehicle, a driving van trailer, was partially derailed 48m beyond the crash site, with the result that its left-hand wheels were running between the rails. By coincidence the train was being propelled by the same Class 91 locomotive as had been involved in the Hatfield accident in 2000. Serious disaster might not have resulted but when the train reached Plasmor Sidings, 515m from the first accident, a rail of the trailing turnout diverted its wheels across towards the down line on which a Class 66 locomotive on the 05.00 Immingham to Ferrybridge coal train was approaching. The report estimated that the leading vehicle was effectively "airborne" for 23m. The closing speed of the two trains was around 142mph, with the passenger train at 88mph and the freight at 54.

Given the high speeds involved, many more might have died but for the strength of modern carriage design. The report noted that "the rolling stock performed adequately in terms of crashworthiness in that survival space was to a large extent maintained". Almost all the passenger train carriages were diverted into the field on the east side of the line whilst the locomotive and two wagons of the coal train were deflected into a garden on the west side with one wagon on top of the locomotive. A woman who lived in a nearby house said it was like "There had been a huge explosion, like an earthquake or a bomb, as I was lying in bed with my husband Charles. It shook the whole house, and even the toothbrushes fell off the handbasin shelf."

The cab unit of the passenger train driving van trailer (DVT)

In 2006 a Plymouth to Edinburgh train was derailed at Copmanthorpe when it hit a car on the track. How the car got to be there was never explained since its driver was killed.
(RAIB)

was severed from the body shell and thrown clear. However, most of the damage was caused by the impact of the freight train on the shells of the passenger coaches, with the bogie of the Class 66 penetrating carriage M at the front of the train; this carriage also rotated 360°. Carriage F suffered severe damage, rotated and turned over. The roofs of the carriages came into contact with an overbridge, causing severe crushing of carriage F in particular. Parts of carriage H punctured the shells of F and E and a bogie from the DVT ended up in the vestibule of D.

Six passengers, of the 99 on board, and four railway staff including the drivers of both the passenger and the coal trains were killed and 82 people injured. Most of the dead passengers were in carriages M, G, F and E. The crash caused huge disruption, the main line not reopening until 13th March. Gary Hart was tried at Leeds and convicted on ten counts of causing death by dangerous driving on 13th December 2001, being sentenced to five years in prison.

Such was the public and political interest in the accident that an interim report was published on 6th March 2001 and a special report on the obstruction of the railway by motor vehicles in February 2002. Great Heck led to major investment in road-rail safety and much was learnt about railway passenger survival – for example, the tables, head rests and arm rests in first class all proved hazardous in crash conditions compared with the seating in standard class. The shells of the carriages and the crush zones in their designs stood up well, but the main risk proved to be their penetration from outside.

After the accident Railtrack issued a writ to recover £11million from Hart's insurers, Fortis Insurance, and further claims were likely from the other railway businesses affected. Fortis indicated that it felt the crash barriers had been inadequate, but nonetheless the court in Leeds imprisoned Hart as it considered his behaviour had caused the accident. Not everyone considered his sentence appropriate, *The Scotsman* carrying an article arguing that jailing him "won't for one

second reduce the chances of such freak accidents occurring again".[26] By October 2003 Fortis had already paid out £22million compensation and was expecting another £12million more, some of which it was seeking to recover from the Highways Agency[27] although it lost this case. Hart was released in 2004.

The accident at Copmanthorpe, a few miles south of York, on the night of 25th September 2006 could easily have been a repeat of the Great Heck disaster – and perhaps this was underlined by the discovery that safety reviews ordered after Great Heck had not been carried out at the spot where this accident occurred. It was remarkable that a Virgin Trains Class 221 diesel unit on a Plymouth to Edinburgh run hit a car on the track at 100mph without any injuries to passengers; the car driver was killed.

Moor Lane was a half-forgotten lane running out of Copmanthorpe on its eastern side, which until 1982 had led to a level crossing and thence across the railway. In 2006 it was signed as a cul-de-sac, but gave the appearance of a narrow country lane as it left the village – there were the standard 'end of speed limit' signs at the end of the lit area. The accident report took care to consider the nature of this road: "The nature of the paving and verges would indicate to a road user that they were driving along a minor road. Outside the speed limit the road surface narrows to little over a car's width, and the road is bordered on both sides by verges of long, uncut grass leading to mature hedges."

In addition, the night was dark with some patchy fog and drizzle. The car left Copmanthorpe and appears to have travelled at 30-40mph, at which speed the driver would have been unable to stop within the sight range of his headlights. For some unknown reason, he reached the end of the road and drove straight through the wooden fence protecting the railway; the front wheels of his car ended up trapped between the rails in the 'four foot' of the down Leeds line. It was not established why the driver took this route, or why he was in Copmanthorpe at all. Alcohol, drugs or illness were all ruled out in the accident report although the inquest heard that the driver was a diabetic.

A witness who heard the car crash through the fence estimated that there was a 30-second delay before the train hit the car. Travelling at 100mph, the train driver had little time to reduce speed and the train effectively cut the car in two. The accident revealed some concerns about the ability of this type of train to withstand an accident, though only three wheelsets were derailed and it kept its alignment. Material from the car passed beneath the train and ruptured three of the train's five fuel tanks, which could have led to serious fire.

A contributory factor to the accident was that checks recommended by the 2003 report on road-rail interfaces had not been carried out – and these specifically referred to the risk of cul-de-sacs. Although a new fence had been installed, it was alleged this was less visible than its predecessor which had been white and the site had not been risk assessed; clearly no protection worthy of the name existed to keep cars off the railway. The York coroner commented on the poor quality of road signs but concluded that "The reason for the presence of Mr. Power on the railway line that day will remain a mystery."[28]

Accidents such as these were not always just the result of vehicles on the line. On 6th March 1922 the up 'Flying Scotsman' ran into a herd of cattle which was believed to have got through a gate that had been left open, south of Goswick[29]. A down parcels train had been brought to a stand because of the hazard and it hid the cattle from the view of the express driver, but the cattle then "dashed in front of the train". The impact derailed the locomotive near Haggerston level crossing but there were no passenger injuries although there were cases of shock. Parts of the animals were spattered all over the front of the locomotive.[30] Passengers took up a collection for the driver and fireman.[31]

FOOTNOTES

1   *The Times*, 21 December 1848
2   Margaret Hutcherson, *Let No Wheels Turn*, Tyne & Wear, 2006.
3   *Manchester Guardian*, 1 July 1926
4   Patrick Renshaw, *Nine Days in May*,
5   *The Times*, 12 July 1926
6   The railway used this spelling although the village itself was spelt Conington at this time, but some earlier histories spell it 'Connington' so perhaps the GNR had just opted for the traditional..
7   J Slack, *The Secret Life of St. Neots Station*, 2010, pps. 57-60
8   Slack, pps70-71, describes Bower's later pioneering work on railway carriage gas lights, which involved close liaison with the GNR although he went bankrupt in 1885.
9   House of Lords Sessional Papers, 1867, vol 27, p.255
10 Accounts and Papers of the House of Commons 1868-9, vol. 21, p.58
11 Thus reports said, but this regulation was not in the 1939 edition held by Michael Back.
12 *Hansard*, 15 March 1944
13 http://www.railwaysarchive.co.uk/docsummary.php?docID+1214; accessed 2 August 2012
14 Col R J Walker, Accident report
15 *Hansard*, 23 June 1962
16 *Hansard*, 18 June 1952
17 *Daily Mail*, 19 May 2009
18 Brooksbank, p. 167
19 *The Times*, 2 March 1948.
20 B W L Brooksbank, *Triumph and Beyond*, Oldham, 1997, p.171

21 One should not leave Connington without mentioning the legendary Connington ghost. This is supposedly another crossing victim, with accounts claiming that a young woman was killed at the crossing in pre-war days. From then on, at the exact time of her death every year, "the levers in the signal box controlling the hand gates would briefly rattle and shake as if somebody down below was trying to get across the line". My correspondent says "You may scoff, as I myself did, but the local signalmen knew of it along the line and the relief signalman who covered the vacancies there was so terrified that he switched the box out at that time, hid in the toilet, and our Operations Manager had to threaten disciplinary action."
22 Correspondents have queried whether this should say Stratford, but the accident report states Stretford.
23 *The Independent*, 1 March 2001
24 *The Guardian*, 14 December 2001
25 *The Guardian*, 14 December 2001
26 *The Scotsman*, 14 December 2001
27 BBC News report, 7 October 2003.
28 BBC, 18 November 2009
29 *Backtrack*, August 2012, p.485.
30 Animals do still get onto railways. The author has a work colleague who is a farmer's wife but travels regularly from an ex-GNR station in Hertfordshire into London. One day, waiting on the platform, an announcement came over the tannoy that trains were being delayed by a bull on the line. As the mood of commuters darkened, she had to ring her husband furtively to tell him that Casanova, *their* bull, was the offender.
31 *The Times*, 7 March 1922

10

CAUSE UNKNOWN

Following the unsatisfactory investigation of the accident at Weston, south of Tuxford, in 1857, an anonymous correspondent wrote to the *Manchester Guardian:* "Everyone acquainted with the elementary principles of dynamics knows that 'accident' has no place in the resultant of bodies (*sic*) acted upon by different forces."

In other and perhaps simpler words, in the physical world nothing can happen by accident – all must have a cause. Therefore, the frequent decision of coroner's juries that persons had died as a result of 'accidental death' in a railway 'accident' can be seen as unscientific. What they mean is that the deaths are not blamed on anyone in particular, or the cause is actually unknown. In recent years, the number of 'cause unknown' accidents is relatively small if, indeed, there are any at all.

One of the reasons for 'cause unknown' in the earlier days was the railway companies' rather cavalier attitudes to 'evidence.' In 1857 the Great Northern was aggressively trying to tap into the Manchester to London traffic, most of which went by way of the London & North Western to Euston. The GNR ran some light, fast trains via Sheffield and Retford and it was one of these that came to grief at Weston, two miles south of Tuxford, on 24th September 1857. Travelling at about 50mph or a little more, the carriages became derailed and detached from the engine just before a bridge over a road. The first two carriages passed over the bridge but then rolled down the embankment to land in a garden, but the other two carriages and the brake van collided with the bridge parapet first, before also going down the embankment and being "smashed to pieces."[1] The press report that the first two carriages "made a complete somersault"[2] must be treated with some doubt, since no-one died in them and they were later hauled back up the bank and rerailed for return to Doncaster! This was reported as "the first fatal passenger accident that has ever occurred on this line".[3]

The deaths were in the last two carriages. The Hon. William Windsor Clive, 20, was killed when he was thrown out of the carriage and his head hit the parapet and the guard had both arms cut off but apparently survived. Three women died, including Letitia Paget who suffered "a most severe fracture of the skull, nearly the whole of the brain escaping". *The Observer* joined in with more details – "the head of one of the ladies killed was crushed quite flat; the face of another was cut in two from top to bottom". A fifth victim, a man, died later. Another man was seen "wandering on the line" after the accident but a day later was referred to as "not having been seen since".

The dead and injured were first taken to the Newcastle Arms in Tuxford, where the coroner also held his inquest. Captain Wynne could not explain it to the coroner – "I am in darkness as to the cause of the accident" he said. However, there were other complaints, including that the communication bell for the guard to attract the driver's attention was not working.

One of the remarkable aspects of this disaster is how soon the GNR recovered. The *Manchester Guardian* reported that other trains were delayed only by "an hour'" The GNR managed to get labourers in from "local factories" to assist with repairing the line. The track had been "raked" and repaired long before Colonel Wynne arrived to investigate for the Board of Trade. There was clearly suspicion in the press – and perhaps in the mind of Wynne – that the GNR had acted too hastily and there were calls for the scene of an accident to be preserved until the Board's man could arrive. On 1st October the editorial of *The Times* complained about the lack of an explanation.

Wynne concluded that the brake van derailed first, but he did not know why. One suggestion was that sudden braking had broken the couplings, but "excessive speed" was the popular view – though no-one could provide any evidence for this and Archibald Sturrock, the locomotive engineer, told the coroner that he had been up to 75mph in similar carriages. In this case then it was 'cause unknown' because accident investigation was in its infancy – or because the GNR had got rid of the evidence.

The disaster at Grantham on 19th September 1906 is one of the most-discussed in the annals of the East Coast Main Line and will perhaps always be so. Driver Fleetwood and Fireman Talbot had taken over the 8.45pm down express from London to Edinburgh at Peterborough, but the reasons for its failure to stop at Grantham went with them into eternity.

As the clock approached 11.00pm, signalman Alfred Day at Grantham South signal box was looking out for the 8.45pm down King's Cross to Edinburgh to arrive in the station, as it was running a little late. As it approached his box behind Atlantic No.276, Day noticed that it seemed to be going rather quickly for a train due to stop at the station but he saw no sparks and heard no noise from the wheels, so later said that "I feel confident the brakes were not applied." Day's observations became part of the folklore of the accident, as he was one of the few people at Grantham to notice Driver Fleetwood and Fireman Talbot: "I noticed the driver and fireman on the engine; they both appeared to be standing looking out of their respective glasses in front of them, but they did not seem to be actually doing anything." Day thought the speed to be 50mph and his telegraph lad also thought there were no brakes applied.

William Knighton was the guard at the front of the train and appears to have been laggardly in his duties. Only when they were passing the South box did he realise there was a problem. "When we passed the South box I noticed that we were going at a terrible speed. I then turned and flew to the vacuum brake handle. I opened the valve and found that there was no vacuum." He thought that the brake had been applied "close on Grantham station" and the wheels were skidding, though other witnesses cast doubt on this testimony. Thomas Rowlett, the rear guard, was convinced that the brakes were on and the

THE TERRIBLE RAILWAY SMASH AT GRANTHAM. Sep. 19/1906.

The cause of the Grantham accident was derailment at speed, but the position of the scene on an embankment and bridge, along with the effects of fire, all contributed.

(GNR Society)

This picture of the Grantham accident shows recovery work on the carriages that went down the embankment.

wheels skidding after passing South box; "The brakes were on, there was not the slightest doubt about that." However, passenger Joseph Glaister, a seasoned traveller, thought there were no brakes.

The express careered on past Grantham Yard signal box, which was at the south end of the up platform, where Isaac Crowson thought "it was going at a terrible rate – I should say 50 miles an hour". He was not entirely certain about the brakes, but thought they were probably not applied, though a passing goods train obscured some of his view.

George Pile, an inspector standing on the station platform, saw no sign of the driver or fireman. As he watched with astonishment as the train ran past, he thought that the steam was off and did not think that brakes had been applied, but thought it was possible that it was skidding. Cecil Cox, a postman waiting on the platform, thought the train came

through faster than the normal 'non-stops' but he also thought the steam was off and the brakes were on – commenting on the sparks.

Further along the platform was George Wilson, a foreman, who had a lucky escape. He crossed the line in front of the train, assuming that it was going to stop, and had a fright when it carried on at high speed. Wilson also did not see Fleetwood or Talbot and thought the train was neither braking nor skidding.

Beyond the end of the down platform was Grantham North signal box, where Richard Scoffin was on duty. He had passed a goods train from the Nottingham line across the down main line and onto the up main line. To do this the points of the down main had been correctly set to the Nottingham branch and Scoffin had left them in this position as he expected the Edinburgh express to stop for at least five minutes. The express, however, ran straight through the platform at about 40mph in

93

his estimate and "did not appear to be checking speed at all". This was not to say that brakes had not been applied – Scoffin commenting that "at the time I thought that the brake must be hard on, and that all the wheels of the train must be skidding". He did not see the driver or fireman.

135 yards north of the down platform's end were the points and a reverse curve onto the Nottingham line which the express took at 40mph or so. The tender derailed first, hitting the parapet of the bridge over Harlaxton Road and dragging the locomotive broadside across the track until it overturned. Knighton recalled "I distinctly remember my vehicle taking the points, and it seemed to go through them all right. I can remember nothing more until I found myself at the bottom of the bank." The train had come to grief when carriages derailed and caught the bridge parapet. The locomotive turned over and its tender went down the embankment, taking the first five of the nine carriages with it, with two coming to rest halfway down. The driver and fireman were killed, nine passengers and a Post Office attendant died at the scene and two other passengers later.

Lifting the locomotive by crane after the Goswick accident of 1907.
(Ken Hoole Collection)

Pile, watching from the station, "heard a noise as of an explosion and immediately afterwards I saw flames shoot up in the air". Two fires started almost immediately, one down by the engine and one up the embankment. The mail van at the front of the train was split apart and later Cecil Cox found Fleetwood and Talbot, dead and badly burnt, buried beneath mail bags.

The wreckage yielded up few clues as to the cause of the disaster. Henry Ivatt reported that the locomotive regulator had been found one third open, but this could easily have been knocked during the accident. There was no reason to believe that the regulator had jammed in an open position.

One of the theories was that Fleetwood had been a drinker, though this theory seems to have originated only in comments made by Talbot to his girlfriend which were themselves without substantiation. The Locomotive Foreman, Goodwin, described Fleetwood as "a very quiet, steady, obliging man, and a capable driver, and one that I could always rely on". The District Locomotive Superintendent called him an "exceptionally reliable driver" and became rather effusive: "As regards his personal character, all I can say is that he was everything I could admire." Talbot's friend, Miss M. Rogers, said that he had told her his driver drank, although she was not certain he meant Fleetwood and the first conversation took place before the men had worked together. They discussed what he would do if his driver was drunk on the engine and Talbot talked about 'stunning' him so that he could take over the controls – which he was quite capable of doing. When cross-questioned, she was hesitant – "I have a sort of an idea that he said something about

stunning." Talbot's friend William Blackburn thought that "he said his driver drank slightly, but it took effect quickly" and also confirmed the discussion about stunning.

Staff at Peterborough all thought Fleetwood had been sober and no-one came forward to say that they had ever seen him inebriated. A former fireman confirmed Fleetwood was careful in his habits and described how he would always whistle when they were approaching the South box if he was driving a stopping train – yet no-one heard any whistle at all on this fateful night.

With Fleetwood's character almost, but not quite, beyond question, attention focussed on Ralph Talbot. He had been a Premium Apprentice at Doncaster, had travelled on engines doing inspection work but had also passed out as a fireman – though this would not have been the career he was expecting. Views started to circulate that Talbot had not been quite up to the job and these were further stirred by the evidence of another Doncaster driver, Richard Cartwright, who had spoken to Fleetwood on the night of the 19th at Peterborough. Cartwright reported "He said a few minutes had been lost the night before, and that someone would have to have the time, he should not have it. He did not say the cause of the time being lost. I cannot say whether he would be fined for losing that eight minutes." Before going on his last journey, Talbot had told Miss Rogers that he had burnt his hand and his left side, and would have to wear a glove perhaps because of a problem with the exhaust ejector. There were also discussions around whether clinker had been left in the firebox, causing Talbot problems.

There was clear evidence that the train did lose time again between Peterborough and Corby.[4]

The story of an argument between the men on the footplate circulated in the press before the inquiry. Joseph Glaister admitted that he had told a reporter about hearing of a fight on the footplate, saying that a man at Grantham station had told him this at 10.00am on 20th September. Apparently, the driver had been heard shouting at various stations including Grantham, but no further evidence of this surfaced.

Another theory was that the men had lost track of where they were or had forgotten they were meant to stop. However, they had worked exactly the same train the previous night, so forgetting the stop seems unlikely, and conditions were not so bad as to hide the many very obvious signs of an approach to Grantham station.

Fleetwood had been off sick with sciatica until 3rd September. He had been off sick three times in the previous year and on one occasion had been taken ill whilst driving to King's Cross, although he had still been able to control the engine and had continued to the end of the journey. However, the GNR 'sick club' records did not show this – they showed an absence with sciatica in 1904, one with mild dyspepsia in 1905 and no entries at all for 1906. Dr. Corbett produced the sick club book at the inquiry to underline his point. However, Fleetwood's mother-in-law, with whom he lived (his wife had died), said that he had been suffering from sciatica for 'practically' the whole of August; he was indeed off work from 2nd August to 1st September during which "he could move about, but with difficulty". He had told her that he had seen Dr. Corbett on 23rd May and also on 23rd June when he had been taken ill whilst driving, but Corbett denied this; all agreed he saw no doctor during his August illness. He took six days off after the 23rd June incident – his holiday entitlement for the year. Fleetwood would have been entitled to draw 9s 6d a week sick pay if he saw the sick club doctor, but this required some 'restrictions' being placed on him. Yet he was able to return to work after four weeks' absence without any medical check at all. Such was the concern about this that Ivatt was recalled and avowed that there was no record of Fleetwood seeing Dr. Corbett since 1904.

Sciatica results in pain in the back and often down the leg, sometimes becoming severe and causing weakness in the muscles. Sciatica can result from standing for long periods, so Fleetwood's profession clearly put him at risk. The issue of why Fleetwood went to such lengths to avoid discussing his illness, to the point of lying to his mother-in-law, was not investigated in any detail and nor was the possibility that the effects of sciatica might have contributed to rumours of Fleetwood drinking which had perhaps reached Talbot in advance of their journeys together.

Von Donop, the inspecting officer, concluded that "a sudden illness of the driver appears certainly the most probable" cause but "it is feared… that the primary cause of this accident must for ever remain a mystery". However, even if Fleetwood had been taken ill, it is still likely that Talbot would have acted to make the train safe, but we will never know what really happened on the footplate of No.276. It is also possible that Talbot took over the controls due to Fleetwood's illness and, in the emergency, made mistakes in his control of the train.

Years later another theory was put forward in discussions between a Mr. Buttery, a former GNR employee at Peterborough, and Leslie Franks, a local railway enthusiast. Buttery's theory was, very simply, that haste in changing engines at Peterborough meant that the vacuum brake was not coupled up properly, leaving the train reliant on only its locomotive brake. This theory had certainly received some airing at the time and on 26th September the *Peterborough Citizen* referred to the "very sensible theory that the regulator refused to act".[5] On 26th September 1906 the *Peterborough Standard* referred to the idea, commenting on the inquiry that "in our opinion the most probable cause of the brake failure did not receive attention and the point still has to be elucidated… we are not unsupported by expert evidence when we say that the probable reason for the driver not being able to bring his engine to a standstill was his or the fireman's inability to apply the brake through a defect in the combination ejector – known amongst drivers as the banjo". Buttery clearly believed that some official cover-up was involved and the tight four-minute changeover at Peterborough certainly laid a premium on efficient work. However, a brake failure would surely have led to the train getting out of control much earlier in the long descent from High Dyke, allowing its driver to at least whistle to give a warning on the approach to Grantham.

Goswick was a small wayside station in Northumberland but it had busy periods, even at night. The night-time trains in August 1908 included a procession of the 10.55pm Edinburgh to London express, the 11.15pm Edinburgh to Newcastle, the 11.10pm slow goods from Tweedmouth to Newcastle and the 11.22pm fitted express goods from Tweedmouth to Leeds – though not necessarily in that order.

Just after midnight on 28th August the signalman at Goswick, William Hay, had already sent the first express through to Beal and the south, then accepted the slow goods and signalled it into the up relief or 'independent' line which ran as a loop to Beal. The Goswick signalman controlled the entrance to this loop line which ran the two miles to Beal, where it rejoined the main line. One of his regular duties was to 'loop' slower trains so that following expresses could pass – often slowing these trains to walking pace as they passed his box although Rule 148 also stipulated that trains entering a loop had to ensure a 'steady passage'. His home signals were protected by a distant, which was visible 1,400 yards away on a clear summer night and which would normally have remained at danger and thus used to caution trains entering the loop.

Knowing that the second express had already left Berwick, Hay prepared to signal the fast goods to follow the slow one along the loop, intending to caution it as to the presence of the other train ahead as it passed his box. Instead he was astonished to see the fast goods come tearing through the little station at "a high rate of speed", perhaps something around 60mph, passing signals set at danger. The signalman "thought the driver had lost control of his engine" but realised the brakes had not been applied.

The locomotive rocked as it took the sharp facing points on the 'independent' line, then it turned right over, crashing at speed into the 12ft ditch beside the line and destroying almost all the wagons in its wake. Hay remembered that "I heard the crash of the accident and there was a sort of flash." Both driver and fireman were killed outright as the engine rolled over and even John Anderson, the guard in his van at the rear of the train, was badly injured; he was unable to give his evidence about the accident for three months. The engine and tender finished upside down in the ditch, buried up to the level of the footplate.

In the aftermath of the disaster there was the confusion over access to the telephone that was typical of the time and had also been a feature in the accident at Retford. Goswick tried to ring Beal to send a warning but the wires had been cut. Northwards, the Scremerston signalman complained that "neither Berwick nor the other operator would give way on the line". The Goswick signalman went down the steps of the box to investigate and found the guard "sitting on his van step", not realising the man had many broken bones. Hay then forgot to send a line obstructed bell signal.

The phenomenon of a fast train coming to grief for no apparent reason was a sensitive issue in 1908, coming on the heels of the disasters at Salisbury on the London & South Western in 1906, Grantham on the Great Northern in 1907 and at Shrewsbury on the London & North Western in October 1907. One early historian explicitly linked them: "Another accident of which little was heard as it concerned a goods train only, and yet which bore a strong resemblance" to the more famous disasters. Here seemed to be another that fitted the pattern, albeit now with a goods train so the usual suspicion about racing to meet competitive timings ought not to have applied. As with other accidents of this type, both driver and fireman were killed as the engine rolled over – so neither lived to explain the driver's apparently reckless speed. As W. H. Raynor, the Inspector, laconically expressed it, "The driver and fireman were both killed so no explanation for their action is forthcoming."[6] Of the nineteen wagons, only two were left upright and nine were utterly destroyed.

What caused this accident? Common sense indicated only three people could know – and two were dead; the other, the Goswick signalman, came under some concerted suspicion but when Anderson, the guard, was able to give evidence he left a clear message that agreed with the signalman's comments about excessive speed. "The train was running fast" Anderson said, with speeds up to about 60mph, and "I do not think that my driver checked speed at all when passing the distant signal."

Despite this, William Hay, the Goswick signalman, still had some explaining to do. He had offered the 11.22pm goods to Beal and the signalman there had wanted Hay to loop it to allow for the express. There was suspicion that Hay had made a late decision to alter his distant signal and change the points for the loop. He explained that he had lowered the up main intermediate signal to allow the goods to pull forwards to the signal box, where he intended to give warning of the other goods standing further up the loop. But it did not stop – so had Hay set the correct signals?

However, the Goswick signals and points were interlocked so the signals could not have been set for the main line in the way that was suggested by some and there was plenty of evidence that the train was travelling excessively fast. It was fitted with vacuum brakes, but they had not been used once after leaving Tweedmouth. Besides, Brown had an unimpressive record – he had three times over-run a signal, once over-run a platform and twice missed stations where he was meant to stop.

The most compelling evidence about the cause of the accident emerged in accounts of a discussion in Tweedmouth goods yard. Driver Brown on the 11.22pm was due to follow the slower 11.10pm in the care of Driver Bennett southwards and got into a discussion with the brake examiner, John Athay – who recalled the conversation later. The brakesman accepted that he had started a debate as to whether the 11.22pm could beat the 11.10pm to Newcastle, which could be done, it was thought, if it was not looped at Goswick – and this was only likely to happen if it was far enough ahead of the next express. "It was I who started a conversation about Brown being able to pass Bennett" he rather plaintively told the enquiry. Brown said that he had known it to be done two or three times, but his fireman doubted this. However, both goods trains left an hour late. In the end, therefore, the best explanation of the accident is that Brown put on speed in order to keep far enough ahead of the following passenger and try to beat Bennett to Newcastle. His speed certainly exceeded the permitted 55mph of his train and, adrenalin flowing, he misread the intentions of the Goswick signalman who had cleared his distant signal for the up independent line. However, Hay did receive some criticism from Colonel von Donop, for he had altered the points to the independent line after he had accepted the 11.22pm, which he should not have done unless it was stationary – although the inspector accepted that all signals except the distant had been at danger until one was cleared to call the train forward.

Forty years later, on 26th October 1947, there was another – and far worse – accident at the same spot when an Edinburgh to London express derailed whilst entering the independent line during a diversion because of engineering work. On this occasion 28 people were killed. This was described in an earlier chapter.

FOOTNOTES

1   *Manchester Guardian*, 25 September 1857.
2   *The Times*, 25 September 1857
3   *The Times*, 25 September 1857
4   Later known as Corby Glen.
5   This theory forms a substantial part of the article in *Great Northern News*, Sept/Oct 2006, by Brian White.
6   W H Raynor, *The Safety of British Railways*, p.140-1